Face to Face

Women Writers on Faith, Mysticism, and Awakening

North Point Press

A division of Farrar, Straus and Giroux

New York

Face to Face

Edited by Linda Hogan and

Brenda Peterson

North Point Press
A division of Farrar, Straus and Giroux
19 Union Square West, New York 10003

The following selections are included by arrangement with the authors: Diane Ackerman, "Imagining the Divine," copyright © 2004 by Diane Ackerman; Susan Biskeborn, "Under My Napkin? In Sky? In Trees?" copyright © 2004 by Susan Biskeborn; Marlene Blessing, "Shoplifting for Jesus," copyright © 2004 by Marlene Blessing; Kim Chernin, "Initiation," copyright © 2004 by Kim Chernin; Suzanne Edison, "Resurrection," copyright © 2004 by Suzanne Edison; Clarissa Pinkola Estés, "Have You Forgotten? I Am Your Mother," copyright © 2004 by Clarissa P. Estés; Rebecca Goldstein, "Looking Back at Lot's Wife," copyright © 2004 by Rebecca Goldstein; Elizabeth Carothers Herron, "Ordinary Mysticism," copyright © 2004 by Elizabeth Carothers Herron; Catherine Johnson, "The Sound of Grace," copyright © 2004 by Catherine Johnson; Mohja Kahf, "Around the Ka'ba and Over the Crick," copyright © 2004 by Mohja Kahf; Rita Kiefer, "Rapture," copyright © 2004 by Rita Kiefer; Marilyn Krysl, "Treatise on Narcissism, Evil, Good, Free Will, and the Persistence of the Idea of the Self," copyright © 2004 by Marilyn Krysl; Demetria Martinez, "Spirit Matters," copyright © 2004 by Demetria Martinez; Susanne Pari, "Ramadan Redux," copyright © 2004 by Susanne Pari; Brenda Peterson, "The Feminine and the *Tao*," copyright © 2004 by Brenda Peterson and Ursula K. Le Guin; Brenda Peterson, "Shall We Gather at the River?" copyright © 2004 by Brenda Peterson; Judith Roche, "The Angels," copyright © 2004 by Judith Roche; Sharman Apt Russell, "Silence," copyright © 2004 by Sharman Apt Russell; Amy Schuring, "Cargo," copyright © 2004 by Amy Schuring; Barbara Sjoholm, "Wonder Voyages," copyright © 2004 by Barbara Sjoholm; Starhawk, "Witchcraft and Women's Culture," copyright © 2004 by Starhawk; Haunani-Kay Trask, "Hi'aka Chanting," copyright © 2004 by Haunani-Kay Trask; Georgiana Valoyce-Sanchez, "Breathing the Ancestors," copyright © 2004 by Georgiana Valoyce-Sanchez; Kate Wheeler, "Taking Vows," copyright © 2004 by Kate Wheeler

Owing to limitation of space, acknowledgments for permission to reprint previously published material can be found on pages 265–267, which constitute an extension of this copyright page.

Library of Congress Cataloging-in-Publication Data
Face to face : women writers on faith, mysticism, and
awakening / edited by Linda Hogan and Brenda Peterson.— 1st ed.
p. cm.
ISBN-13: 978-0-86547-558-8
ISBN-10: 0-86547-558-X (hardcover : alk. paper)
1. Spiritual biography. 2. Women and religion. I. Hogan, Linda.
II. Peterson, Brenda, date.

BL72.F33 2004
204—dc22   2003028111

Designed by Cassandra J. Pappas

www.fsgbooks.com

1 3 5 7 9 10 8 6 4 2

For now we see through a glass darkly; but then face to face: now I know in part; but then shall I know even as also I am known.

—I CORINTHIANS 13:12

We are closer to the gods than we ever thought possible.

—JOY HARJO
"Songline of Dawn"

Contents

At One with the World

God in the Art of the Everyday

Practicing

Preface

Women have long gazed, face to face, upon the divine. We have found holiness reflected in nature and in the familiar faces of those we love. Often we discover a distinctly personal mysticism in the everyday and the minute. Our steady attention to ordinary revelations, to the overlooked and the powerless, to the "most humble matter," as the Catholic novelist Flannery O'Connor said of her vision, gives us a unique perspective—we are as awakened by revelations of *this* world as of another. We can also find our spiritual guidance embodied right here on Earth.

The feminine focus in this anthology is on the living present, on the Zen-like "here and now," on the blessings of nature, and on restoring a balance to traditions that have often denied the feminine. For the past two thousand years, women have wielded little official power in the Vatican, the mosque, the fundamentalist Christian traditions. Even in the twenty-first century, women still cannot be ordained as Catholic or Mormon priests, and they must cover their faces or be beaten in certain Muslim fundamentalist countries. There has never been a female Dalai Lama or a recognized female pope. In the three most widespread religions—Islam, Judaism, and Christianity—women

are not yet equal to men or recognized alongside them for their visionary and inspirational powers.

But women are not without spiritual authority. There have been
women shamans, sibyls, prophets, ministers, mystics, revolutionaries.
For millennia, indigenous women's societies have given tribes counsel
and inspiration. "There were always the women," Paula Gunn Allen
writes here, in "Where I Come from Is Like This," "who dance and
sing and remember and hold within their hearts the dream of their ancient peoples—that one day the woman who thinks will speak to us
again, and everywhere there will be peace."

We begin this anthology with stories of spiritual legacies—from
Mohja Kahf's trying to practice her Muslim heritage in a small Indiana
farming town to the Yoruba primal ocean goddess Yemaya in Flor Fernandez Barrios's Cuban childhood—in the section "Heritage and
Beyond." And naturalist Terry Tempest Williams struggles with a patriarchal Mormon faith while finding refuge in her family's tradition of
strong women and an abiding bond with the land: "As a people and as
a family, we have a sense of history. And our history is tied to land . . .
I was raised to believe in a spirit world, that life exists before the earth
and will continue to exist afterward, that each human being, bird, and
bulrush, along with all other life forms, had a spirit life . . ."

From today's perspective, it is difficult to imagine that for almost
two thousand years the highest spiritual authority was feminine. Our
second section, "God the Mother," explores the time before the great
patriarchal religions, when mystery traditions of the Greek oracles
flourished. Of the more than 260 practicing oracles in ancient Greece,
the Delphic oracle was the most sacred. Even in a culture that ele-
vated men, the Greek oracle's great seer, or Pythia, was always a
priestess, and her power held the ancient world in thrall. It was Pythia
whose mystical visions poets, scholars, and philosophers such as
Sophocles, Plutarch, Plato, Homer, Pindar, and Pythagoras consulted.
Socrates claimed the great priestess Diotema of Mantinea as his spiritual mentor. Sadly, these thousand-year-old traditions of feminine
gnosis, a way of knowing the world, were systematically destroyed and
lost in the Roman and later Christian conquests. Feminine spiritual
authority, such as the Greek oracles and the earth-centered pagan tra-

ditions, was conquered by the warrior traditions of a Yahweh who would "have no other gods before him."

But these sacred traditions of the goddess and the seer were never completely lost, and today they are flowering again. In her revolutionary book *The Gnostic Gospels*, author Elaine Pagels asks, "What Became of God the Mother?" as she brings to light new interpretations of the Nag Hammadi texts rediscovered in 1945. These ancient writings suggest that in the gnostic traditions "women were considered equal to men, they were revered as prophets, and they acted as teachers, traveling evangelists, healers, priests, and even bishops . . . Given such research, the history of Christianity never could be told in the same way again." In fact, Pagels has led the way in an explosion of gnostic scholarship, much of it offering evidence that Mary Magdalene was an important apostle of the church. It was to Mary Magdalene, after all, that Christ is said to have revealed himself first after the Resurrection. Commenting on this groundbreaking research in the winter of 2003, Phyllis Tickle, a contributing religion editor at *Publishers Weekly*, notes that this twenty-first-century revival of interest in Mary Magdalene goes far beyond questions of the role of women in the church. "This is the pursuit of the divine feminine," Tickle writes, "a kind of yearning that infects both genders: it wishes to find in the divine parent that wholeness that is the feminine and masculine together."

As we selected essays and poetry for this anthology, we found that women have always been bridges between cultures, between humankind and nature, between often warring faiths. Our stories seem to be centered in birth, not death; in contemplation rather than conquest; in compassion more than in judgment. We often follow a more private, inward path, rather than forcing upon others evangelical dogma. The original meaning of the word *sacrifice* is "to make sacred," but we can make sacred without focusing only on sacrifice. We can sing, dance, study, and include all other sentient beings in our definition of holy. We can "imagine the divine," as poet Diane Ackerman writes here, "Like the sky, heaven begins / at one's feet. Look down. / When the here and now / becomes the there and then . . ." Ackerman was the first to respond to our call for submissions, and her poem has been a "true north" by which we have navigated our way through years of reading and choosing selections for *Face to Face*.

In our third section, "At One with the World," we hear women seeking and finding the divine in every particle of nature. Here psychologist and author Kim Chernin seeks spiritual regeneration on a kibbutz: "Every time I walked off the kibbutz, into the fields and hills that surrounded it, I responded to the landscape with a growing rapture, as if I were returning home after thousands of years of absence." And in "The Great Without," coeditor Linda Hogan concludes, "The cure for soul loss is in the mist of morning, the grass that grew a little through the night, the first warmth of sunlight, the waking human in a world infused with intelligence and spirit." Here, too, are nature writers Alison Hawthorne Deming and Jane Goodall finding epiphany in the company of bumblebees and chimpanzees.

The women in this collection have not constructed elaborate "kingdoms in heaven," or rules, or judgments and punishments for infidels. Perhaps because we have often been marginalized, outside religious power, we have found a more subtle and everyday path—a practice gathered together in this fourth section, "God in the Art of the Everyday." With our concerns of mothering and nurturing, we have a unique perspective on creation and the divine in daily life. Contributor Susan Biskeborn tries to answer her daughter's question about where a loved one has disappeared to after death: "Where she go? Under my napkin? . . . In sky? In trees?"

Molly Peacock is a poetic architect of a "soul house," which offers "A place to grow in, but not outgrow. / Not emptiness, but emptiedness. A source." Demetria Martinez finds that the daily contemplative art of writing fiction teaches her that "the writer who cannot love the color gray, who cannot embrace a world that is less than black and white, will not last long."

Ursula K. Le Guin has taken the *Tao Te Ching* to heart since she was a girl and finds it a book that "speaks to women. Lao Tzu feminized mysteries in a different way from anybody else. These are not 'feminine mysteries,' but he makes mystery itself a woman . . . And the most mystical passages in the book are the most feminine." After a dialogue with Le Guin about Le Guin's new rendition of this ancient text, coeditor Brenda Peterson rediscovers in Taoism echoes of her own childhood story of seeking spirit in water, "Shall We Gather at the River?"

Our final section is called "Practicing," and the writers here include in their worship both traditional and unorthodox visions. Buddhist Kate Wheeler takes her vows, and Georgiana Valoyce-Sanchez turns to her ancestors for divine guidance. Sharman Apt Russell muses upon the discipline of Quaker silence. Native Hawaiian poet Haunani-Kay Trask dances to the deity of the forest, Hi'iaka, Pele's sister.

Starhawk, with her scholarship on Wicca traditions and her visionary book *The Spiral Dance*, has reignited pagan practice and reverence for the heaven here on Earth. Like many indigenous traditions, paganism celebrates through ritual, dance, and traditional herbal medicines the healing power of connecting humans with our earthly home. Both traditions offer earthbound narratives, sacred geographies, and wise women. They revere the holy places of mountains, rivers, forest, plants, hearth, and kitchen table. A striking element in many indigenous, pagan, and priestess feminine traditions is the emphasis on joy and humor and the genius of the human body. Even sex is sacred, as contributor Deena Metzger shows in "Re-Vamping the World: On the Return of the Holy Prostitute." "If we become world reaching to the gods, then love is essentially a spiritual act that redeems the world," Metzger writes in this groundbreaking vision. "It is to commit oneself to eros, bonding, connection, when the world values thanatos, separation, detachment. The Holy Prostitute was Everywoman . . ."

In all three anthologies we have edited on women in the natural world, we have sought to bring to light often overlooked but important feminine knowledge. We collected this feminine gnosis in *Intimate Nature: The Bond Between Women and Animals*, and we gathered women's invaluable knowledge of plants in *The Sweet Breathing of Plants*. When we first conceived *Face to Face*, we wanted to know how women envision spirit. We imagined a new testament for a new century—stories with a feminine view. In this final collection, we see perhaps the most need of that feminine balance. Just as our stories of spirit can inspire and make us more whole, they can also separate, damn, and destroy us.

We bring this collection out in a post-9/11 world, a world discovering, as Arab-American poet Naomi Shihab Nye writes, that "it is only kindness that makes sense anymore." In our new century, patriarchal religions seem to be at war in a new and terrorizing way. As religions clash, it is not just crusaders and spiritual soldiers who are dying; it is our children, our future. We hope in this collection to make a bridge between traditions, add to a growing dialogue, and discover another way that is more about seeking divine wholeness than any victory in a holy war, that is more grounded in the beauty of this life than an afterlife, and that finds not judgment but one of the most beloved visions of any faith—acceptance. And recognition that we stand before spirit, just as we stand before one another, face to face.

LINDA HOGAN
BRENDA PETERSON

Heritage and Beyond

Around the Ka'ba and Over the Crick

Mohja Kahf

Over by the "crick" out back, scuffing the chain-link fence and dashing through a couple of neighbors' backyards was the shortcut to the bus stop when I was in the sixth grade at Van Buren Elementary School in the small farming town of Plainfield, Indiana. The "crick" was tiny but beautiful to us; blue-green dragonflies zigzagged over it and creepy "crawdads" crawled in the muddy bank. But as a Muslim in Plainfield, the chasm I traveled each day between school and home was wider than the little creek my brother and I hopped on the way to school . . .

Dogging the early years of our life in Plainfield, Indiana, was a lawsuit filed by the "Concerned Citizens of Hendricks County." Though most Plainfielders were decent folks who went about their own business, this ad hoc group was formed specifically to oust from its site the Islamic Society of North America (ISNA), the organization for which my father worked and for which we had moved to Plainfield.

Neighboring towns in our concerned citizens' county, such as Danville and Morrisville, were reputed to be Ku Klux Klan enclaves. We were reminded of this by the graffiti that regularly defaced ISNA property. Daughters of those pursuing the lawsuit would goad me in the girls' room about the progress of the case, and Klansmen's boys would boast to me about their vandalism . . .

When I was in junior high, one of those "Americans" who would brag about spray-painting "KKK" on the Islamic Society's placard was a gorgeous football player, and it gave me goose-bumps to be faced with him. In that heartbeat that lasts an eternity for a teenage girl, I would be entranced by his halo of blond hair and chiseled features. Then he'd open his mouth and say crude, hateful things right at me, and I realized that I wasn't even a girl to him, just an undifferentiated enemy. My religious community, for its part, expected me to see his being a non-Muslim male as the sole significant factor defining my interaction with him and preferred that I had no interaction with him at all. And I complied, except for brief moments when some other possibility seemed imaginable. Yet, these were the encounters that characterized this period of my life: Beauty overtaken by ugliness too quickly for it to operate as beauty should. My two worlds refused to meet . . .

The derision was especially sharp when it came to the way I dressed. After making *hajj*, the pilgrimage to Mecca to the Ka'ba, the holiest place on earth for Muslims, with my family during the seventh grade, I had decided to wear the head scarf associated with conventional Islamic notions of womanly propriety. Contemporary Muslim discourse calls this dress *hijab*. Choosing hijab helped junior-high-school-me marshal the resources of my family and faith community. In fact, my parents were so proud of me that I am still running into relatives in the Arab world who heard about my *hijab* . . .

"You're in America now," the be-jeaned girls and boys would jeer, flipping their Farrah Fawcett and Fonzie hair. "Whyn't you dress like everybody else?" "It's a free country!" I'd retort. With *hijab* as an alternative, I could reject their Barbie-and-Ken teenage conformity. The headcloth reminded me that even if no one in Plainfield connected with me, there were whole worlds of people, thousands of whom had thronged around me at the Ka'ba, with whom I did have a connection, with whom I was real and legitimate and belonged . . . With *hijab*, then, I shored up my identity—far too entirely. With supreme naïveté, I believed I could pin my self-formation upon this already overloaded bit of fabric. I suppose, given the circumstances, it worked: the scarf did its job; it helped me navigate through a sea wherein I could have broken down psychologically and capsized.

Years later, I met a beautiful person who, just by being who she is, has taught me volumes about being a human being, a friend, and a Muslim. An Arab-American like me—although from a very different type of family—she had grown up only a few dozen miles away from Plainfield. "Surely you visited the ISNA farm," I asked, delighted at the common ground we'd trodden, unbeknownst to each other.

"I went to look at books a few times," she said. "I always slunk out quickly, feeling uncomfortable."

"Why ever so?" I asked, completely surprised.

"I don't think they approved of the way I dressed or looked. They seemed to disapprove of the kind of Muslim I was," she explained.

Maybe it was because she did not wear the head scarf that the folks at the ISNA did not feel she was quite kosher—so to speak. Whatever was the cause, I began to see that every closed place has its shadows. My one-time haven could be, in its turn, a cold and intolerant place for certain others who were outside a carefully drawn circle. And it is easiest, I learned, to remain silent about the dark spots in one's own community—and one's self.

. . . In those days, I was a Muslim with a capital "M." As a young woman, I was far from questioning the structure of an us-versus-them opposition, even as I fought for an end to the harassment. Some ways of battling discrimination and bigotry can also stunt your own spiritual growth, block the imagination, and keep you at the level of parrying blows and living angry, exhausted, and defensive.

My family moved to New Jersey when I began the tenth grade. After physically leaving Plainfield, Indiana, I slowly began to leave it in other ways: emotional, intellectual, and spiritual. At Passaic Valley

High, in a student body almost entirely made up of second-generation Polish- or Italian-Americans, there was yet another lesson in store for me. I learned that being different was not so different after all . . .

"Hey, so do you also eat, like, *yabra'* 'n' shit?" Marlene says to me, snapping her gum as we change into gym sneakers. I start with delighted recognition when I hear her use the word for stuffed grape leaves, Syrian-style. I am also shocked at the casual cussing, and from a girl with Arab ancestry! "Americans," I always thought, were the ones who used profanity, not "us." Here in this New Jersey high school, I had my first encounter with Arab Christians, with children of interfaith marriages, and with new mixtures of identity that had not occurred to me. I would now have to rearrange all my mental charts and binary oppositions.

"*Yabra'* 'n' shit." How cool, how tough, how exquisitely an expression of both Arabness *and* Americanness, how totally Jersey. I could do this!—maybe. In reality, I was ill-prepared to explore friendships across cultural or religious boundaries, first dipping in a toe, then bounding back from the shoreline. Now that my social scene permitted new kinds of opportunities for friendships, it turned out that I had a poverty of personal resources for engaging "the Other," those outside the particular conservative Muslim identity which I then embraced. It was the nourishing "spring rain" of such friendships that would finally enable my stunted little soul to grow beyond the rigid dichotomies to which I held fast.

When I could allow myself to love, it would be friendship that would reveal human beauty—beauty that surely must be a reflection of the Divine. Maybe that is why, in the poetry of Islamic mysticism, one of the poet's code words for God is "The Friend." "Fundamentally, all loves relate and refer to the True Beloved," writes Muzzaffer Ozak in *The Unveiling of Love*. "However," he continues, "the manifestations appear variously. . . ."

Intellectually, I began to learn how to connect the jagged halves of my two worlds when I entered college. I went to a school with a long-standing commitment to the development of women's potential. There, in the form of feminist theory and civil-rights movement history, I learned that the individual is embedded in ideological structures, and the knowledge which comes from personal experience is not just an irrelevant, slightly shameful burden to be shed at the threshold of real, objective knowledge. In graduate school, I came back down from the deterministic extremes of this idea that the individual is defined solely by larger structures toward a more pragmatic medium ground.

I was not sure how to reconcile all this progressive thought, particularly the feminist part, with Islam as I knew it, but I decided to hang on to both sides, including the *hijab*, and let things work themselves out gradually. Insight would come, I felt, through intuition and experience, not through more theory. Or, to quote Ghazali, the twelfth-century Muslim who details his journey from traditional belief through the stages of skepticism, theology, philosophy, and finally veering toward mysticism, "It became clear to me that the last stage could not be reached by mere instruction, but only by transport, ecstasy, and the transformation of the moral being."

This kind of engaged self-transformation, I am embarrassed to admit, was a new frontier for me. You mean being "religious" is not merely a matter of conforming to massive rule books handed down by generations of legalistic scholars? I actually have to think about things like "manifesting the beauty Divine" in the here and now, not just follow a crime-and-punishment logic to please a Grand Inquisitor God? Years of imbibing a rather confident missionary stance made me wary of more easy talk of God. The beauty part I could understand, however: poetry, song, music, glorious Form. Yes, these are paths to another dimension; yes, I want to go to that planet.

Spiritually, what I have been experiencing since leaving Plainfield, and leaving and leaving, is a slow draining of silt, layer after layer of the sediment of racism, sexism, and prejudice—my own. Every time I think I have finished with the last layer I find another. I have glimmers that in doing so I am making room for some beautiful dimension of reality that has escaped me, even though the emptying out can be wrenching, especially on my relationships.

I wonder what it might be like to become a muslim with a small "m," turning toward the etymological root of the word: the giving over of one's self, surrendering to the Divine—as opposed to the social-religious community that currently owns the label of Muslim with a capital "M" and carries with it all the accumulated historical doctrines and assumptions about what being a Muslim should entail. The contemporary liberationist Farid Esack explores this question in his book *Qur'an, Liberation, and Pluralism*, showing how the Qur'an uses the terms "islam" and "muslim" in far more dynamic ways than traditional Muslim thinking allows. After all, there are no capital letters in Arabic, the language of the Qur'an. To seek the living manifestation of spiritual and ethical values themselves, regardless of the label they come under, is to discover unexpected kinship with persons from utterly different social and religious backgrounds. In this view, faith is no longer a matter of allegiance to a specific community or identity, but a ceaseless search for the beautiful ways to realize the human potential in every given age and place. "Every new encounter with ourselves and others, every deed that we do or refuse to do, is a step in our perpetual transformation," Esack says. There's that word again—transformation.

The spiritual path before me is still dim. All I know for certain is that it lies in the direction of love. Somewhere, a dragonfly, blue or green—both or neither—moults through metamorphosis after metamorphosis, preparing to swoop over a zigzaggy creek and into the whitehot flame of an unimaginable beauty.

FROM *Refuge*

Terry Tempest Williams

I n Mormon culture, that is one of the things you do know—
history and genealogy. I come from a family with deep roots in
the American West. When the expense of outfitting several
thousand immigrants to Utah was becoming too great for the
newly established church, leaders decided to furnish the pioneers
with small two-wheeled carts about the size of those used by apple
peddlers, which could be pulled by hand from Missouri to the Salt
Lake Valley. My ancestors were part of these original "handcart com-
panies" in the 1850s. With faith, they would endure. They came with
few provisions over the twelve-hundred-mile trail. It was a small sacrifice in the name of religious freedom. Almost one hundred and fifty
years later, we are still here.

I am the oldest child in our family, a daughter with three younger
brothers: Steve, Dan, and Hank.

My parents, John Henry Tempest III and Diane Dixon Tempest,
were married in the Mormon Temple in Salt Lake City on Septem-

ber 18, 1953. My husband, Brooke Williams, and I followed the same tradition and were married on June 2, 1975. I was nineteen years old.

Our extended family includes both maternal and paternal grandparents: Lettie Romney Dixon and Donald "Sanky" Dixon, Kathryn Blackett Tempest and John Henry Tempest, Jr.

Aunts, uncles, and cousins are many, extending familial ties all across the state of Utah. If I ever wonder who I am, I simply attend a Romney family reunion and find myself in the eyes of everyone I meet. It is comforting and disturbing, at once.

I have known five of my great-grandparents intimately. They tutored me in stories with a belief that lineage mattered. Genealogy is in our blood. As a people and as a family, we have a sense of history. And our history is tied to land.

• • •

I was raised to believe in a spirit world, that life exists before the earth and will continue to exist afterward, that each human being, bird, and bulrush, along with all other life forms, had a spirit life before it came to dwell physically on the earth. Each occupied an assigned sphere of influence, each has a place and a purpose.

It made sense to a child. And if the natural world was assigned spiritual values, then those days spent in wildness were sacred. We learned at an early age that God can be found wherever you are, especially outside. Family worship was not just relegated to Sunday in a chapel.

Our weekends were spent camped alongside a small stream in the Great Basin, in the Stansbury Mountains or Deep Creeks. My father would take the boys rabbit hunting while Mother and I would sit on a log in an aspen grove and talk. She would tell me stories of how when she was a girl she would paint red lips on the trunks of trees to practice kissing. Or how she would lie in her grandmother's lucerne patch and watch clouds.

"I have never known my full capacity for solitude," she would say.

"Solitude?" I asked.

"The gift of being alone. I can never get enough."

The men would return anxious for dinner. Mother would cook

over a green Coleman stove as Dad told stories from his childhood—
like the time his father took away his BB gun for a year because he
shot off the heads of every red tulip in his mother's garden, row after
row after row. He laughed. We laughed. And then it was time to bless
the food.

After supper, we would spread out our sleeping bags in a circle,
heads pointing to the center like a covey of quail, and watch the Great
Basin sky fill with stars. Our attachment to the land was our attachment to each other.

White Pelicans

LAKE LEVEL: 4209.09′

The Refuge is subdued, unusually quiet. The spring frenzy of
courtship and nesting is absent, because there is little food and habitat
available. Although the species count remains about the same, individual numbers are down. Way down. This afternoon, I watched a
white-faced ibis nest float alongside a drowned cottonwood tree.
Three eggs had been abandoned. I did not see the adults.

A colony-nesting bird survey has been initiated this spring by the
Utah Division of Wildlife Resources to monitor changes in population
and habitat use of selected species affected by the rising Great Salt
Lake.

The historical nesting grounds on the islands of Great Salt Lake
are gone, with the exception of a California gull colony on Antelope
Island and the white pelicans on Gunnison. This means colony
nesters are now dependent upon the vegetation surrounding the lake
for their livelihood.

Great blue herons, snowy egrets, cattle egrets, and double-crested
cormorants use trees, tall shrubs, or man-made structures for nesting.

Franklin gulls, black-crowned night herons, and white-faced
ibises nest in emergent vegetation such as bulrushes and cattails.

American avocets, black-necked stilts, and other shorebirds are
ground nesters who usually scrape together a few sticks around
clumps of low-lying vegetation such as salt grass and pickleweed.

Don Paul, waterfowl biologist for the Division of Wildlife Resources, anticipates that the white-faced ibis and Franklin gull populations will be the hardest hit by the flood.

"Look around and tell me how many stands of bulrush you see?" He waves his hand over the Refuge. "It's gone, and I suspect, so are they. We should have our data compiled by the end of the summer."

I turn around three hundred and sixty degrees: water as far as I can see. The echo of Lake Bonneville lapping against the mountains returns.

The birds of Bear River have been displaced; so have I.

• • •

Nothing is familiar to me any more. I just returned home from the hospital, having had a small cyst removed from my right breast. Second time. It was benign. But I suffered the uncertainty of not knowing for days. My scars portend my lineage. I look at Mother and I see myself. Is cancer my path, too?

As a child, I was aware that my grandmother, Lettie, had only one breast. It was not a shocking sight. It was her body. She loved to soak in steaming, hot baths, and I would sit beside the tub and read her my favorite fairy tales.

"One more," she would say, completely relaxed. "You read so well."

What I remember is my grandmother's beauty—her moist, translucent skin, the way her body responded to the slow squeeze of her sponge, which sent hot water trickling over her shoulders. And I loved how she smelled like lavender.

Seeing Mother's scar did not surprise me either. It was not radical like her mother's. Her skin was stretched smooth and taut across her chest, with the muscles intact.

"It is an inconvenience," Mother said. "That's all."

When I look in the mirror and Brooke stands behind me and kisses my neck, I whisper in his ear, "Hold my breasts."

Whistling Swan

LAKE LEVEL: 4208.35´

The snow continues to fall. Red apples cling to bare branches.

I just returned from Tamra Crocker Pulfer's funeral. It was a reunion of childhood friends and family. Our neighborhood sat on wooden benches row after row in the chapel. I sat next to Mother and wondered how much time we had left together.

• • •

Walking the wrackline of Great Salt Lake after a storm is quite different from walking along the seashore after high tide. There are no shells, no popping kelp or crabs. What remains is a bleached narrative of feathers, bones, occasional birds encrusted in salt and deep piles of brine among the scattered driftwood. There is little human debris among the remote beaches of Great Salt Lake, except for the shotgun shells that wash up after the duck-hunting season.

Yesterday, I walked along the north shore of Stansbury Island. Great Salt Lake mirrored the plumage of immature gulls as they skimmed its surface. It was cold and windy. Small waves hissed each time they broke on shore. Up ahead, I noticed a large, white mound a few feet from where the lake was breaking.

It was a dead swan. Its body lay contorted on the beach like an abandoned lover. I looked at the bird for a long time. There was no blood on its feathers, no sight of gunshot. Most likely, a late migrant from the north slapped silly by a ravenous Great Salt Lake. The swan may have drowned.

I knelt beside the bird, took off my deerskin gloves, and began smoothing feathers. Its body was still limp—the swan had not been dead long. I lifted both wings out from under its belly and spread them on the sand. Untangling the long neck which was wrapped around itself was more difficult, but finally I was able to straighten it, resting the swan's chin flat against the shore.

The small dark eyes had sunk behind the yellow lores. It was a whistling swan. I looked for two black stones, found them, and placed them over the eyes like coins. They held. And, using my own saliva as my mother and grandmother had done to wash my face, I washed the swan's black bill and feet until they shone like patent leather.

I have no idea of the amount of time that passed in the preparation of the swan. What I remember most is lying next to its body and imagining the great white bird in flight.

I imagined the great heart that propelled the bird forward day after day, night after night. Imagined the deep breaths taken as it lifted from the arctic tundra, the camaraderie within the flock. I imagined the stars seen and recognized on clear autumn nights as they navigated south. Imagined their silhouettes passing in front of the full face of the harvest moon. And I imagined the shimmering Great Salt Lake calling the swans down like a mother, the suddenness of the storm, the anguish of its separation.

And I tried to listen to the stillness of its body.

At dusk, I left the swan like a crucifix on the sand. I did not look back.

. . .

There is something unnerving about my solitary travels around the northern stretches of Great Salt Lake. I am never entirely at ease because I am aware of its will. Its mood can change in minutes. The heat alone reflecting off the salt is enough to drive me mad, but it is the glare that immobilizes me. Without sunglasses, I am blinded. My eyes quickly burn on Salt Well Flats. It occurs to me that I will return home with my green irises bleached white. If I return at all.

The understanding that I could die on the salt flats is no great epiphany. I could die anywhere. It's just that in the forsaken corners of Great Salt Lake there is no illusion of being safe. You stand in the throbbing silence of the Great Basin, exposed and alone. On these occasions, I keep tight reins on my imagination. The pearl-handled pistol I carry in my car lends me no protection. Only the land's mercy and a calm mind can save my soul. And it is here I find grace.

It's strange how deserts turn us into believers. I believe in walking in a landscape of mirages, because you learn humility. I believe in living in a land of little water because life is drawn together. And I believe in the gathering of bones as a testament to spirits that have moved on.

If the desert is holy, it is because it is a forgotten place that allows us to remember the sacred. Perhaps that is why every pilgrimage to the desert is a pilgrimage to the self. There is no place to hide, and so we are found.

In the severity of a salt desert, I am brought down to my knees by its beauty. My imagination is fired. My heart opens and my skin burns in the passion of these moments. I will have no other gods before me.

Wilderness courts our souls. When I sat in church throughout my growing years, I listened to teachings about Christ in the wilderness for forty days and forty nights, reclaiming his strength, where he was able to say to Satan, "Get thee hence." When I imagined Joseph Smith kneeling in a grove of trees as he received his vision to create a new religion, I believed their sojourns into nature were sacred. Are ours any less?

There is a Mormon scripture, from the Doctrine and Covenants section 88:44–47, that I carry with me:

> The earth rolls upon her wings, and the sun giveth
>   his light by day, and the moon giveth her light
>   by night, and the stars also give their light, as
>   they roll upon their wings in their glory, in the
>   midst of the power of God.
> Unto what shall I liken these kingdoms that ye may understand?
> Behold all these are kingdoms and any man who
>   hath seen any or the least of these hath seen God
>   moving in his majesty and power.

I pray to the birds.

I pray to the birds because I believe they will carry the messages of my heart upward. I pray to them because I believe in their existence, the way their songs begin and end each day—the invocations and benedictions of Earth. I pray to the birds because they remind me of what I love rather than what I fear. And at the end of my prayers, they teach me how to listen.

• • •

Dawn to dusk. I have spent the entire day with Mother. Lying next to her. Rubbing her back. Holding her fevered hand close to my face. Stroking her hair. Keeping ice on the back of her neck. She is so uncomfortable. We are trying to work with the pain.

Her jaw tightens. She cramps. And then she breathes.

I am talking her through a visualization, asking her to imagine what the pain looks like, what color it is, to lean into the sensation rather than resisting it. We breathe through the meditation together.

The light begins to deepen. It is sunset. I open the shutters, so Mother can see the clouds. I return to her bedside. She takes my hand and whispers, "Will you give me a blessing?"

In Mormon religion, formal blessings of healing are given by men through the Priesthood of God. Women have no outward authority. But within the secrecy of sisterhood we have always bestowed benisons upon our families.

Mother sits up. I lay my hands upon her head and in the privacy of women, we pray.

Yemaya

Flor Fernandez Barrios

C armen was our Afro-Cuban nanny. Her ancestors were slaves brought by the Spaniards to Cuba from Africa around 1800 to work on their sugar plantations and mills. Carmen lived with my grandparents for many years. I was told by my Grandfather José that when Carmen was young, maybe nineteen, she appeared one day at their door looking for work. My Grandmother Petra, who didn't believe in having maids, was hesitant at first to take the stranger into the family.

"*Señora*," Carmen said, with eyes that were pleading, "I have been knocking on doors all day long, and no one seems to need the working hands of this *negra*. Please give me a chance, I promise you'll be happy with my work."

"Look," Grandmother said, showing Carmen her strong and rough hands from her hard work in the house and the farm, "I have worked the land, I have cooked and taken care of all my children and husband without ever needing any maids in this house. My husband José thinks I'm a stubborn woman for not wanting any help, but I come

from a place where my own mother raised all of us kids, all on her own
and—"

"*Señora*," Carmen interrupted, "you have a good heart. You are
not like the other rich ladies in town. You work like a man in the fields
and like a *negra*, at home with your children."

"How do you know that?" Grandmother asked, somewhat perplexed by this young woman's knowledge of her life.

"This is a small town. People talk and they say what they see and
that's what they say about you, *Señora* Petra," Carmen said, lowering
her eyes, a little embarrassed by her disclosure. "Besides, *Señora*, your
hands are just like the hands of my mother," Carmen said, very wisely
stealing my grandmother's heart.

Carmen stayed with my grandparents, helping them with the
chores around the house. She was an excellent cook who delighted the
family with special recipes such as her *congri*, black beans and rice
cooked in coconut milk, or her famous *ropa vieja*, shredded beef in a
mild sauce of tomatoes, green peppers, garlic, onions, and other ingre-
dients that Carmen never revealed to anyone, not even to Grandmother Petra. She became best friends with my mother, who was just
a couple of years younger than her. When my mother married and I
was born, Carmen moved into our household and became part of my
family. She helped my mother take care of me, and later my brother.

My memories of Carmen are many. As a young child I remember
her putting me to sleep with her ancient, sweet, and loving lullabies,
arru ru mi niña, arru ru mi amor duermete pedazo de mi corazón, while
she held me in her arms, close to her voluptuous, dark goddess body.
It was like being embraced by the ocean, feeling the warm waves of
love and tenderness from her skin on my tiny, fragile body.

"*Niña*," she used to say, "you better go to sleep now, because if
you don't the moon is going to be upset, and she is not going to come
around tomorrow night with her silver rays. It will be very, very dark."

I remember going to sleep and thinking about the moon and her
powers. Yes, I thought of the moon as a woman. During the hot nights
of the summer, Carmen used to tell my brother and me stories about
the slaves that worked so hard on the sugar plantations, and how they
kept themselves happy by drumming and singing at night. She also

told us scary stories about ghosts and spirits that haunted old Spanish houses in the town where I grew up, and how when people go inside these houses they heard voices and sounds and they saw things being moved around by invisible hands.

"You are not supposed to disturb those spirits. People that go inside those houses end up suffering illness and terrible accidents," she said to us every time she told us the stories. "Like the man who went inside one of the houses, looking for old money buried in the ground. He found an old ceramic jar with many gold coins. He took them and a few months later he became very ill and the doctor in town was never able to diagnose his problem. He lost lots of weight and his skin turned yellow like the gold coins. He died slowly in great misery and pain. He died of ghost illness."

Carmen was very well known in our town for her healing powers and her capacity to be a medium. She was able to diagnose illnesses and prescribe herbs and remedies for those that sought her help. She was a *curandera*, or healer. Carmen had a special room in the back of our house where she practiced her ancient African Yoruba religion and medicine. I used to love going into Carmen's room when she was away, and exploring all the different magical plants that she kept for her practice. In one corner was an altar with her favorite saints—Saint Lazarus and Saint Barbara. For Saint Lazarus, she kept offerings of a large Cuban cigar and a little glass containing the best Cuban rum. For Saint Barbara, she kept a candle and a red apple. Every time I visited this sanctuary I felt an aura of protection and magic, as well as mystery, and sometimes I felt fear of the unknown powers Carmen professed to have.

My first experience with Carmen's practice as a medium was when I was seven years old. A woman from our neighborhood, Francisca, came to visit Carmen one morning. She had a look of worry on her face, and she was very pale and ill-looking to me. She was also coughing nonstop. My brother and I were playing on the patio, near the fountain across from Carmen's place, and I could see Francisca and Carmen engaged in what appeared to be a very secret conversation that immediately captured my attention. I heard Carmen say something like "The spirits will help us find out." That was more than enough for me to leave my game of army soldiers to figure out what was going on between the two women. Victor was disappointed and wanted to hide with me, but I sent him away with the promise that I would play with him later.

"The spirits," I said to myself, and quickly proceeded to a spot close to the window on the opposite side of the wall where Carmen had her altar. From my hideout behind the gardenia tree I could see inside. I was careful not to make any noise. My heart was beating very fast in anticipation and in fear that Carmen could see me. She had warned me many times not to go around this area when she was doing her healing work with friends or other people, but this time my curiosity was stronger than my fear. I wanted to find out once and for all what she was doing in there with the so-called "spirits."

I could see Carmen seated in front of the altar, and Francisca seated next to her. Carmen took one of the cigars from the altar and, after lighting it, proceeded to puff smoke everywhere around the room and over Francisca. Then she sat across from Francisca, and closing her eyes, softly sang words I couldn't understand—they were from another language. Soon Carmen began to sing louder and call out names and her face began to be transformed, as well as her voice. She looked and sounded angry—her frowning forehead, and mouth twisted with lips firmly pressed against each other. She got up from her chair and began to move around the room, again puffing on her big cigar and blowing smoke around, especially over Francisca. I couldn't figure out what was going on. I couldn't recognize any of the words. Carmen's voice became softer at this point, as she passed her dark hands over Francisca's body without touching her skin. It was as if she were cleansing something in the air and pulling some invisible thing from the woman's body.

At this point, Carmen's body started shaking and her words grew unintelligible. Words turned into deep sounds, like the roar of some wild beast. Carmen was sweating. She dropped to the floor, her body shaking all over.

At the same moment that Carmen fell, Francisca began to cry intensely, almost hysterically.

"Oh my God!" I whispered to myself, and I thought, What should

I do, should I call my mother and get help? I was ready to run to the house when I heard a voice inside myself saying, "Stop and be quiet." I immediately began to feel calm, very calm and peaceful. It was as if a warm current of energy were moving like a wave from the bottom of my spine all the way to the top of my head. Almost as if Carmen's big arms were holding me and rocking me to sleep. At that moment I realized that all the time I had been there by the window, Carmen knew it. She knew it! Why didn't she send me away like other times? Having no answer, I stood there with my eyes fixed on the two women inside the room. Now things were quiet; Francisca was no longer crying or screaming. She was calmly seated in her chair, and Carmen was getting up from the floor with a soft smile on her dark, round face. When Carmen was up on her feet, the two women looked at each other, and then embraced in silence for a few seconds.

"*¿Dime Francisca, como te sientes?*" asked Carmen, looking into the eyes of her friend.

"Ay, *negra*, it was hard. I thought that I was going to die, but now I feel better, as if the whole world has been lifted from my shoulders," said Francisca, taking Carmen's hands into her own.

Carmen went to the altar and quietly picked some of the dry herbs she had placed inside a clay pot and gave some in a little bundle to Francisca with instructions on how to prepare tea with it. "*Mira*, Francisca, these are very healing herbs for your problem. Make a tea and drink it in the morning and at night before going to bed, and come back and see me in a couple of days."

Francisca thanked Carmen and left the room. I could see that she was no longer pale and she was moving more energetically than when she arrived. Then I saw Carmen coming toward my window. She stood there on the other side of the wall with her hands resting on her wide hips, looking right out at me. For a second I thought I was going to faint from fear. I was expecting the worst.

"Teresa," Carmen called me, "come inside, quick."

I thought about running away, but I knew I would have to face her sooner or later. As I walked slowly to the door, I saw that Victor was still gone, so it was just me and Carmen. I could feel my legs shaking and my heart racing faster and faster with every step I took.

"Teresa, what were you doing spying on this *negra* from that window?"

"I'm sorry, Carmen," I said in a very low voice. "I'll never do it again, I promise. I was just trying—" And before I could finish Carmen interrupted me.

"You are just a very curious child," she said, smiling. I was surprised she wasn't angry with me. "Come sit down, child."

"Aren't you mad at me, Carmen?"

"No, I am not, but I want to warn you that if I ever catch you again spying on me I will have to tell your mama, so she can decide how to punish you."

"No, please Carmen, don't tell Mami," I begged, knowing already she was not going to do anything. Carmen adored me and she had a heart the size of Cuba.

"*Mira*, Teresa, I want to say something to you. What you saw today is nothing to play with. These things I do are very sacred. You never want to upset the spirits that come to help me do my work with people. They don't like to be disturbed or annoyed in any way," Carmen said seriously, without taking her dark eyes off me.

"What would happen if they got upset? Who are they anyway?"

"They will come to your room at night and pull your toes when you're asleep. They will hide your toys and play tricks on you."

"Who are these spirits, Carmen?"

"They are ancient ones who have already passed on into the realm of the dead. They are good spirits who continue helping us on this earth when, and only when, we need them."

"What was happening to you when you had your eyes closed and you were talking some strange language and making scary sounds?"

Carmen shifted in her chair, as if she was beginning to get impatient with my questions. "Teresa, when I close my eyes in front of my altar, it is like when you white people go to church and pray to your favorite saints. I'm asking the spirits for help. They come and talk to me."

"How do they talk to you?"

"Just imagine my body being like a drum or a guitar. When they come, they play with my vocal cords, making the sounds I need to hear, or sometimes they even talk to the person I'm helping, like in the case of Francisca. That is how they communicate with me."

"How do you know when the spirits come?"

"You want to know everything, don't you?" Carmen said, smiling at me and patting me on the head. "Most of the time it's just a feeling. When they enter the room, I feel like a cool breeze is coming from the ocean. Other times, the vibrations of their essence are so strong that my body shakes. Occasionally, I can see their image. They may take the human form they had before they died."

Carmen learned much of what she knew from both her mother and her grandmother, who learned from their own people, *Africanos*, who brought to Cuba their spirituality and religion.

"My people," Carmen said, "were strong and wise. They found ways to disguise their spirits or Yoruba deities by giving them names from the Catholic Church. That way, they were able to continue practicing their rituals."

I thought about the way Cubans call the name of Saint Barbara after seeing lightning in the sky during a storm. She is Shango, the main *orisha* of fire, lightning, and thunder. Carmen taught me about other saints and corresponding *orishas* such as: Oshun, equivalent to La Virgen de la Caridad del Cobre; Yemaya, to the Lady of Regla; Babalue, to our healing Saint Lazarus.

A few days after my experience with Carmen in her healing room, she invited me to go to a *Bembe* with her. A day before the *Bembe*, Carmen called me into the kitchen, where she was peeling plantains to make *tachinos* for lunch. The plantains are sliced, fried in hot oil till soft, then allowed to cool down so they can be pressed in between brown paper to form a kind of flat, round medallion shape, and then are thrown back in the frying pan until golden brown. The plantains are crunchy with somewhat of a sweet taste. Cubans eat *tachinos* plain or with black beans and rice.

Carmen was, as usual, having a good time by herself, singing along with the songs on the radio and dancing around as she picked up pots and pans from the cabinets. Carmen's hips were like ocean waves coming and going, or like the palm trees swaying to the gentle wind with softness and beauty.

"Sit down, *niña*," Carmen said as she handed me a knife. "Help me peel these plantains while we talk." She turned off the radio and sat next to me. "First of all, I want you to promise me to behave. I don't want you to be wandering off and disappearing from my sight," she said as she poked me on my right shoulder with her index finger.

"I promise, Carmen."

"This *Bembe* is to celebrate one of Rufino's children's birthday, his *santo*. What you're going to see is people drumming and dancing for the saints or *orishas*. I'm telling you this now, so you won't be asking all kinds of questions in the middle of everything." She paused and got up to check the rice she was cooking on the stove.

"Now let me tell you about the drums. These drums are used to call the *orishas* to come down and to inhabit the dancers' bodies. In this dance something very special happens, the *orishas* inside us come out to dance and a union of the human and the Divine takes place. This brings healing for the group." Carmen paused. She looked at me straight in the eye and proceeded in a very solemn tone. "You must not talk to anyone about this *Bembe*. The CDR has given Rufino permission to have a simple birthday celebration. Nothing about a *Bembe*, so you better seal your mouth, *niña*, otherwise we all end up behind bars."

"Why, Carmen? What's wrong with having a *Bembe*?" I asked.

"*Mira, mija.* That *barbudo* doesn't want any kind of religion in this country," she said, referring to Fidel Castro and to his nasty beard. "*Bembe* is part of the Afro-Cuban religion. *Ese desgraciado*, he has declared," Carmen said slowly, emphasizing the word, "that religion causes antirevolutionary attitudes among the people. So we are back to the times of slavery. Once more in the history of this country, we have to keep our deities well disguised."

I was very excited when Saturday finally arrived and Carmen and I walked down the street toward the outskirts of town. Rufino and his family lived in a modest white brick house, surrounded by palm, orange, avocado, lemon, and plantain trees. There was an atmosphere of celebration in the house. Rufino and his wife Caridad greeted us at the door. Several friends of Carmen had already arrived and were talking about the *fiesta* and expressing their hope and desire that the *orishas* would descend, and that the *milicianos* would stay away from that part of town.

Rufino invited everybody onto the patio, where some drummers were already tuning their drums. I was fascinated by the beauty of these drums, their differences in sizes and shapes and the smoothness of the wood and the skins. I was wishing deep inside that I could play them. Carmen said, reading my mind, "These drums are very special. It takes many years of training to play them. Each drum has a function. See that big drum there? That's the mother drum."

I walked to the mother drum, softly touching the stretched hide with my hands.

"Mother drum," Carmen continued, "does all the talking while the other, smaller drums keep the basic rhythms."

The drummer sitting behind the mother drum, a toothless black man with white hair, maybe fifty years old, smiled at me. "I'll let you play later," he said, and made a signal to the other two men. Carmen pulled me away from the drums to another side of the patio.

Soon, just as she said, the mother drum began to talk, followed by the other two drums, penetrating and loud. Carmen lowered her mouth to my ear and whispered, "The drums are asking Elegua to open the path for us. Elegua is the messenger, the Lord of the Roads, the gatekeeper. It is important to call Elegua first, otherwise he may get upset and not open the doors to the *orishas*."

The drums continued playing, calling the different *orishas* with changing rhythms, or toques, according to the saint being called. In the midst of all the pounding sounds and loud voices, Carmen tried hard to let me know what was going on.

"Now they're calling Ogun, the warrior of iron, the hunter," and she continued naming each one of them for me as the drums changed. "Obatala, the *orisha* of calm and clarity; Oshun, the goddess of the rivers; Babalue, Saint Lazarus the healer; Yemaya, the goddess of the sea."

People were moving their feet, hips, and shoulders rhythmically. Finally, Shango, the king of thunder, was called and some of the participants started to dance frenetically, as if they had been struck by lightning. They were jerking their bodies and throwing their arms into the air. Some were jumping and others were rolling on the ground. Rufino was shaking a rattle and chanting in a deep voice words I didn't understand. Carmen explained to me that he was greeting the *orishas* in the ancient Yoruba language. Several members of the crowd joined him. By then, the group of dancers were very excited and deeply involved in their dances, which are supposed to be an impersonation of the *orishas*.

An older black man moved across the patio as Ogun, pretending to be hunting in the forest. Next to him, Oshun moved softly in a sensuous dance of love. By her side was Yemaya, the *orisha* of the sea, with undulating hips that were inviting and provocative. I was fascinated by Yemaya's movements. I wanted to go and dance with her. I asked Carmen if I could and she said it was okay, so I moved shyly into the crowd. At first, I was very conscious of the way I was dancing, but slowly all my fears and self-awareness disappeared and I found myself right next to Yemaya and Oshun.

The more I danced the more I felt possessed by a deep wave of energy carrying me to a place in my imagination, somewhere by the ocean. My body was floating in the clear, warm waters of the Caribbean. There was no fear at all. The sea was like a safe womb, where I could relax and move effortlessly. "I am water, I am water," I heard my voice repeating. I'm a big wave crushing the shore in the winter, I thought. I am the calm surf caressing the coastline in the summer. In my belly, all kinds of colorful tropical fish were swimming and marine plants were growing.

In the midst of all the drums, I heard the voice of Yemaya singing to me, and she was rocking me in her watery arms. She was so beautiful in her white and blue cotton dress decorated with shells. Yemaya was singing ancient songs in the same Yoruba language Rufino had spoken earlier. I imagined Yemaya dancing in the waters with her body, radiating a rainbow of colors. She was dancing in the waters and laughing. I heard her say to me: "It is not magic! It is dancing with life, it is living . . . knowing death, it is walking the path of a woman." She smiled at me, and then continued. "Soon, you'll be a woman and you must learn the ways of the waters." She paused. I saw her pulling out one of the shells from her dress, a tiny conch shell that she handed to me.

"I'll tell you a story," she said. "Once there was a woman who forgot her path. She got tangled in the old pain of so many years and of so many generations. The woman became old and her face filled with wrinkles. She went to sit by the ocean, where she told her story over and over, but no one listened. With time, tiredness occupied the woman's mind and heart and her dark hair turned to salt and her lips were sealed by the cold wind of the winter.

"Then . . . one day, a song was heard coming from the sea. People ran to the shore trying to find who was playing the music. To their surprise, a beautiful woman emerged from the water. She was young, with dark long hair and clear eyes. Her wet skin was brown like the earth and she wore a dress made from silky silver threads from the moon. The woman spoke to the people: 'I bring new dreams and songs, I bring new dreams and songs . . .' "

The woman's voice was echoing in my mind when I finally opened my eyes. I found myself in a corner of the patio, still dancing to the beat of the drums. There were people all around me moving and singing to the *orishas*. I was confused by my experience with Yemaya. Did I fall asleep? What happened? All I could remember was wanting to dance and then . . . Nothing made sense. I ran away from the crowd and went inside the house. There by the altar was Carmen lighting some tall white and blue candles. My first impulse was to go and talk to her, but then, as I looked into the flame of the candle, I saw Yemaya dancing in the waters again. She said, "This is between you and me. It is your dream and not Carmen's."

As Carmen and I walked home that evening, we were quiet. I could feel that somehow Carmen knew about my experience, but she also knew how important it was for her not to ask me any questions. I figured it was going to take me a very long time, if ever, to understand my encounter with Yemaya.

Wonder Voyages

Barbara Sjoholm

O nly a narrow channel separates the small island of Iona from the Isle of Mull in the Inner Hebrides. From the ferry dock at Fionnphort on Mull, I could see the whole shape of Iona across the water. The slant of afternoon light made it look devoid of greenery; it seemed all rock—burnt ocher and old rose—less like an inhabited island than a stepping-stone to a farther place. It seemed to rise from the grape-gold sea like the first in a string of western paradise isles the medieval Irish were so enamored of: the Island of the Little Cat, the Island of the Stone Door, the Island of Women, the Blessed Isle. We waiting passengers could have been monks here at the edge of the Hebrides—monks in Gore-Tex habits, true, but still, like pilgrims long ago, in search of something across the water.

I, too, was searching. I was on the trail of the spiritual voyagers whose stories were found in old tales and religious legends from around the Irish and Hebridean seas. In Cornwall the year before, in a pamphlet about Cornish saints, I'd come across the story of St. Ia. The daughter of a Munster chieftain, St. Ia missed the ship in Ireland that was to take her and her fellow missionaries over the Irish Sea to pagan England. As she stood on the shore, distraught, she spied a giant leaf floating by and stepped into it, whereupon it turned into a boat and carried her to the west of Cornwall. She came ashore at St. Ives, which is named for her.

At first I thought this tale of spiritual seafaring was a singular oddity, but in my reading, I began to come across more references to saints and anchoresses who sailed, drifted, and rowed across the northern seas. A medieval life of the sixth-century saint Budoc tells how his mother, Azenor, was placed in a cask on the Breton coast by her enemies. Adrift for many months, she gave birth to Budoc at sea and eventually washed up with him on Irish shores. He was educated there before setting off as a missionary to Cornwall, where he founded a church near Falmouth, St. Budock. He eventually made his way back to Brittany (on a floating stone) and ended up bishop of Dol.

Like Azenor, many of the female votaries in medieval writings were accidental tourists. The legend of St. Sunniva, which would reappear in my northward travels, exemplified this martyred drift. Sunniva was the daughter of an Irish king, who, rather than surrender her virtue to a Viking chief, set off with her retinue in three ships, none of which had oars, sails, or rudders. It wasn't just the urgency of her escape that made her forgo such navigational trappings; no, Sunniva elected to place her trust in God, who let her cruise on the high seas all the way to the Norwegian coast. Sunniva and her companions came ashore on the island of Selje, but even there, their trials were not over. More Vikings threatened them and they hid in a cave, which was promptly buried in a landslide.

There are charming illustrations in medieval manuscripts that show little tonsured monks setting off in their saucer-shaped boats for new worlds. "Wonder voyages" these travels were called. The monks of those days, wrote one seventeenth-century author, seemed "born under a traveling planet." What of the nuns and holy women who were also born under a traveling planet? There seemed no better place to ask this question than the tiny island of Iona in the Inner Hebrides. Fifteen hundred years ago, St. Columba had left Ireland seeking the "white martyrdom" of exile in order to found a monastery. Unlike more ascetic Christian monastics who fled temptation and searched out barren isles in the midst of the ocean's solitude to pray and fast, St. Columba meant to create a community in Iona. He succeeded so well that Iona became one of the most important Christian centers in the Celtic world. Before the Vikings began the raids that would eventually destroy the abbey and force many of the monks back to Ireland, Iona was so busy with pilgrims that, at one time, the resident monks limited visitors to high clergy and kings and at other times instituted rules that visits could last no longer than three days and three nights.

St. Columba's vision of community is still alive; many of my companions waiting for the ferry were a Birkenstockish set, most likely connected with the Iona Community, a progressive Protestant movement that began as an experiment within the Church of Scotland and now includes a worldwide congregation devoted to service. The Iona Community, with its yearlong program of retreats and conferences, has been greatly responsible for making Iona a spiritual stop for pilgrims again.

Our ferry set off for the fifteen-minute crossing. The channel water became lighter, more aqua; we created lace as we cut through the current. The island grew greener but retained its gilding. It was a lambent light that glided over the few buildings and the pastures. The abbey seemed lit from within. The Reverend MacLeod had begun its rebuilding in 1938. He invited young ministers to come and reconstruct the thirteenth-century ruins of the Benedictine monastery, which had itself been constructed on the site of St. Columba's first abbey. I stood at the railing and took in the vision of bare-shouldered Iona sunning herself in a gold-glanced sea, but even as I watched, a mist came up and hid the sun. By the time we'd docked and I'd put on my pack and set off on foot for the hotel, the gilded light had waned.

. . .

Agatha had come to Iona for "spiritual refreshment," as she did every year from her home in the north of England. A widow with a smooth dark bouffant and the steely blue eyes of a retired schoolmistress, she had been seated across from me at the hotel's restaurant. Most visitors to Iona are day-trippers on bus tours and there are few hotels and restaurants. This hotel provided breakfast and dinner as part of the price and reserved the right to seat single people together.

Agatha showed the opaque, persistent politeness that had often unnerved me with British women of her class. "Spiritual refreshment" seemed an odd phrase coming from her, but it was uttered in such crisp tones that it lost any New Age fuzziness it might have had. "The first thing you'll want to do is attend the abbey service tonight at nine. It's very informal, no need to dress"—she gave a glance at my slacks and no-iron shirt, the best I had with me on this trip—"and tomorrow you'll of course want to take the walking tour of the island. They go every Wednesday and it lasts all day. It's an *an toras*, the Gaelic for a journey along a set route, with rituals at every stop."

I'd arranged my trip to Iona precisely so that I could go on the Wednesday walk, but hearing Agatha describe it, I wondered if I'd be up to spending the whole day with others. Furtively, my eyes sought the other tables around the room. Other strangers had been placed together; they seemed to be having a delightful time getting to know each other. Next to us, two men, one with an Australian accent, the other Indian, were telling each other animated stories of their travels. Why couldn't I sit with them?

Agatha was not a full-fledged member of the Iona Community but a longtime supporter. She spoke of her work with the elderly in her Anglican church at home while we were served a healthy if not particularly adventurous meal.

She asked me what church I went to. I stumbled a little as I confessed, "I grew up a Christian Scientist, but now I'm a Buddhist—sort of a Buddhist . . ."

"Many Eastern believers come to Iona, too," she reassured me. "The community is nothing if not ecumenical." She paused over her vegetarian lasagna, and her expression softened. "Are you on a spiritual search, dear?"

I probably was, but the expression horrified me. "No," I said. "I'm writing a book, a travel book about women and the sea." I told her about St. Ia and about Azenor, imprisoned in the cask, and about St. Ursula, who set out with eleven thousand virgin companions in eleven ships. There were nunneries and hermitages all through the Hebrides, I told her. "On the Monach Isles off North Uist was a nunnery with strong connections to Iona. I've read that the nuns who lived there were excellent rowers; they used to take large boats across the Sound of Monach to North Uist to collect peat for fuel. Right here on Iona are the ruins of a nunnery."

Agatha listened without speaking. "It sounds to me," she said, "that it *is* a bit of a spiritual quest." She got up without having dessert, pulling her cardigan close around her thin, straight shoulders. "Shall I see you at the service later?"

"Maybe." I thought that I should go up to my room and meditate at least, but I was so tired that, shortly after lying down upstairs to read, I fell asleep. After an hour or two I woke up, still disoriented from jet lag and the work of getting to Iona. So far, whatever I'd hoped to find on this island wasn't visible; the community almost felt claustrophobic—too neat, too precious, a tidy spiritual reconstruction for contemporary seekers who still wanted their comforts. I wandered outside. The sky was pale violet. Venus had risen. It wasn't the fault of Iona that I felt so out of step; it was the unsettled state of my own faith. Agatha's innocent questions about my religious beliefs troubled me.

The church I'd grown up in, Christian Science, was fiercely religious but hardly traditionally Christian. A nineteenth-century zealot, Mary Baker Eddy, was our leader; Jesus was a healer, not a martyr on the cross, and God was our Father-Mother, neither vengeful nor stern, but a kindly presence. The earth and all of us who lived here were made in God's image and it was a perfect world and we were the perfect children of God; there was no evil, sickness, or death. My grandparents had made their living as practitioners—healers—in Battle Creek, Michigan. My mother, having been brought up in the church, was even more determined in her loyalty to Mrs. Eddy's dogmatism than her parents. When she discovered a lump in her breast, she suffered a crisis of faith so severe it sent her into mental illness. After she died two years later, my father took my brother and me out of the

Christian Science Sunday school and tried to make us Lutherans. I'd lost interest in spirituality completely until seven or eight years ago when I began to write a memoir about my childhood religion. It was then that I began to meditate and to explore Buddhism, mostly of the Tibetan variety.

One of the things that most appealed to me about Buddhism initially was its essential dictum, the first noble truth: *Life is suffering.* It was a healthy change from Mrs. Eddy's rule that suffering did not exist; and given what I'd experienced growing up, it was healing to recognize that pain and death touched all of us, and were not to be feared but accepted. Yet even though I began to think of myself as a Buddhist, I found I was still profoundly influenced by my Judeo-Christian tradition. Tibetan ritual and worship—indeed, the very iconography of the East—seemed to leave me cold. Statues of the Buddha, before whom my fellow meditators bowed and prayed, stirred nothing in me. When I traveled in Italy, however, I found myself one day in Padua, weeping at Giotto's paintings of the Crucifixion and Resurrection. The overtone chanting of Tibetan monks I found dull, even a little annoying, while Gregorian chant sent my spirits upwards. The Book of Isaiah was dearer to me than the Diamond Sutra. I hadn't known I had these preferences, perhaps these prejudices, until some years after I took up with the dharma, when I began to realize that temples and Tibetan monasteries were fine, but I felt more myself, more spiritually alive, in a cathedral.

Just choose a path. Don't be so picky, I kept telling myself. Go to church if you want, but keep up the sitting every day. It will get clearer what you're doing. Yet Christian Science had left its peculiar mark. Eastern in its insistence on the unreality of the physical world; pragmatically American in its no-nonsense emphasis on results; feminist, authoritarian, austere, and gentle, it seemed to have abandoned me between East and West, comfortable nowhere. I'd gone only so far with Buddhism, then had seemed to lose interest, though I still meditated and often thought of Pema Chödrön's teachings on compassion when I was impatient or irate. The few times I'd gone to a church service over the years, I'd been bored, resistant to the often hectoring tone of the sermon. Yet I had to acknowledge that I'd been a deeply religious child and was religious still, unbelieving often, but always yearning and invariably curious about manifestations of the spirit, whether in church, in myth, or in the starry universe above.

• • •

Bells called me to the abbey service at nine. I sat expectantly, hoping for absolution for having been wanting in spirit so much of the day. I was ready to try to be part of the community here for an evening. The abbey church filled with women in long dresses and Birkenstocks, with men in beards and boots. A young woman with a waterfall of black hair appeared at a podium, took the microphone, and in a Dutch accent began explaining what was in store this evening. A special service for healing, she said. Her voice was firm, but the podium was to the side and she looked away from the congregation as she spoke. The desire for connection I'd brought to this event began to leak away. My little chair felt hard. The woman next to me smelled of depression, while on the other side a man beat time, more or less correctly, to the hymns with his foot. His wife looked annoyed and tugged at his arm. I didn't know the songs or prayers. I liked to hear the King James version in a stone church like this, especially the psalms. I would have settled for an ordinary Church of Scotland service. But there was none of that here. Only some flat-footed prayers and songs that called for the congregation to respond. A group of women of all ages began to circle and sway behind the podium; their arms flailed as they danced and shuffled forward and back. A flute warbled unconvincingly.

It was a user-friendly service, as remote from medieval pageantry as it could be. Now those who wished to invite healing were asked to come forward and kneel, and place their hands on each other's shoulders. Agatha made her way down to the front, regimental shoulders shuddering a little from emotion. Was she ill, was she in great sorrow? Why hadn't I given her a chance? Why hadn't I opened up to her? There was some weeping, of a restrained sort, and much hugging. It was obvious that the congregation was quite moved by all this, and I felt churlish in refusing to join in, much less to soar, to ask in such a public way for healing. If there had only been a choral group, a soprano allowing her voice to echo through the vaulted abbey. What should religious ceremony consist of? I slipped out while the healing was still in progress and made my way back to the ruins of the nunnery. The smell of earth, with a delicate hint of sea salt in it, reassured me slightly. Spirit was still alive here, my spirit, too.

It was dark now, more indigo than pitch, but stars were visible, bright as foam in the celestial ocean. I began to think of a legend I'd discovered recently, the story of St. Ursula and her eleven thousand virgin companions. Like St. Brendan the Navigator, who made several wonder voyages through the Hebrides and perhaps as far north as Iceland, Ursula's legend began in the tenth century, reaching its greatest popularity in the fifteenth, when Memling in Bruges and Carpaccio in Venice painted their tremendous cycles of her life and martyrdom. According to this legend, St. Ursula was a Christian princess who was asked in marriage by a king's son who followed the old religion. As she didn't want to marry a pagan, she requested three years to prepare for the marriage, hoping perhaps he would change his mind or convert in the meantime. She set off in a ship with a thousand servant women, and each of her ten handmaids also had a ship with a thousand servant women. "Ursula sailed away with them on the blue seas in eleven elegantly furnished galleys. For three years they went thus merrily sailing," writes Sabine Baring-Gould in volume twelve of his sixteen-volume *Lives of the Saints*. Here we lose track of Ursula, learning only that she "taught herself the seaman's art" and was "cast on barbarous shores." Where did she go and what did she learn of the seaman's art? Was it to steer into the wind, shape a course, navigate by the stars, dance a hornpipe?

The rich vermilion- and jade-tinted ocher scenes in Carpaccio's paintings are long on the pageantry of ships but short on details of Ursula's life as sea-roving fiancée. Most of the focus is on her martyrdom, for when her ship was blown into the mouth of the Rhine, she went to Cologne, where she and all her women companions were killed by Huns. The painting in the cycle I like best shows Ursula sleeping neatly alone in a four-poster bed with a hand cupped to her ear. An angel stands at the entrance of her room, and at the foot of the bed, on the floor, is a small dog. The joy of the painting is in the details: the pair of green slippers by the bed, an open book on a table, two feathery potted plants in a window. The women in Memling's paintings are more pearlike and severe. In one, Ursula stands larger than life with her cloak open surrounding and protecting some of the virgin companions who will shortly be martyred with her. She looks like a pregnant whippet with a double litter of puppies.

Contemporary historians trace the legend of St. Ursula to the fact of a fifth-century martyrdom that took on the quality of hagiographic hyperbole when the number eleven was incorrectly written down as eleven thousand. There had been a massacre of Christians in Cologne by Huns. Bones had been found. The massacre story, the bones, and the transposition of a Roman numeral or two made for one of the more fraudulent stories of an age much given to exaggeration. St. Ursula was removed from the approved list of Catholic saints some time ago.

But other scholars have suggested a different origin for the worship of Ursula. Ursula, they suggest, is a Christianized form of the Saxon goddess Ursel, whose name is associated with the she-bear. It is the title of Artemis Calliste, who, as Ursa Major, ruled all the stars until she was ousted by Zeus. Ursel's most important shrine was in Cologne, and as the city became Christianized, a new story was invoked to explain Ursel's popularity, a story more in line with women's lesser role in the scheme of the universe. Sabine Baring-Gould tells us that the Teutons worshipped Isis in the form of a ship that was carried in her honor through the countryside. Gradually guilds grew up in the Middle Ages called "The Skiffs of St. Ursula." Isis was called Urschel or Hörsel by the Teutons, Freya by the Norse. Baring-Gould writes, "The goddess Hörsel was, in fact, the moon deity, gliding in her silver skiff over the blue sea of the sky, accompanied by her train of stars." In this version of Ursula as a great goddess, a she-bear, she is a moon deity and her eleven thousand companions are her children, or stars.

• • •

I grew cold and eventually found my way back to the abbey. The congregation had vanished, leaving only a few of us in solitude. I sat in the pew, cozy in my sweater and the silence, and noticed I felt happier than I had all day. I often had that sense in a church, some emotional repose, some ease of mind and spirit. When Bachelard asked himself to name the chief benefit of a house to a human being, he answered, "The house shelters daydreaming, the house protects the dreamer, the house allows us to dream in peace."

The corollary, that a church might shelter us as we dreamed of God, was not necessarily an original thought (the builders of Chartres and the Cistercian monasteries understood it well), but for the first time, here in Iona's ancient abbey, it didn't seem so odd to me to acknowledge the particular pleasure I took in simply sitting inside a church. I might not think of God, exactly; I might not pray, do penance, or participate in the rituals (preferring, in fact, no rituals to be in process), but I felt deeply at home, in harmony with the universe. A church was an abode for my soul; it housed me while my spirit dreamed.

This line of thought, that there was a value in spiritual reverie, was hardly what I'd been trying to practice as a homeschooled Buddhist, where the primary lesson of meditation is to learn to quiet one's mind, to free it from obsessive desires, useless imaginings, distractions of all sorts. Yet reveries and daydreams had been, since childhood, an immense source of nourishment and joy. I liked to be where I was not, to let my mind drift, to be inattentive in my walks, to be physically unpresent in the service of a roaming imagination. Buddhism had taught me much about mindfulness and letting go of attachments and expectations, but I realized now, as I sat in the pew watching the candles flicker in front of the altar, that I'd never been entirely convinced that suffering and longing were the natural result of an undisciplined mind and must be chastised and controlled. Indeed, I associated my daydreams with amplitude and harmony, a voluptuous contentment. In spite of books, classes, and sitting practice, the admirable tenets of Buddhism hadn't quite penetrated. I was hardly a Christian, either, in spite of finding solace in certain passages in the Bible, in spite of sobbing at Giotto's touching imagery of pain and resurrection. I had no faith; perhaps I didn't want any. I didn't believe in hell or salvation, confession or Communion. "I don't believe. I *know*," said Jung. But I was content not to know, simply to sit in the interior of a sacred place, a perpetual church-sitter, lost in reverie.

One by one the others slipped out, leaving me alone in the church, with a surprising response to Agatha's question of what church I went to. I went to all churches, all temples, all sacred spaces. I came and sat and listened and walked on. Why call myself anything except a pilgrim, occasionally at rest?

Where the Past Takes Us

Colleen J. McElroy

When I was eight, I saw the movie *The Song of Bernadette*, starring Jennifer Jones. Eight is an impressionable age, at least for me it was. *When I was eight*, I say. *When I was eight* . . . Perhaps when I was eight, the world started to come into focus. I passed from being merely a child, to being someone who observed and made decisions. What I do know is that the time has become fixed in my memory as magical, a time that I now assume was the beginning of my personal "age of reason"—or at least, the age when I began to seek reason.

I am sure part of that quest was triggered by the fact that in 1943 the world was at war, and most of the men in my family, including my father, were in the military, while women, like my mother, worked long hours at defense plant jobs. It was a time when everyone needed something outside of the life they knew, a force that could lead them toward what was beautiful and good. As I watched Bernadette ascend into heaven, a choir of angels bathing her in golden light, I believed I had glimpsed that force. I was too young to think of it as spiritual, but

I was certainly moved, moved enough to declare that I intended to become a Catholic. Only one member of my family was Catholic, my aunt Jennie, the rebel. Everyone else was bare-bones Methodist, not as fire-and-brimstone as the Baptists, not as physical as the sanctified Holy Rollers. Except for the tiny cups of sweet grape wine on sacrament days, and palms on Palm Sunday, Methodists' beliefs were simple and direct, "just a call to the gospel," as my grandmother would say.

I suspect that in those days, had I used the words *spirituality* or *faith*, they would have been synonymous with religion. Certainly I carried that movie image of the angels lifting Bernadette to the tune of golden harps through some six years of Catholicism. I went to confirmation classes and confession, said the Stations of the Cross, and prayed with my rosary every Sunday. Only my mother questioned why I needed a different-colored rosary for each Sunday outfit. And only one priest questioned the elaborate stories I concocted for the confessional, at eight and nine, truly unable to conjure up any sins of my own that were worthy of penance. I was among the faithful. On Sundays, I walked my grandmother to the Methodist church on the corner, then took the bus to the Catholic church across town. I held my rosary tight and made sure my lace kerchief stayed reverently in place on the crown of my head. And no doubt, I dreamed of Bernadette.

But during the week, I listened to my grandmother singing gospels as she set about cooking on the spindly-legged gas stove where the oven door held the drawing of a chicken hatching from an egg. I memorized every word to "The Old Rugged Cross," "Go Down, Moses," "When the Roll Is Called Up Yonder," and "Amazing Grace," her favorite. As I sat in that kitchen, inhaling the odors of beef or chicken, blueberry dumplings or apple pies wafting from the oven, I also listened to her stories about the family—how they had dispersed with the Emancipation, how she and her sister, Ethel, had relied on each other. But I was drawn especially to her tales of spirits, "souls who still walk among us though we can't see them." In my grandmother's stories, death was not an end but a journey that left restless souls wandering, and good souls returning to help the living. She used those tales to instill in me the wisdom of the old folks. In doing so, I believe she may have taught me a deeper faith than the one I so diligently practiced with brightly colored rosaries and communion lace. Most important, my grandmother allowed me to ask questions: when did it happen and where, and who-all was there? If I doubted the outcome, she'd tell me to wait, for the true answers would come to me when I needed them. In church, there was only one answer, and the questions were both asked and answered by the priest.

For six years, I kept to my routine: Mass on Sundays, my grandmother's stories during the week. I besieged her with questions and dutifully recited the catechism. But one day, when I was nearly fourteen and thought of myself as logical, I dared to ask a priest, "What happens if you're born on a mountain in Tibet and you've never heard of Catholicism?" "You go straight to hell" was the answer I received. It was as if the closing credits had just appeared on the skyline, as if once again Bernadette had received her calling, leaving me behind to watch, awestruck, as the heavens opened to accept her. How could I join her if only coincidence of birth separated me from those who were blessed?

To my surprise, my grandmother did not embrace me as the prodigal come home, but rather as the confused child I was, trying to come to terms with belief. Instead of carting me back to the Methodist church, she told more stories as she let me find my own way toward understanding.

As I grew from questioning child to doubt-filled adult, my grandmother's sense of spirituality, her faith that we are linked because we share a history of family and place, sustained me. This is not to say that I was always conscious of her guidance, or that I always recognized it as guidance. I only know that I absorbed her stories, that I willingly suspended disbelief when they were tales of ghosts and spirits, and that I eagerly embraced them when they were traceable to family that had come before me. For her stories gave me something that organized religion—Methodist or Catholic—could not provide: a sense of belonging for a black child surviving in white America, a sense of faith. Indeed, what is faith but a belief that we can imagine a presence outside of ourselves that guides us, be it family, nature, or God? I suspect it is a godliness of family and nature. This sense of direction took hold somewhere in the eighth year of my life, and when I started writing, continuously surfaced in my poetry.

I began writing in the sixties, and my first poems were written in protest. I did not set out to become a protest poet, but I did protest the appropriation of African-American culture—the ethos of family and place—by white writers who only had a surface knowledge of difference. Theirs was a kind of exploration into the "melting pot," too often ill-conceived if well-meaning. These poets, with their ambitious poems about the black and white of American culture, did not—and perhaps could not, given the racial segregation of the period—share my sense of faith in family and place any more than the priest who had dismissed my question about Catholicism could see any other point of view.

It was hardly an accident that I titled my first collection of poems *Music from Home*. How could it have been otherwise when I was about the business of re-creating those stories my grandmother shared? My memories of my grandmother's voice revolved around stories and songs, gospels that for her were an expression of faith and unity through a common spirit. They served as a way of praying when she was not in church, an ordinary, everyday presence of spirituality. The images in my poems were designed to recapture that commonality of faith. In my poetry, my grandmother becomes the mythic grandmother, her mother (my great-grandmother), and all those who were assigned to the fields or the plantation house. But she is also the grandmother I knew, married to my grandfather, who serves, for me, as a symbol of how to survive in the world outside of the family home. While my grandfather, who was decidedly secular, developed a hard edge that enabled him to cope with the world but left little patience for any form of religion, my grandmother came to terms with the world through religion. Through her stories, she gave me a way of constructing a kind of faith that was not entirely dependent on what a priest might tell me. Her way of shaping a story has lent a spiritual quality to my poetic voice.

I am convinced that we as writers share a hunger to be something more than a brief flicker in time, a hunger for continuity and the sense that what we are doing now comes out of what others have done before us. As a writer, I indulge myself in tradition, and a belief that tradition, this sense of myself in the universe, has been passed down to me as cultural memory. In a way, I am still asking, What happens to belief if you were born somewhere else? During my adult life, I have traveled to countries my grandmother could have scarcely imagined. With the exception of India and Antarctica, I have circled the globe. In 1993, I went to Madagascar on a Fulbright to research the oral tradition. More than once, I found myself caught in that space between family and stranger, especially when I was mistaken for Malagasy, my facial features reminding someone of a Betsileo or Bara friend, or a Sakalava neighbor. Of course, I only needed to attempt a few words in Malagasy, laminated by my midwestern accent, for anyone to recognize that I was a *vahiny*, a foreigner. Nevertheless, I was asked, sometimes simply because I resembled a friend who had recently immigrated to the West, if I were the child or perhaps the grandchild of that person. And always, even when I was asked how far I had traveled and how long I would stay, I was an outsider made to feel welcome.

That was how I felt the morning of the *famadihana*, a ceremony for the ancestors—a stranger in a world that was at once familiar and foreign, a *vahiny* who was as moved by this gathering as I would have been by a wake held by my own family. I remembered my grandfather's wake, the relatives who had journeyed to St. Louis from all over the United States, the mixture of joy and sadness as we shared a meal of my grandfather's favorite food and listened to stories of his life, both truth and fiction. It was our way of acknowledging that my grandfather had passed on and would no longer be a part of our lives except in memory.

But for *famadihana*, which loosely translates into "turning the bones," there are no somber clothes, no women veiled in black or men in stiff suits. Children played games of tag, and grown-ups made preparations to properly greet the ancestors. There was an air of expectancy, an urgency to get on with the business of the day. When the diviner and the family elder arrived, all idle conversation ceased. Even the children who had been playing catch-me games in the driveway moved closer to their parents who were standing near the tomb. The family elder, M. Razanatsimba, with his salt-and-pepper hair and neatly trimmed mustache, reminded me of one of my father's army buddies. M. Razanatsimba moved with the ease of authority that no one questioned. In the United States, he and the diviner might simply have been friends, on their way to someone's house or to a meeting to discuss the political issues of the day, but in Madagascar, they were charged with the governance of a ritual, one that linked the generations. As the tomb was opened, the diviner began to speak.

"He is addressing the ancestors," my translator, Tiana Tsizana, told me. "He tells them that we are their descendants and not as wise as they are. He is apologizing for disturbing them, but he asks them to be patient with us. He tells them that they will be taken to a new place. He says the ancestors are wise, and if we are careful, they have much to tell us."

Everyone wanted to look into the newly opened tomb, to add their voices to the comments already filling the air. As I watched the men about to enter the tomb, I realized a few people were looking my way, not staring but rather checking my reaction. I smiled. They smiled back. I was measuring that line between friend and stranger again, but at the unspoken invitation of several people, I moved forward and looked into the tomb. The air that greeted me was cool and dry and smelled of earth, like moss or leaves turning to mulch. The room was dark, unlit even by the rays of sunlight breaking through the last traces of fog. But I felt no sense of uneasiness, no dread of spirits about to rise and take hold of me. Instead, I sensed a kind of peacefulness, as if I had been invited into the parlor of a house reserved for very special guests. I leaned forward for a closer look. The walls seemed carved out of the earth itself, with niches along the sides and a corridor down the middle for easy passage, the space seemingly measured with an exacting fit for several generations of the family. There were no labels, no conventional tombstones, only the dim outlines of bodies wrapped in *lamba-menas*, with the outer shrouds woven of sisal. I stepped back from the opening and watched as the men began the procession of ancestors. They started with the eldest.

When I asked, "How can they know who is lying where?" the elder replied, "You see, everyone has a role. The men will lift each one from the tomb. They must all be greeted and offered new *lambas*, silk ones to honor them. Each one, each one will have a new *lamba* and a place in the new tomb."

The procession moved swiftly, the men placing the oldest ancestors in the laps of three or four of the youngest descendants seated on the ground, their legs stretched out in front of them. As soon as one body was positioned in the laps of the family, the men returned to the tomb for the next one. This process was broken only once, when they removed the remains of an infant who had been buried outside of the tomb because it had not lived long enough to be considered an ancestor. In order to make the journey to the new tomb, the child was nestled in the arms of its deceased father, who would now be its guardian in the world of the ancestors. Soon there was a lineup, twelve ancestors in all, and the family seated on the ground, cradling them like students at their desks, or worshippers in church pews.

At the site of the new tomb, we had lunch, and the family paid their respects to various ancestors, telling them of recent events, of regrets and desires, of unions and rapprochements. Then the family began the processional that would usher the ancestors home. The musicians offered music and the women their songs of loss and family and trust. The family carried newly shrouded bodies on their shoulders like pallbearers at a wake. Seven times they circled the tomb. The bandleader flamboyantly directed the musicians, who played the music of storytellers and dancers. The mood was both serious and upbeat. Some complained about the weight of an ancestor, the difficulty of carrying their burdens, feet first, seven times in a circle that seemed to widen and shrink erratically. "We must confuse them so that they don't get up and wander away from the tomb," Tiana said. The trumpet player all but drowned out her words. The drummer kept everyone moving. When the family saw my camera, they smiled and laughed, beckoned me to join them. "I should have taken a lighter load," someone called. Someone else waved at me. And a *ramatoa*, an older woman, begged the forgiveness of the ancestors for such laughing disrespect. But for that time, while the ancestors took one more outing in the sun, while the diviner entrusted everyone with the responsibility of family and God, while the elder made sure the bodies would be properly placed within the tomb, everyone—with all the music and laughter and singing—everyone was in accord.

At no time are the ancestors excluded from Malagasy life. At an elegant dinner party at the home of a professor at the University of Madagascar, the host, a business executive, included the ancestors in the first toast of the evening by offering the first few drops of wine in the northeast corner of the house. "For the ancestors," he said. And while no one made further mention of ancestors, I felt their presence, not unpleasantly but understandably, throughout the evening.

It was one of the times during my visit when I found myself considering how far away I was from home. In the United States, the dead are locked in memory and beseeched to "rest in peace." They have "passed over," "passed away." They are out of our lives. Only as an adult had I brought my ancestors back into the realm of the living through my writing. And only when I began to write about them did I realize how much I had learned from my grandmother during my childhood.

In an article titled "Writers and Faith," the poet Marilyn Nelson says that poetry can be thought of as a form of prayer, "a way of connecting with something beyond myself." I would take it one step further and say that poetry is a form of redemption, a way of bringing the past into focus. It is my attempt to retrieve my grandmother's sense of what the past tells me. Throughout my writing, I have woven her stories, both mythical and real, into the fabric of prose and verse. These are the poems that I must write, my house of echoes, where I have learned to listen to my grandmother's spirits.

Shall We Gather at the River?

Brenda Peterson

*I*t was the summer that fireworks fell into my eye, the summer I sat on a wasp's nest in my granddaddy's attic, the summer I accidentally killed his two hound pups by dressing them in dolls' clothes and settling them in shade that changed to brutal sunlight. It was my ninth summer, when my eyes glowed in the night with fire and phosphorescent medicine, when I shed my wasp-poisoned skin, when I understood that I was capable of harming what I most loved, that was when my grandfather took me down to the river with all the other sinners to meet God.

Current River runs through my fire-and-brimstone childhood like a balm. Boasting one of America's fastest-flowing currents, this river flows from the southern Missouri Ozarks all the way down to the hardscrabble hills of Arkansas. Its spring-fed water is so warm it rarely freezes. Every summer, the river carried my family on our daylong float trips. In a flotilla of giant inner tubes strung together with rope and long, idling legs, we cousins, aunts, and uncles rode downriver, gossiping about each other all the way.

My wayward Uncle Lloyd, the one who drank alcohol, sprawled in his inner tube like a river god, smoking Lucky Strikes and greeting other floaters.

"Hey, sweet gals," he'd nod to a bikini-clad knot of nearby floaters. "Have mercy on a sinner."

My uncle could bum Budweiser and smokes all the way down the wide waterway. But according to my grandfather, Uncle Lloyd couldn't find mercy in Current River.

"How come the river won't give Uncle Lloyd any mercy?" I asked. "Everyone gives him whatever he asks for."

"Because he's asking for all the wrong things," Grandfather said and spat a wad of tobacco ominously near my bare foot. "Why you think we get baptized in this river?" He fixed me with his black eyes, stroking his beard stubble as if he were both judge and jury.

Grandfather was the town's sheriff, and we used to play checkers in his small jail with his prisoners—usually repentant drunks or "disorderlies." He also often gathered us cousins into his battered pickup to cruise the backwoods roads, rounding up votes for his antidrinking campaign. He'd park outside a speakeasy or still and deliver righteous campaign speeches that sounded like a sermon. To his grandchildren, he was the closest thing to a biblical god we could imagine. When he talked to us, we listened up.

"The river don't give God's mercy . . . not unless you ask." With a meaningful glare at me, he concluded, "If'n I was you, I'd be down on my knees 'bout now."

After Grandfather had discovered his hound pups dead of sunstroke, dressed in my dolls' clothing, he had stood completely still. Instead of yelling at me, he'd taken up his whittling knife and slashed at a piece of lodgepole pine. I believed I deserved the dreaded strap. But this silence was worse.

Surely I needed some mercy. But how was I to ask for it from both my grandfather and this mighty river?

When Grandfather announced that he was taking me to the river, no one said a word in my defense. My step-grandmother, Vergie, just nodded and said, "I'll be right along, Ralph."

Why was Vergie lollygagging when I needed her most? I was terrified. No cousins, no inner tubes. Just Grandfather, the rapids, and me.

"What's at the river?" I gathered all my courage to ask as we roared down dirt roads to Current River.

"Almighty God," he said.

As a small scholar of Scripture, I knew only too well that it was water that Yahweh once used to destroy the whole world. I had never been afraid of Current River, but we were all frightened of our grandfather—a man who thought nothing of castrating a juvenile pup with his pocketknife. A man who had broken the heart of his first wife, my grandmother, and taken up with Vergie, a passionate and self-employed beautician. Although they would be married for more than thirty years before his death, there are some in my family who still refer to Vergie as "that other woman."

"You just sit here on the riverbank and it'll all come clear to you," Grandfather promised.

The thought occurred to me that Grandfather might drown me here and nobody would know. Another soul lost in the fierce rapids. Maybe I deserved to die after what I'd done. *Judgment is mine, sayeth the Lord.* Some part of me even longed for penance.

How often had I nuzzled those hound pups, sung them lullabies, cuddled them? They were my living doll babies. Because of me, they were dead. I could hardly stand to be around myself. Surely Grandfather would give me the most terrible punishment of my nine years.

We sat there on the riverbank in complete silence. Closing my eyes, I listened to the strong voice of the rapids, the singing leaves of the thirsty cottonwoods, the drone of mosquitoes and dipping of dragonflies.

I don't ever remember another time when I was alone with my grandfather. "What am I waiting for, Grandpa?" I finally broke our silence in a small voice.

"Well, young'un, what we're all waitin' for." He grinned and spat tobacco onto his hand, then roughly smeared spittle on the wasp stings along my arms.

I stared at my grandfather in surprise. His Seminole, French-

Canadian Indian, and Swede blood lent his high-boned face a dark and mysterious power. I was surprised by my grandfather's seeming patience with me now. His less gruff manner was usually reserved for his animals and his fishing. At retirement, Grandfather had bulldozed a lake in his ample front yard and every night hauled in catfish for Vergie to fry up with hush puppies, butter beans from her garden, and a sinfully delicious blueberry cobbler.

Maybe it was Vergie who had hinted to Grandfather to take his bewildered granddaughter to Current River alone. My cousins and I adored Vergie just as she was resented by some of the adults. It was Vergie who gave us well-water baths in a steaming tin tub in her farmhouse kitchen, who delicately plucked ticks from our raggedy heads after horse riding in the piney woods, who sang us lullabies and gossiped about dead bodies in the morgue all made fit for heaven by her "beautification."

I once asked Vergie if God had a wife or mother or daughter, since they seemed sorely missing in the Old and New Testaments.

With her healing herbs, her beauty parlor potions, her quick wit, Vergie was more pagan than even she knew. "You're the Scripture gal," she teased me, just as she was teasing my thin hair into a storm of dark blond ringlets, held in a beehive by blue goo called Dippity-Do and a steady mist of hair spray so foul-smelling I had a choking fit. "Any mention of God's kinswomen in the Bible?"

"Not many," I admitted. "I've looked for them everywhere, but except for Eve and that Ruth and Naomi, and maybe Deborah the Jewish judge and Mary Magdalene . . ." I paused, and considered, "Of course there was Jezebel . . ."

"Now, I bet she was a lot of fun, don't you?" Vergie laughed and slapped my knee. "Probably just having too good a time for her own good."

When I gazed up at this grandmother I claimed like blood kin, squinting though the haze of hair spray she aimed at me good-humoredly, I had one of my first epiphanies: I believed right then and there, holding court in her garage beauty shop, Chez Vergie, that she would have made a very fine wife of God. Or maybe just a misunderstood, high-spirited Jezebel.

"Don't know if God is really a woman," Vergie was fond of telling me. "But I do believe he needs to find hisself a better half."

God the Father definitely needed the civilizing and kindly help-mate of a wife and mother, I thought. Noah had one; so did Abraham, the patriarch who would obediently almost slay his own son; unforgiving Lot and long-suffering Job and, of course, Adam—the man my grandfather believed was "henpecked."

We all knew that for all his bluster, Grandfather somehow needed Vergie. He loved her desperately, still acting even after decades together like a suitor. She was stunningly beautiful. Black-blue hair curled in a "France coif," perfect Modigliani face and olive skin with the brightest fuchsia lipstick in the county. There were family rumors that Vergie was a mulatto, and surely her dusky elegance was the unspoken envy of many townswomen. To me, she was more enthralling than any movie star. I wanted so much to be like Vergie that I allowed her to perm my wild cowlicks into tight coils "fit for eternity," as she often promised her elderly beauty clients. Years younger than my grandfather, Vergie would sometimes cajole him as he lounged idly on the sofa, "See that old thang? That *used* to be your grandfather!"

Since Vergie was so much a part of my grandfather's life, I was unnerved that she did not accompany us to meet God at the river. Maybe my punishment was too horrible for her to witness?

"She'll be along," Grandfather promised. "She's got business here with the river like everybody else."

The business, I soon realized to my great relief, was baptismal. One of Vergie's kinsfolk had been saved after some skullduggery that no one talked about. What had Vergie's kinsman done? I wondered, as a small gathering of church people began joining us on the riverbank. They were all clothed in homemade choir robes flapping like fresh laundry on the summer breeze.

Someone pulled a rough burlap baptismal gown over my head and it scratched my wasp stings. But I did not cry out, accepting the painful sack like a penitent.

"Don't go torturing her no more!" Vergie appeared out of the crowd and in an instant rid me of my burlap gown.

She wore her "fancy face"—skillfully etched eyebrows, Loretta

Young lips, and an artfully twirled French twist. Her high heels did not even sink in the mud. "Ralph"—she turned to my grandfather— "this young'un's swolled up with wasp venom, she's got an eye full of sparklers from those blasted fireworks, and she's in her own hell from killing your pups. No more meanness in the family now!"

Grandfather shrugged and then did something shocking and wonderful. He winked down at me. Never in his life had my grandfather winked at anybody but Vergie. I considered this akin to a biblical sign.

"Thank you, ma'am." I hugged Vergie. We kids had been taught not to call her *Grandmother*, for fear of offending some of the relatives who still believed Vergie a fallen woman.

"Nevermine," she told me. "Lord knows, you've seen some small suffering this summer. Now, let the river show you her real miracles."

Her. Vergie had called this river female. The power of naming rivers and mountains was usually given to men, patriarchs of Bible and family. They called female their boats, their cars, and the prey they shot for supper. But no one in my knowledge had given this feminine pronoun to a body of water. Maybe this was a holy place where the Father God in heaven met and mingled with his wifely waters here on Earth?

I settled myself on the riverbank and Vergie leaned forward in a lawn chair my grandfather had set up for her. "I can make over most anything," she confided as we watched the baptismal procession—all the sinners in their burlap robes floating toward the river. "Except for meanness and stinginess. Just can't ease meanness from a face with all the makeup in this world."

To Vergie, God wanted folks to get "beautified," both body and soul. The way she talked about God, you'd think He'd also gone to beauty school and had his own shop to help sinners with their spiritual makeovers. Vergie didn't dwell on the crucifixion of his Son, like most other adults. Instead, Vergie liked to tell the story of Mother Mary taking her broken-down son off the cross. "It's always the women do the death chores—washing the poor old bodies, primping them to be angels in heaven."

"Do you . . ." I hesitated as I watched an old man sinner splash out of the river after his baptismal. "Do you think I'm still going to heaven—after what I did to those little pups?"

Vergie said nothing for a long time. "It's not right what you did, young'un." She laid a large hand on my shoulder. "Those little pups died because you didn't pay them no mind. Most evil is like that. It's forgetting 'bout anybody but yourself."

Tears suddenly streamed down my chin and dropped onto the riverbank. This talking to from Vergie was worse than Grandfather's anger. I had disappointed the grandmother whom I so loved. I was worse than any sinners here. Even Current River would not wash away my shame.

"But," Vergie lifted my face to hers, "you didn't do this terrible thing on purpose. That's the really big sin, sister. *Wanting* to hurt somebody."

Now on the muddy riverbank as a procession of white-robed penitents paraded past us to the very edge of the Current River, Vergie began a rousing chorus of "Shall We Gather at the River?"

> "Yes, we'll gather at the river
> The beautiful, the beautiful river
> Gather with the saints at the river,
> That flows by the throne of God."

Even with my bandaged, burned eye, I could see the world more clearly now. I was touched by the stream of believers floating into the river, their rough gowns flowing up around them like the flotsam of their sins, while they fell trustingly backward into the currents. A miracle happened right then and there—I forgot my own misery.

"Now, honey," Vergie whispered and took my arm. "Looks like you need some savin'."

I let Vergie take my hand. To my surprise she did not deliver me to my grandfather or the white-robed minister. She walked me away from the baptismal gathering and down to a favorite "putting-in" place for our family float trips.

From her large tapestry bag, Vergie took out my red swimsuit, a bottle of Coca-Cola, and my battered Keds. She kissed me on the forehead, her scent of Chanel No. 5 and hairspray clinging like sweet humidity. Then Vergie stepped back from me. "Now, child," she said, "*float.*"

As soon as I stepped into the river, the current knocked me down. But I was a strong swimmer. Vergie waved me on and called out, "We'll fetch you down at the covered bridge."

Floating fast, I stared at the blue sky, trusting the river to carry me as always. She rocked me along so safely, my body unclenched and rested on the warm water. For hours I floated, watching the summer clouds above. I swear some of them were shaped like the little hound pups, passing by, passing over.

When at last I reached the covered bridge, my grandfather waded into Current River to snatch my relaxed body from the fast-moving water.

"Good," he said, noting that I still held my empty Coca-Cola bottle in one hand. "You didn't litter the river none."

It was the closest he ever came to forgiving me. As I shivered in the pickup's front seat between my grandfather and Vergie riding back to their farm, Vergie took up humming the chorus, "The beautiful, the beautiful river . . ." Grandfather joined in with his growling bass and I listened to them singing together like two old angels—their voices a little wobbly and off-key.

Where I Come from Is Like This

Paula Gunn Allen

I

Modern American Indian women, like their non-Indian sisters, are deeply engaged in the struggle to redefine themselves. In their struggle they must reconcile traditional tribal definitions of women with industrial and postindustrial non-Indian definitions. Yet while these definitions seem to be more or less mutually exclusive, Indian women must somehow harmonize and integrate both in their own lives.

An American Indian woman is primarily defined by her tribal identity. In her eyes, her destiny is necessarily that of her people, and her sense of herself as a woman is first and foremost prescribed by her tribe. The definitions of woman's roles are as diverse as tribal cultures in the Americas. In some she is devalued, in others she wields considerable power. In some she is a familial/clan adjunct, in some she is as close to autonomous as her economic circumstances and psychological traits permit. But in no tribal definitions is she perceived in the same way as are women in western industrial and postindustrial cultures.

In the west, few images of women form part of the cultural mythos, and these are largely sexually charged. Among Christians, the madonna is the female prototype, and she is portrayed as essentially passive: her contribution is simply that of birthing. Little else is attributed to her and she certainly possesses few of the characteristics that are attributed to mythic figures among Indian tribes. This image is countered (rather than balanced) by the witch-goddess/whore characteristics designed to reinforce cultural beliefs about women, as well as western adversarial and dualistic perceptions of reality.

The tribes see women variously, but they do not question the power of femininity. Sometimes they see women as fearful, sometimes peaceful, sometimes omnipotent and omniscient, but they never portray women as mindless, helpless, simple, or oppressed. And while the women in a given tribe, clan, or band may be all these things, the individual woman is provided with a variety of images of women from the interconnected supernatural, natural, and social worlds she lives in.

As a half-breed American Indian woman, I cast about in my mind for negative images of Indian women, and I find none that are directed to Indian women alone. The negative images I do have are of Indians in general and in fact are more often of males than of females. All these images come to me from non-Indian sources, and they are always balanced by a positive image. My ideas of womanhood, passed on largely by my mother and grandmothers, Laguna Pueblo women, are about practicality, strength, reasonableness, intelligence, wit, and competence. I also remember vividly the women who came to my father's store, the women who held me and sang to me, the women at Feast Day, at Grab Days, the women in the kitchen of my Cubero home, the women I grew up with; none of them appeared weak or helpless, none of them presented herself tentatively. I remember a certain reserve on those lovely brown faces; I remember the direct gaze of eyes framed by bright-colored shawls draped over their heads and cascading down their backs. I remember the clean cotton dresses and carefully pressed hand-embroidered aprons they always wore; I remember laughter and good food, especially the sweet bread and the oven bread they gave us. Nowhere in my mind is there a foolish woman, a dumb woman, a vain woman, or a plastic woman, though the Indian women I have known have shown a wide range of personal style and demeanor.

My memory includes the Navajo woman who was badly beaten by her Sioux husband; but I also remember that my grandmother abandoned her Sioux husband long ago. I recall the stories about the Laguna woman beaten regularly by her husband in the presence of her children so that the children would not believe in the strength and power of femininity. And I remember the women who drank, who got into fights with other women and with the men, and who often won those battles. I have memories of tired women, partying women, stubborn women, sullen women, amicable women, selfish women, shy women, and aggressive women. Most of all I remember the women who laugh and scold and sit uncomplaining in the long sun on feast days and who cook wonderful food on wood stoves, in beehive mud ovens, and over open fires outdoors.

Among the images of women that come to me from various tribes as well as my own are White Buffalo Woman, who came to the Lakota long ago and brought them the religion of the Sacred Pipe which they still practice; Tinotzin, the goddess who came to Juan Diego to remind him that she still walked the hills of her people and sent him with her message, her demand, and her proof to the Catholic bishop in the city nearby. And from Laguna I take the images of Yellow Woman, Coyote Woman, Grandmother Spider (Spider Old Woman), who brought the light, who gave us weaving and medicine, who gave us life. Among the Keres she is known as Thought Woman who created us all and who keeps us in creation even now. I remember Iyatiku, Earth Woman, Corn Woman, who guides and counsels the people to peace and who welcomes us home when we cast off this coil of flesh as huskers cast off the leaves that wrap the corn. I remember Iyatiku's sister, Sun Woman, who held metals and cattle, pigs and sheep, highways and engines and so many things in her bundle, who went away to the east saying that one day she would return.

II

Since the coming of the Anglo-Europeans beginning in the fifteenth century, the fragile web of identity that long held tribal people secure has gradually been weakened and torn. But the oral tradition has prevented the complete destruction of the web, the ultimate disruption of tribal ways. The oral tradition is vital; it heals itself and the tribal web by adapting to the flow of the present while never relinquishing its connection to the past. Its adaptability has always been required, as many generations have experienced. Certainly the modern American Indian woman bears slight resemblance to her forebears—at least on superficial examination—but she is still a tribal woman in her deepest being. Her tribal sense of relationship to all that continues to flourish. And though she is at times beset by her knowledge of the enormous gap between the life she lives and the life she was raised to live, and while she adapts her mind and being to the circumstances of her present life, she does so in tribal ways, mending the tears in the web of being from which she takes her existence as she goes.

My mother told me stories all the time, though I often did not recognize them as that. My mother told me stories about cooking and childbearing; she told me stories about menstruation and pregnancy; she told me stories about gods and heroes, about fairies and elves, about goddesses and spirits; she told me stories about the land and the sky, about cats and dogs, about snakes and spiders; she told me stories about climbing trees and exploring the mesas; she told me stories about going to dances and getting married; she told me stories about dressing and undressing, about sleeping and waking; she told me stories about herself, about her mother, about her grandmother. She told me stories about grieving and laughing, about thinking and doing; she told me stories about school and about people; about darning and mending; she told me stories about turquoise and about gold; she told me European stories and Laguna stories; she told me Catholic stories and Presbyterian stories; she told me city stories and country stories; she told me political stories and religious stories. She told me stories about living and stories about dying. And in all of those stories she told me who I was, who I was supposed to be, whom I came from, and who would follow me. In this way she taught me the meaning of the words she said, that all life is a circle and everything has a place within it. That's what she said and what she showed me in the things she did and the way she lives.

Of course, through my formal, white, Christian education, I discovered that other people had stories of their own—about women, about Indians, about fact, about reality—and I was amazed by a number of startling suppositions that others made about tribal customs and beliefs. According to the un-Indian, non-Indian view, for instance, Indians barred menstruating women from ceremonies and indeed segregated them from the rest of the people, consigning them to some space specially designed for them. This showed that Indians considered menstruating women unclean and not fit to enjoy the company of decent (nonmenstruating) people, that is, men. I was surprised and confused to hear this because my mother had taught me that white people had strange attitudes toward menstruation: they thought something was bad about it, that it meant you were sick, cursed, sinful, and weak and that you had to be very careful during that time. She taught me that menstruation was a normal occurrence, that I could go swimming or hiking or whatever else I wanted to do during my period. She actively scorned women who took to their beds, who were incapacitated by cramps, who "got the blues."

As I struggled to reconcile these very contradictory interpretations of American Indians' traditional beliefs concerning menstruation, I realized that the menstrual taboos were about power, not about sin or filth. My conclusion was later borne out by some tribes' own explanations, which, as you may well imagine, came as quite a relief to me.

The truth of the matter as many Indians see it is that women who are at the peak of their fecundity are believed to possess power that throws male power totally out of kilter. They emit such force that, in their presence, any male-owned or -dominated ritual or sacred object cannot do its usual task. For instance, the Lakota say that a menstruating woman anywhere near a yuwipi man, who is a special sort of psychic, spirit-empowered healer, for a day or so before he is to do his ceremony will effectively disempower him. Conversely, among many if not most tribes, important ceremonies cannot be held without the presence of women. Sometimes the ritual woman who empowers the ceremony must be unmarried and virginal so that the power she channels is unalloyed, unweakened by sexual arousal and penetration by a male. Other ceremonies require tumescent women, others the presence of mature women who have borne children, and still others depend for empowerment on postmenopausal women. Women may be segregated from the company of the whole band or village on certain occasions, but on certain occasions men are also segregated. In short, each ritual depends on a certain balance of power, and the positions of women within the phases of womanhood are used by tribal people to empower certain rites. This does not derive from a male-dominant view; it is not a ritual observance imposed on women by men. It derives from a tribal view of reality that distinguishes tribal people from feudal and industrial people.

Among the tribes, the occult power of women, inextricably bound to our hormonal life, is thought to be very great; many hold that we possess innately the blood-given power to kill—with a glance, with a step, or with a judicious mixing of menstrual blood into somebody's soup. Medicine women among the Pomo of California cannot practice until they are sufficiently mature; when they are immature, their power is diffuse and is likely to interfere with their practice until time and experience have it under control. So women of the tribes are not especially inclined to see themselves as poor helpless victims of male domination. Even in those tribes where something akin to male domination was present, women are perceived as powerful, socially, physically, and metaphysically. In times past, as in times present, women carried enormous burdens with aplomb. We were far indeed from the "weaker sex," the designation that white aristocratic sisters unhappily earned for us all . . .

Of course, my mother's Laguna people are Keres Indian, reputed to be the last extreme mother-right people on earth. So it is no wonder that I got notably nonwhite notions about the natural strength and prowess of women. Indeed, it is only when I am trying to get non-Indian approval, recognition, or acknowledgment that my "weak sister" emotional and intellectual ploys get the better of my tribal woman's good sense. At such times I forget that I just moved the piano or just wrote a competent paper or just completed a financial transaction satisfactorily or have supported myself and my children for most of my adult life.

Nor is my contradictory behavior atypical. Most Indian women I know are in the same bicultural bind: we vacillate between being dependent and strong, self-reliant and powerless, strongly motivated and hopelessly insecure. We resolve the dilemma in various ways: some of us party all the time; some of us drink to excess; some of us travel and move around a lot; some of us land good jobs and then quit them; some of us engage in violent exchanges; some of us blow our brains out. We act in these destructive ways because we suffer from the societal conflicts caused by having to identify with two hopelessly opposed cultural definitions of women. Through this destructive dissonance we are unhappy prey to the self-disparagement common to, indeed demanded of, Indians living in the United States today. Our situation is caused by the exigencies of a history of invasion, conquest, and colonization whose searing marks are probably ineradicable. A popular bumper sticker on many Indian cars proclaims: "If You're Indian You're In," to which I always find myself adding under my breath, "Trouble."

III

. . . As a Roman Catholic child I was treated to bloody tales of how the savage Indians martyred the hapless priests and missionaries who went among them in an attempt to lead them to the one true path. By the time I was through high school I had the idea that Indians were people who had benefited mightily from the advanced knowledge and superior morality of the Anglo-Europeans. At least I had, perforce, that idea to lay beside the other one that derived from my daily experience of Indian life, an idea less dehumanizing and more accurate because it came from my mother and the other Indian people who raised me. That idea was that Indians are a people who don't tell lies, who care for their children and their old people. You never see an Indian orphan, they said. You always know when you're old that someone will take care of you—one of your children will. Then they'd list the old folks who were being taken care of by this child or that. No child is ever considered illegitimate among the Indians, they said. If a girl gets pregnant, the baby is still part of the family, and the mother is too. That's what they said, and they showed me real people who lived according to those principles.

Of course the ravages of colonization have taken their toll; there are orphans in Indian country now, and abandoned, brutalized old folks; there are even illegitimate children, though the very concept still strikes me as absurd. There are battered children and neglected children, and there are battered wives and women who have been raped by Indian men. Proximity to the "civilizing" effects of white Christians has not improved the moral quality of life in Indian country, though each group, Indian and white, explains the situation differently. Nor is there much yet in the oral tradition that can enable us to adapt to these inhuman changes. But a force is growing in that direction, and it is helping Indian women reclaim their lives. Their power, their sense of direction and of self will soon be visible. It is the force of the women who speak and work and write, and it is formidable.

Through all the centuries of war and death and cultural and psychic destruction have endured the women who raise the children and tend the fires, who pass along the tales and the traditions, who weep and bury the dead, who are the dead, and who never forget. There are always the women, who make pots and weave baskets, who fashion clothes and cheer their children on at powwow, who make fry bread and piki bread, and corn soup and chili stew, who dance and sing and remember and hold within their hearts the dream of their ancient peoples—that one day the woman who thinks will speak to us again, and everywhere there will be peace. Meanwhile we tell the stories and write the books and trade tales of anger and woe and stories of fun and scandal and laugh over all manner of things that happen every day. We watch and we wait.

Women of God

Mary Gordon

For the whole of what I would call my childhood I wanted to be a nun. In my box of treasures, alongside my Dale Evans cowgirl outfit and my cutouts of Grace Kelly, I kept my favorite book, *The Nuns Who Hurried*, and my favorite doll, a stiff, coiffed figure in a habit of black silk. I enjoyed my cowgirl outfit and my cutouts very much, but the nun doll and the nun book had a special shimmer. They made me feel exalted and apart.

The Nuns Who Hurried was hand-lettered, more a pamphlet than a book. I have kept it for nearly fifty years. Its pages are yellow now. Some of the letters in the text are drawings in themselves. On the cover the word "Hurried" slants forward, rushing, like the figures of the rushing nuns below the word. The attribution, "By One of Them," seemed to me wonderfully sly.

A large part of the book is really an annotated list of the kinds of nuns who rise with alacrity at the sound of the bell that calls them to morning prayer, an irresistible list of occupations: contemplating nuns (my plan for myself), teaching nuns, comforting nuns, visiting nuns, catechetical nuns. I know I read this book myself, rather than having it read to me, because with it is associated my first pleasure in the solitary ecstasy of words as words. I learned the joy of the sound of the word "catechetical" from this book, and that it meant having to do with instruction in the faith. I followed the rhythm of the final, menial categories—"the ones who cooked and played the organ and fixed the altar"—with the headlong intoxication of a gavotte or a downhill run.

The catechetical nun is pictured with a half-naked child whose hair suggests that he is black (or Negro, as we would have said then), but his face, like the others' (because the drawings are only line drawings, and therefore the figures are only outlined), is the color of the page. The catechetical nun follows the missionary nun, pictured standing beside a bicycle in front of a grass hut. Her page says, "THE MISSIONARY NUN HURRIED—Because she thought of all the little and big PAGANS all over the country just waiting in the darkness of ignorance for the LIGHT of the world to dawn over them—And she wanted to be filled with this divine LIGHT so that it would shine out to all she met—And then to help that stubborn old heathen who needed special prayers."

Each of these nuns is smiling, the smile a single, quick, upturning curve. The point of the book is that they are smiling because their lives are intensely meaningful. *All their hurrying is in order to complete their work for the love and glory of God.* And they are smiling in part because their lives are a charming joke. They may look like plain, unlovely workhorses, but they are brides of Christ, *sposae Christi*, and they share in the romance invoked by the "NUN WHO COOKED": she "HURRIED—Because she loved this time of audience with her KING and LORD—So much of her time must be spent in the royal kitchen getting the meals—But she still liked to think that it was CINDERELLA who won the PRINCE after all—wasn't it?"

The last page shows a group of kneeling nuns surrounded by a text that says, "They PRAY AND PRAY that WE will hurry up and start loving GOD REALLY AND TRULY—Because—they just can't bear the thought of all of us NICE PEOPLE not getting to heaven after ALL their hurrying—!"

We are all nice and they are all happy—a vision as simple and perfect as the line drawings with their blank centers. A quick look, not lingering and not close.

My devotion to my nun doll is memorialized in a photograph of me at four years old. I remember—in a vague, dim way that makes it seem like an image pulled from a memory before birth—the occasion of the photograph. The official photograph—as if I were royalty. As in royal photographs, the iconography was fixed. The child or children posed with their favorite toys—or their favorite presentable toys. The chewed-up blanket, the moldy teddy, would be kept from sight.

It is the night before the great event. My mother is on the telephone. I am in bed, but my heart is racing: tomorrow is the day of the photograph. I want to look pretty. I take the nail scissors from the bedside table and cut my hair. I can only imagine what kind of job I must have done at four years old. I remember only the snip-snip sound of the scissors—exhilarating, entirely productive. And then my mother's screams.

And then what? A blank. The next morning the photographer arrives. He is wearing a tan suit and brown shoes and a red bow tie, and I, with my formal sense as rigid as a Versailles courtier's, know this is all wrong, and that his taste is not to be trusted. I remember the stiff blue-corduroy jumper I am wearing, and the lace of the white blouse underneath it, irritating to the soft skin of my neck. I do not remember all the barrettes my mother stuck all over my head, trying to conceal the damage I had wrought, though I could see them later in the photograph. I don't remember the look on the photographer's face when he asked me what toy I'd like to be photographed with, and I produced my nun doll: uncuddleable, something to be looked at and admired rather than held. I now understand that the photographer must have thought he had been paid to photograph a freak, a child with her uneven hair held in place by multiple barrettes, a child holding a nun doll. Did I cut my hair because I knew nuns were shorn and I wanted to be like them?

I know that my father wanted me to be a nun. He was a Jewish convert; perhaps this accounted for his romanticism. He died when I was seven, but I remember his saying, with real pride, "My daughter will be either a nun or a lady of the night." He was a man of extremes.

I didn't know what a lady of the night was. It sounded glamorous, but no more glamorous than the image of a nun. He and I had a party piece about nuns. He would say, "Honey, what do you want to be when you grow up?" And I would say, without skipping a beat, "A contemplative."

I knew exactly what I meant. I knew, even at four and five, what contemplation was: Silence and prayer. Union with God. I had knelt beside my parents in the dim light of early-morning masses. I knew as many prayers and hymns as nursery rhymes. More. I dreamed of First Communion, believing those who said it would be the happiest day of my life. And I had had a glimpse of a real contemplative, a glimpse that would press itself into the hot wax of my imagination—an indelible image marking a life devoted to the creation of images.

We were visiting the convent of Mary Reparatrix, on East Twenty-ninth Street in Manhattan. The Sisters of Mary Reparatrix were a contemplative order. They specialized in retreats for working women. This was my mother's connection to them: she made their retreats. Their habits were sky-blue.

I went into the chapel with my parents. From the back I could see one of the nuns kneeling in prayer. Her form was impeccable: back straight, hands folded, head bowed for the inspiration of the Holy Ghost. A beam of light fell on her. And I knew that saturation in pure light was the most desirable state in the world.

Ramadan Redux

Susanne Pari

My father was a religious man, probably more religious than he would have been had he not been an immigrant from Iran and married to an American woman. He carried the heavy responsibility of passing on beliefs and traditions to his four half-breed children. So when I was fourteen and said I wanted to do the Ramadan fast with him, he was very pleased. I had an ulterior motive. I thought fasting would seem exotic to my friends at school; they'd never heard of Iran or Islam until I told them about it. Really. This was in the seventies.

That first night, my father got me out of bed at four in the morning. I stumbled to the dining room, where my father removed our plates from beneath the bubble top of an electric warming tray. My mother had earlier arranged chicken cutlets, rice, and a mound of overcooked peas on our plates—this was what everyone had eaten for dinner the night before. My father sat in his flannel pajamas and leather slippers, his plate and glass of water before him. I sat to his right and contemplated my food. My stomach churned.

"I'm not hungry," I said, shoving the food around with my fork, feeling shy and nervous and wary of showing my aggravation; my father and I hardly ever shared a quiet room together.

"It is the first night," he said, loading his mouth with a balanced forkful of meat, rice, and vegetable. "You will get used to it. Eat. What you don't eat now will haunt you tomorrow."

He was right. Skipping breakfast was a cinch, but by lunchtime I was salivating over the odor of cafeteria food and grinding my teeth at the sound of soda cans being opened. I fell asleep during Spanish class and had a dry coughing fit in geometry. What's worse, nobody at school seemed even mildly interested in my sacrifice to ritual. To them, my fasting wasn't exotic, just weird.

But I was determined to continue. I joined my father for the following middle-of-the-night meal. Again, I had little appetite. He frowned. "Eat and I will tell you a story," he said. I was shocked. My father cultivated traditional patriarchy: that meant instilling fear, maintaining distance, and speaking to us in lecture form. Storytelling was a woman's job. I swallowed a spoonful of lamb stew and immediately took another mouthful.

Each evening at sundown, we broke our fast, first sipping boiled water from a small tea glass, then slurping hot rice cereal, and finally gorging ourselves on warm gingerbread with goat's cheese and honey. And my father continued to tell me stories of his childhood. Of the children snuggling their legs together to stay warm around a charcoal brazier covered with a thick quilt. Of the homing pigeons he bred on the roof. Of his beloved wet nurse, his uncle the carpet maker, and his younger brother whom he bribed with two rials to accompany him to the outhouse in the middle of the dark night. And of his own father, who beat him, and his frail and seemingly dutiful mother whose secretive machinations allowed him to sneak out to the cinemas on Thursday nights.

That winter when I was fourteen, I managed to fast for only four days. One afternoon, I inadvertently popped a chocolate chip cookie crumb into my mouth. Our Iranian housekeeper threw her head back and laughed at my pout of deep guilt and self-disappointment. "It is okay," she said. "You are American girl." Well, I'd had my flirtation with religious ritual.

I thought my father would be angry, disappointed at the very least. He wasn't. "You did well," he said. "You learned about hunger, sacrifice, willpower." True. But mostly, I'd learned about him. And now, when I look up at a cobalt blue sky decorated with the brilliant white crescent of the new moon and one gleaming star, I think of the simplicity of that Islamic ritual I once practiced. I am not a Muslim anymore. The Islamic Revolution did that for me. The brutality of a fundamentalist theocracy drove me, in shame and anger, away from my religion. The simplicity is gone, devoured by sanctimonious, power-passioned men in robes and turbans. I keep my faith personal, write my own book of commandments, and create those simple, meaningful rituals—the whisper of a prayer memorized from the Qur'an, the planting of a hyacinth flower on the first day of spring, the burning of wild rue incense to bless the house—gentle and quiet rituals so like that Ramadan thirty years ago, when I first began to know my father.

God the Mother

What Became of God the Mother?
Conflicting Images of God in Early Christianity

Elaine H. Pagels

*U*nlike many of his contemporaries among the deities of the ancient Near East, the God of Israel shares his power with no female divinity, nor is he the divine Husband or Lover of any.[1] He scarcely can be characterized in any but masculine epithets: King, Lord, Master, Judge, and Father.[2] Indeed, the absence of feminine symbolism of God marks Judaism, Christianity, and Islam in striking contrast to the world's other religious traditions, whether in Egypt, Babylonia, Greece, and Rome or Africa, Polynesia, India, and North America. Jewish, Christian, and Islamic theologians, however, are quick to point out that God is not to be considered in sexual terms at all. Yet the actual language they use daily in worship and prayer conveys a different message and gives the distinct impression that God is thought of in exclusively *masculine* terms. And while it is true that Catholics revere Mary as the mother of Jesus, she cannot be identified as divine in her own right: if she is "mother of God," she is not "God the Mother" on an equal footing with God the Father.

Christianity, of course, added the trinitarian terms to the Jewish description of God. And yet of the three divine "Persons," two—the Father and Son—are described in masculine terms, and the third—the Spirit—suggests the sexlessness of the Greek neuter term *pneuma*. This is not merely a subjective impression. Whoever investigates the early development of Christianity—the field called "patristics," that is, study of "the fathers of the church"—may not be surprised by the passage that concludes the recently discovered, secret *Gospel of Thomas*: "Simon Peter said to them [the disciples], 'Let Mary be excluded from among us, for she is a woman, and not worthy of Life.' Jesus said, 'Behold I will take Mary, and make her a male, so that she may become a living spirit, resembling you males. For I tell you truly, that every female who makes herself male will enter the Kingdom of Heaven.' "[3] Strange as it sounds, this only states explicitly what religious rhetoric often assumes: that the men form the legitimate body of the community, while women will be allowed to participate only insofar as their own identity is denied and assimilated to that of the men.

Further exploration of the texts which include this *Gospel*—written on papyrus, hidden in large clay jars nearly 1,600 years ago—has identified them as Jewish and Christian gnostic works which were attacked and condemned as "heretical" as early as A.D. 100–150. What distinguishes these "heterodox" texts from those that are called "orthodox" is at least partially clear: they abound in feminine symbolism that is applied, in particular, to God. Although one might expect, then, that they would recall the archaic pagan traditions of the Mother Goddess, their language is to the contrary specifically Christian, unmistakably related to a Jewish heritage. Thus we can see that certain gnostic Christians diverged even more radically from the Jewish tradition than the early Christians who described God as the "three Persons" or the Trinity. For, instead of a monistic and masculine God, certain of these texts describe God as a dyadic being, who consists of *both* masculine and feminine elements. One such group of texts, for example, claims to have received a secret tradition from Jesus through James, and significantly, through Mary Magdalene.[4] Members of this group offer prayer to *both* the divine Father and Mother: "From Thee, Father, and through Thee, Mother, the two immortal names, Parents of the divine being, and thou, dweller in heaven, mankind of the mighty name."[5] Other texts indicate that their authors had pondered the nature of the beings to whom a single, masculine God proposed, "Let us make mankind in our image, after our likeness" (Gen. 1:26). Since the Genesis account goes on to say that mankind was created "male and female" (1:27), some concluded, apparently, that the God in whose image we are created likewise must be both masculine and feminine—both Father and Mother.

The characterization of the divine Mother in these sources is not simple since the texts themselves are extraordinarily diverse. Nevertheless, three primary characterizations merge. First, a certain poet and teacher, Valentinus, begins with the premise that God is essentially indescribable. And yet he suggests that the divine can be imagined as a dyad consisting of two elements: one he calls the Ineffable, the Source, the Primal Father; the other, the Silence, the Mother of all things.[6] Although we might question Valentinus's reasoning that Silence is the appropriate complement of what is Ineffable, his equation of the former with the feminine and the latter with the masculine may be traced to the grammatical gender of the Greek words. Followers of Valentinus invoke this feminine power, whom they also call "Grace" (in Greek, the feminine term *charis*), in their own private celebration of the Christian eucharist: they call her "divine, eternal Grace, She who is before all things."[7] At other times they pray to her for protection as the Mother, "Thou enthroned with God, eternal, mystical Silence."[8] Marcus, a disciple of Valentinus, contends that "when Moses began his account of creation, he mentioned the Mother of all things at the very beginning, when he said, 'In the beginning, God created the heavens and the earth,' "[9] for the word *beginning* (in Greek, the feminine *arche*) refers to the divine Mother, the source of the cosmic elements. When they describe God in this way, different gnostic writers have different interpretations. Some maintain that the divine is to be considered masculo-feminine—the "great male-female power." Others insist that the terms are meant only as metaphors—for, in reality, the divine is *neither* masculine nor feminine. A third group suggests that one can describe the Source of all things in *either* masculine or feminine terms, depending on which aspect one intends to stress.[10] Proponents of these diverse views agree, however, that the divine is to be understood as consisting of a harmonious, dynamic relationship of opposites—a concept that may be akin to the eastern view of *yin* and *yang* but remains antithetical to orthodox Judaism and Christianity.

A second characterization of the divine Mother describes her as Holy Spirit. One source, the *Secret Book of John*, for example, relates how John, the brother of James, went out after the crucifixion with "great grief," and had a mystical vision of the Trinity: "As I was grieving . . . the heavens were opened, and the whole creation shone with an unearthly light, and the universe was shaken. I was afraid . . . and behold . . . a unity in three forms appeared to me, and I marvelled: how can a unity have three forms?" To John's question, the vision answers: "It said to me, 'John, John, why do you doubt, or why do you fear? . . . I am the One who is with you always: I am the Father; I am the Mother; I am the Son.' "[11] John's interpretation of the Trinity—as Father, Mother, and Son—may not at first seem shocking but is perhaps the more natural and spontaneous interpretation. Where the Greek terminology for the Trinity, which includes the neuter term for the spirit (*pneuma*), virtually requires that the third "Person" of the Trinity be asexual, the author of the *Secret Book* looks to the Hebrew term for spirit, *ruah*—a feminine word. He thus concludes, logically enough, that the feminine "Person" conjoined with Father and Son must be the Mother! Indeed, the text goes on to describe the Spirit as Mother: "the image of the invisible virginal perfect spirit. . . . She became the mother of the all, for she existed before them all, the mother-father [matropater]."[12] This same author, therefore, alters Genesis 1:2 ("the Spirit of God moved upon the face of the deep") to say, "the Mother then was moved."[13] The secret *Gospel to the Hebrews* likewise has Jesus speak of "my Mother, the Spirit."[14] And in the *Gospel of Thomas*, Jesus contrasts his earthly parents, Mary and Joseph, with his divine Father—the Father of Truth—and his divine Mother, the Holy Spirit. The author interprets a puzzling saying of Jesus in the New Testament ("whoever does not hate his father and mother is not worthy of me") by adding: "Whoever does not love his father and his mother in my way cannot be my disciple; for my [earthly] mother gave me death but my true Mother gave me the Life."[15] Another secret gnostic gospel, the *Gospel of Phillip*, declares that whoever becomes a Christian "gains both a father and a mother."[16] The author refers explicitly to the feminine Hebrew term to describe the Spirit as "Mother of many."[17]

If these sources suggest that the Spirit constitutes the maternal element of the Trinity, the *Gospel of Phillip* makes an equally radical suggestion concerning the doctrine that later developed as the virgin birth. Here again the Spirit is praised as both Mother and Virgin, the counterpart—and consort—of the Heavenly Father: "If I may utter a mystery, the Father of the all united with the Virgin who came down"[18]—that is, with the Holy Spirit. Yet because this process is to be understood symbolically, and not literally, the Spirit remains a virgin! The author explains that "for this reason, Christ was 'born of a virgin'"—that is, of the Spirit, his divine Mother. But the author ridicules those "literal-minded" Christians who mistakenly refer the virgin birth to Mary, Jesus' earthly mother, as if she conceived apart from Joseph: "Such persons do not know what they are saying; for when did a female ever impregnate a female?"[19] Instead, he argues, virgin birth refers to the mysterious union of the two divine powers, the Father of the All with the Holy Spirit.

Besides the eternal, mystical Silence, and besides the Holy Spirit, certain gnostics suggest a third characterization of the divine Mother as Wisdom. Here again the Greek feminine term for wisdom, *sophia*, like the term for spirit, *ruah*, translates a Hebrew feminine term, *hokhmah*. Early interpreters had pondered the meaning of certain biblical passages, for example, Proverbs: "God made the world in Wisdom." And they wondered if Wisdom could be the feminine power in which God's creation is "conceived"? In such passages, at any rate, Wisdom bears two connotations: first, she bestows the Spirit that makes mankind wise; second, she is a creative power. One gnostic source calls her the "first universal creator";[20] another says that God the Father was speaking to her when he proposed to "make mankind in our image."[21] The *Great Announcement*, a mystical writing, explains the Genesis account in the following terms: "One Power that is above and below, self-generating, self-discovering, its own mother; its own father; its own sister; its own son: Father, Mother, unity, Root of all things."[22] The same author explains the mystical meaning of the Garden of Eden as a symbol of the womb: "Scripture teaches us that this is what is meant when Isaiah says, 'I am he that formed thee in thy mother's womb' [Isaiah 44:2]. The Garden of Eden, then, is Moses' symbolic term for the womb, and Eden the placenta, and the river which comes out of Eden the navel, which nourishes the fetus."[23] This teacher claims that the Exodus, consequently, symbolizes the exodus from the womb, "and the crossing of the Red Sea, they say, refers to the blood." Evidence for this view, he adds, comes directly from "the cry of the newborn," a spontaneous cry of praise for "the glory of the primal being, in which all the powers above are in harmonious embrace."[24]

The introduction of such symbolism in gnostic texts clearly bears implications for the understanding of human nature. The *Great Announcement*, for example, having described the Source as a masculo-feminine being, a "bisexual Power," goes on to say that "what came into being from that Power, that is, humanity, being one, is found to be two: a male-female being that bears the female within it."[25] This refers to the story of Eve's "birth" out of Adam's side (so that Adam, being one, is "discovered to be two," an androgyne who "bears the female within him"). Yet this reference to the creation story of Genesis 2—an account which inverts the biological birth process, and so effectively denies the creative function of the female—proves to be unusual in gnostic sources. More often, such sources refer instead to the first creation account in Genesis 1:26–27 ("And God said, let us make mankind in Our image, after Our image and likeness . . . in the image of God he created him: male and female he created them"). Rabbis in Talmudic times knew a Greek version of the passage, one that suggested to Rabbi Samuel bar Nahman that "when the Holy One . . . first created mankind, he created him with two faces, two sets of genitals, four arms, and legs, back to back: Then he split Adam in two, and made two backs, one on each side."[26] Some Jewish teachers (perhaps influenced by the story in Plato's *Symposium*) had suggested that Genesis 1:26–27 narrates an androgynous creation—an idea that gnostics adopted and developed. Marcus (whose prayer to the Mother is given above) not only concludes from this account that God is dyadic ("Let *us* make mankind") but also that "mankind, which was formed according to the image and likeness of God [Father and Mother] was masculo-feminine."[27] And his contemporary, Theodotus, explains: "the saying that Adam was created 'male and female' means that the male and female elements together constitute the finest production of the Mother, Wisdom."[28] We can see, then, that the gnostic sources which describe God in both masculine and feminine terms often give a similar description of human nature as a dyadic entity, consisting of two equal male and female components.

All the texts cited above—secret "gospels," revelations, mystical teachings—are among those rejected from the select list of twenty-six that comprise the "New Testament" collection. As these and other writings were sorted and judged by various Christian communities, every one of these texts which gnostic groups revered and shared was rejected from the canonical collection as "heterodox" by those who called themselves "orthodox" (literally, straight-thinking) Christians. By the time this process was concluded, probably as late as the year A.D. 200, virtually all the feminine imagery for God (along with any suggestion of an androgynous human creation) had disappeared from "orthodox" Christian tradition.

What is the reason for this wholesale rejection? The gnostics themselves asked this question of their "orthodox" attackers and pondered it among themselves. Some concluded that the God of Israel himself initiated the polemics against gnostic teaching which his followers carried out in his name. They argued that he was a derivative, merely instrumental power, whom the divine Mother had created to administer the universe, but who remained ignorant of the power of Wisdom, his own Mother: "They say that the creator believed that he created everything by himself, but that, in reality, he had made them because his Mother, Wisdom, infused him with energy, and had given him her ideas. But he was unaware that the ideas he used came from her: he was even ignorant of his own Mother."[29] Followers of Valentinus suggested that the Mother herself encouraged the God of Israel to think that he was acting autonomously in creating the world; but, as one teacher adds, "It was because he was foolish and ignorant of his Mother that he said, 'I am God; there is none beside me.' "[30] Others attribute to him the more sinister motive of jealousy, among them the *Secret Book of John*: "He said, 'I am a jealous God, and you shall have no other God before me,' already indicating that another god does exist. For if there were no other god, of whom would he be jealous? Then the Mother began to be distressed."[31] A third gnostic teacher describes the Lord's shock, terror, and anxiety "when he discovered that he was not the God of the universe." Gradually his shock and fear gave way to wonder, and finally he came to welcome the teaching of Wisdom. The gnostic teacher concluded: "This is the meaning of the saying, 'The fear of the Lord is the beginning of wisdom.' "[32]

All of these are, of course, mythical explanations. To look for the actual, historical reasons why these gnostic writings were suppressed is an extremely difficult proposition, for it raises the much larger question of how (i.e., by what means and what criteria) certain ideas, including those expressed in the texts cited above, came to be classified as heretical and others as orthodox by the beginning of the third century. Although the research is still in its early stages, and this question is far from being solved, we may find one clue if we ask whether these secret groups derived any practical, social consequences from their conception of God—and of mankind—that included the feminine element? Here again the answer is yes and can be found in the orthodox texts themselves. Irenaeus, an orthodox bishop, for example, notes with dismay that women in particular are attracted to heretical groups—especially to Marcus's circle, in which prayers are offered to the Mother in her aspects as Silence, Grace, and Wisdom; women priests serve the eucharist together with men; and women also speak as prophets, uttering to the whole community what "the Spirit" reveals to them.[33] Professing himself to be at a loss to understand the attraction that Marcus's group holds, he offers only one explanation: that Marcus himself is a diabolically successful seducer, a magician who compounds special aphrodisiacs to "deceive, victimize, and defile" these "many foolish women"! Whether his accusation has any factual basis is difficult, probably impossible, to ascertain. Nevertheless, the historian notes that accusations of sexual license are a stock-in-trade of polemical arguments.[34] The bishop refuses to admit the possibility that the group might attract Christians—especially women—for sound and comprehensible reasons. While expressing his own moral outrage, Tertullian, another "father of the church," reveals his fundamental desire to keep women out of religion: "These heretical women—how audacious they are! They have no modesty: they are bold enough to teach, to engage in argument, to enact exorcisms, to undertake cures, and, it may be, even to baptize!"[35] Tertullian directs yet another attack against "that viper"—a woman teacher who led a congregation in North Africa.[36] Marcion had, in fact, scandalized his "orthodox" contemporaries by appointing women on an equal basis with men as priests and bishops among his congregations.[37] The teacher Marcillina also traveled to Rome to represent the Carpocratian group, an esoteric circle that claimed to have received secret teaching from Mary, Salome, and Martha.[38] And among the Montanists, a radical prophetic circle, the prophet Philumene was reputed to have hired a male secretary to transcribe her inspired oracles.[39]

Other secret texts, such as the *Gospel of Mary Magdalene* and the *Wisdom of Faith*, suggest that the activity of such women leaders challenged and therefore was challenged by the orthodox communities who regarded Peter as their spokesman. The *Gospel of Mary* relates that Mary tried to encourage the disciples after the crucifixion and to tell them what the Lord had told her privately. Peter, furious at the suggestion, asks, "Did he then talk secretly with a woman, instead of to us? Are we to go and learn from *her* now? Did he love her more than us?" Distressed at his rage, Mary then asks Peter: "What do you think? Do you think I made this up in my heart? Do you think I am lying about the Lord?" Levi breaks in at this point to mediate the dispute: "Peter, you are always irascible. You object to the woman as our enemies do. Surely the Lord knew her very well, and indeed, he loved her more than us." Then he and the others invite Mary to teach them what she knows.[40] Another argument between Peter and Mary occurs in *Wisdom of Faith*. Peter complains that Mary is dominating the conversation, even to the point of displacing the rightful priority of Peter himself and his brethren; he urges Jesus to silence her—and is quickly rebuked. Later, however, Mary admits to Jesus that she hardly dares to speak freely with him, because "Peter makes me hesitate: I am afraid of him, because he hates the female race." Jesus replies that whoever receives inspiration from the Spirit is divinely ordained to speak, whether man or woman.[41]

As these texts suggest, then, women were considered equal to men, they were revered as prophets, and they acted as teachers, traveling evangelists, healers, priests, and even bishops. In some of these groups, they played leading roles and were *excluded* from them in the orthodox churches, at least by A.D. 150–200. Is it possible, then, that the recognition of the feminine element in God and the recognition of mankind as a male and female entity bore within it the explosive social possibility of women acting on an equal basis with men in positions of authority and leadership? If this were true, it might lead to the conclusion that these gnostic groups, together with their conception of God and human nature, were suppressed only because of their positive attitude toward women. But such a conclusion would be a mistake—a hasty and simplistic reading of the evidence. In the first place, orthodox Christian doctrine is far from wholly negative in its attitude toward women. Second, many other elements of the gnostic sources diverge in fundamental ways from what came to be accepted as orthodox Christian teaching. To examine this process in detail would require a much more extensive discussion than is possible here. Nevertheless, the evidence does indicate that two very different patterns of sexual attitudes emerged in orthodox and gnostic circles. In simplest form, gnostic theologians correlate their description of God in both masculine and feminine terms with a complementary description of human nature. Most often they refer to the creation account of Genesis 1, which suggests an equal (or even androgynous) creation of mankind. This conception carries the principle of equality between men and women into the practical social and political structures of gnostic communities. The orthodox pattern is strikingly different: it describes God in exclusively masculine terms and often uses

Genesis 2 to describe how Eve was created from Adam and for his fulfillment. Like the gnostic view, the orthodox also translates into sociological practice: by the late second century, orthodox Christians came to accept the domination of men over women as the proper, God-given order—not only for the human race, but also for the Christian churches. This correlation between theology, anthropology, and sociology is not lost on the apostle Paul. In his letter to the disorderly Corinthian community, he reminds them of a divinely ordained chain of authority: As God has authority over Christ, so the man has authority over the woman, argues Paul, citing Genesis 2: "The man is the image and glory of God, but the woman is the glory of man. For man is not from woman, but woman from man; and besides, the man was not created for the woman's sake, but the woman for the sake of the man."[42] Here the three elements of the orthodox pattern are welded into one simple argument: the description of God corresponds to a description of human nature which authorizes the social pattern of male domination.

A striking exception to this orthodox pattern occurs in the writings of one revered "father of the church," Clement of Alexandria. Clement identifies himself as orthodox, although he knows members of gnostic groups and their writings well; some scholars suggest that he was himself a gnostic initiate. Yet his own works demonstrate how all three elements of what we have called the "gnostic pattern" could be worked into fully "orthodox" teaching. First, Clement characterizes God not only in masculine but also in feminine terms: "The Word is everything to the child, both father and mother, teacher and nurse. . . . The nutriment is the milk of the father . . . and the Word alone supplies us children with the milk of love, and only those who suck at this breast are truly happy. . . . For this reason seeking is called sucking; to those infants who seek the Word, the Father's loving breasts supply milk."[43] Second, in describing human nature, he insists that "men and women share equally in perfection, and are to receive the same instruction and discipline. For the name 'humanity' is common to both men and women; and for us 'in Christ there is neither male nor female.' "[44] Even in considering the active participation of women with men in the Christian community Clement offers a list—unique in orthodox tradition—of women whose achievements he admires. They range from ancient examples, like Judith, the assassin who destroyed Israel's enemy, to Queen Esther, who rescued her people from genocide, as well as others who took radical political stands. He speaks of Arignole the historian, of Themisto the Epicurean philosopher, and of many other women philosophers, including two who studied with Plato and one trained by Socrates. Indeed, he cannot contain his praise: "What shall I say? Did not Theano the Pythagoran make such progress in philosophy that when a man, staring at her, said, 'Your arm is beautiful,' she replied, 'Yes, but it is not on public display.' "[45] Clement concludes his list with famous women poets and painters.

If the work of Clement, who taught in Egypt before the lines of orthodoxy and heresy were rigidly drawn (ca. A.D. 160–80), demonstrates how gnostic principles could be incorporated even into orthodox Christian teaching, the majority of communities in the western empire headed by Rome did not follow his example. By the year A.D. 200, Roman Christians endorsed as "canonical" the pseudo-Pauline letter to Timothy, which interpreted Paul's views: "Let a woman learn in silence with full submissiveness. I do not allow any woman to teach or to exercise authority over a man; she is to remain silent, *for* [note Gen. 2!] Adam was formed first, then Eve and furthermore, Adam was not deceived, but the woman was utterly seduced and came into sin."[46] How are we to account for this irreversible development? The question deserves investigation which this discussion can only initiate. For example, one would need to examine how (and for what reasons) the zealously patriarchal traditions of Israel were adopted by the Roman (and other) Christian communities. Further research might disclose how social and cultural forces converged to suppress feminine symbolism—and women's participation—from western Christian tradition. Given such research, the history of Christianity never could be told in the same way again.

NOTES

1. Where the God of Israel is characterized as husband and lover in the Old Testament (OT), his spouse is described as the community of Israel (i.e., Isa. 50:1,

54:1–8; Jer. 2:2–3, 20–25, 3:1–20; Hos. 1–4, 14) or as the land of Israel (cf. Isa. 62:1–5).

2. One may note several exceptions to this rule: Deut. 32:11; Hos. 11:1; Isa. 66:12 ff; Num. 11:12.

3. *The Gospel according to Thomas* (hereafter cited as *ET*), ed. A. Guillaumount, H. Ch. Puech, G. Quispel, W. Till, Yassah 'Abd-al-Masih (London: Collins, 1959), logion 113–114.

4. Hippolytus, *Refutationis Omnium Haeresium* (hereafter cited as *Ref*), ed. L. Dunker, F. Schneidewin (Göttingen, 1859), 5.7.

5. *Ref*, 5.6.

6. Irenaeus, *Adversus Haereses* (hereafter cited as *AH*), ed. W. W. Harvey (Cambridge, 1857), 1.11.1.

7. Ibid., 1.13.2.

8. Ibid., 1.13.6.

9. Ibid., 1.18.2.

10. Ibid., 1.11.5–21.1, 3; *Ref*, 6.29.

11. *Apocryphon Johannis* (hereafter cited as *AJ*), ed. S. Giversen (Copenhagen: Prostant Apud Munksgaard, 1963), 47.20–48.14.

12. *AJ*, 52.34–53.6.

13. Ibid., 61.13–14.

14. Origen, *Commentary on John*, 2.12; *Hom. On Jeremiah*, 15.4.

15. *ET*, 101. The text of this passage is badly damaged; I follow here the reconstruction of G. MacRae of the Harvard Divinity School.

16. *L'Evangile selon Phillipe* (hereafter cited as *EP*), ed. J. E. Ménard (Leiden: Brill, 1967), logion 6.

17. *EP*, logion 36.

18. Ibid., logion 82.

19. Ibid., logion 17.

20. *Extraits de Théodote* (hereafter cited as *Exc*), ed. F. Sagnard, Sources Chrétiennes 23 (Paris: Sources Chrétiennes, 1948).

21. *AH*, 1.30.6.

22. *Ref*, 6.17.

23. Ibid., 6.14.

24. *AH*, 1.14.7–8.

25. *Ref*, 6.18.

26. Genesis Rabba 8.1, also 17.6; cf. Leviticus Rabba 14. For an excellent discussion of androgyny, see W. Meeks, "The Image of the Androgyne: Some Uses of a Symbol in Earliest Christianity," *History of Religions* 13 (1974): 165–208.

27. *AH*, 1.18.2.

28. *Exc*, 21.1.

29. *Ref*, 6.33.

30. *AH*, 1.5.4; *Ref*, 6.33.

31. *AJ*, 61.8–14.

32. *Ref*, 7.26.

33. *AH*, 1.13.7.

34. Ibid., 1.13.2–5.

35. Tertullian, *De Praescriptione Haereticorum* (hereafter cited as *DP*), ed. E. Oethler (Lipsius, 1853–54), p. 41.

36. *De Baptismo* 1. I am grateful to Cyril Richardson for calling my attention to this passage and to the three subsequent ones.

37. Epiphanes, *De Baptismo*, 42.5.

38. *AH*, 1.25.6.

39. *DP*, 6.30.

40. *The Gospel according to Mary*, Codex Berolinensis, BG, 8502,1.7.1–1.19.5, ed., intro., and trans. G. MacRae, unpublished manuscript.

41. *Pistis Sophia*, ed. Carl Schmidt (Berlin: Academic-Verlag, 1925), 36 (57), 71 (161).

42. 1 Cor. 11:7–9. For discussion, see R. Scroggs, "Paul and the Eschatological Woman," *Journal of the American Academy of Religion* 40 (1972): 283–303; R. Scroggs, "Paul and the Eschatological Woman: Revisited," *Journal of the American Academy of Religion* 42 (1974): 532–37; and E. Pagels, "Paul and Women: A Response to Recent Discussion," *Journal of the American Academy of Religion* 42 (1972): 538–49.

43. Clement Alexandrinus, *Paidegogos*, ed. O. Stählin (Leipzig, 1905), 1.6.

44. Ibid., 1.4.

45. Ibid., 1.19.

46. 2 Tim. 2:11–14.

Looking Back at Lot's Wife

Rebecca Goldstein

*I*t was one of the stories from Genesis that most frightened me as a child: the story of Lot's wife.

She was told not to look, and she looked; and her punishment came swift and horrible. Frozen in the moment of her transgression, exposed to the eyes of all in her act of rebellion, she was transformed into a spectacle of salt, reduced to an element vaguely ridiculous, as if to turn back any motion of pity in us. And for what? She was told not to look, and she looked.

"Why did she look?" I asked the second-grade Hebrew-school teacher, who was telling the story.

"It doesn't matter *why* she looked," my teacher answered. "God said not to look, and she looked. She thought she could get away with it, but of course she couldn't. Nobody can get away with anything. God sees all."

That God sees all was a lesson my teacher was anxious to impress upon us at any opportunity, and it was a lesson that I, as a child, accepted without question. It was clear that God's seeing all was a consequence of God's being God. My teacher's response therefore seemed to me irreproachable so far as its theology went. It was on the level of human psychology that I felt it falling short.

Specifically, I didn't believe that Lot's wife had thought that she could get away with it. I wouldn't have thought so, and I was a mere child, living in pallid, nonbiblical days. In vivid contrast was the picture of Lot's wife: fleeing the accursed city, the shrieks of the damned in her ears, and in her nostrils the sickening stink as heaven's fire and brimstone came raining down behind her. (What *was* brimstone?)

God had warned that he would come, and he had come: in the version, embellished by rabbinical tradition, told to us by my teacher, his very Presence had descended, along with a host of twelve thousand angels of destruction. It wasn't the moment in which to think that one could get away with very much of anything.

I wasn't about to press the issue any farther with my teacher, but I was fairly certain that whatever it was that had made Lot's wife look back in her flight was in the nature of an overwhelming compulsion (a concept with which children tend to be well acquainted): the sort of irresistible urge that makes the whole question of whether or not one is going to get away with it pretty much beside the point.

What therefore seemed to me very much to the point was the question I had put to my teacher: what forced Lot's wife to look back, and—even more to the point—would I have felt driven to do exactly the same?

You begin to see why the story frightened me. Up to now in Genesis, the villains had been recognizably villainous—a brother who killed a brother, egomaniacs who brazenly questioned God's authority and erected claims to their own imagined supremacy.

But looking where one is told not to look?

Had Lot's wife, I wondered, looked back simply because she had been told not to do so, as I unfailingly sneaked a peek while standing between my mother and sisters in our pew in the synagogue during the recitation of the priestly blessing that was said on the holidays?

I had been warned by my mother, and again by my older sister, to avert my eyes from the *bimah*, where the priests were chanting their spooky melody, lest I be blinded by the Presence descending upon their upraised hands. Beneath my lowered lids I could see my two sisters turned dutifully away, facing the back of the synagogue, as all the congregation was turned away, many of the men covering their heads with their prayer shawls, as the priests themselves were doing.

Did Lot's wife and I share the same perversity of nature that compelled us to take stupid risks for no very good reason at all, for no reason that really went beyond the risk itself? And was it for this that her punishment had come swift and horrible?

Or was it rather for the whisper of a doubt, soft but irrepressible, that is perhaps always spoken in such actions as looking where one is told not to look? Were there moments in history during which God simply would not tolerate the *existence* of the skeptic?

The symbolic significance of the gesture of looking back wasn't lost on me. A child's knowledge of nostalgia is one of the mysteries of childhood. Perhaps it wasn't so much that there were moments forbidding doubt as that there were places that merited no sense of attachment. Was it the regret and longing she had directed back to her home in Sodom that had drawn God's wrath down on her?

And yet another sort, a meaner sort, of motive behind her action suggested itself, one that would remove her to a safer distance from myself: a kind of cold enchantment with the drama of death.

The summer we had spent at the seashore I had seen for myself how the crowd had gathered around the boy who had been pulled unconscious from the ocean, and how the voice and face of this crowd had quickened with a strange excitement, as if it were almost glad for the event.

Did Lot's wife have such a strong taste for the theater provided by others' tragedy that she could not keep herself from stealing a glimpse of the flaming spectacle? And was it for this that she herself had been turned, most appropriately, into the stuff of tragic spectacle?

Voyeurism or skepticism, nostalgia or bravado: who was Lot's wife, and what had moved her to look back and risk all?

· · ·

When I came home from school that evening, I immediately went to my father with my questions. I asked him whether we knew the name of Lot's wife, and I asked him why she had looked back.

My father went to his bookshelf and took down one of his huge tomes, leafed through it for a while, returned it to the shelf, took down another book, and read. After a while he said to me:

"According to this midrash her name was Irit (some say Idit). She and Lot had four daughters. There were the two daughters who fled together with their parents out of Sodom, but there were also two other daughters, who were already married to Sodomite men. When Lot warned these two sons-in-law that Sodom was about to be destroyed, they laughed and said, 'There is music and festivity in the city, and you speak about destruction!'

"According to this midrash, Irit had pity on her two older daughters, who were left behind with their husbands. She turned around to see if they were following her and she saw the Presence and was turned to salt."

My father and I stared at each other for a few moments.

"This is only one midrash," my father finally said. "I'll see if I can find some other interpretations that will make things clearer to us."

My father was telling me that he, too, was confused by the story of Lot's wife. And from his confusion I knew many things. I knew, first of all, that in looking back at Irit, he, too, looked back with pity. But far more importantly, I knew from his confusion that my father, just like Irit, would also have looked back to see if all his daughters were following . . .

• • •

My father did come up with several more midrashim regarding Lot's wife. One of the midrashim tried to explain why it was salt, of all things, that she became.

Irit, said this midrash, always used to skimp on the salt in the food she served. When the two messengers, who of course were angels, came to Lot's house to warn him of the imminent destruction, he ordered his wife to serve them a meal, and this time to salt the food properly. So she went around borrowing salt from all the neighbors, in this way spreading the word that the household had visitors, which was a species of persons dangerously unwelcome in the sinful town of Sodom. Because of her action a crowd of evil intent soon gathered around Lot's house, demanding that they be allowed to have a go at the strangers. The inhabitants of the house were only saved because of the angels, who blinded the men, young and old, who stood at the entrance. The blindness began with the young because it was they who had instigated the mob.

My father simply offered me this midrash, without suggesting that he thought it supplied the final resolution to the conflict we both felt on looking back at Lot's wife.

. . .

On the one hand, I still remember my father's admission of confusion about Irit's fate, and the knowledge and comfort I gathered from his confusion. On the other hand, my father never could work up any enthusiasm for the luminous vision of the life of pure reason I tried to paint for him. I argued that it was the life that was the most consistent and thus right. He agreed with me that it was consistent, but he wouldn't agree that it was right. In fact he thought it was all wrong. He thought it was right for human life to be subject to contradictions, for a person to love in more than one direction and sometimes to be torn into pieces because of his many loves. I suspect he even felt a little sorry for any great man of ideas who had cut himself off, so consistently, from what my father saw as the fullness of human life.

But now, only recently, I've discovered a commentary on the story of Lot's wife that I wish I might have been able to talk over with my father.

Rabbi David Kimchi (a thirteenth-century exegete known by the acronym Radak) points out that in Genesis it is sulfur and fire that are said to have rained down on Sodom. But in Deuteronomy, when Moses, before dying, warns the children of Israel not to repeat the sins of the past, he speaks of sulfur and *salt* as having been poured onto the doomed city. In the course of explaining the discrepancy, Radak says that in fact all the people of Sodom became pillars of salt. The outcome of the physical devastation wrought upon Sodom was that the place itself became sulfur, while the people became salt.

Hence, at least if one follows Radak, it seems that Lot's wife was not the spectacular aberration I had always thought. Her fate was continuous with those who had been left behind. Suddenly I felt the whole story of Lot's wife shifting.

She was told not to look and she looked, says the Bible. And her punishment came swift and horrible, added my teacher, following the traditional interpretation I, too, had thought inevitable. But I read the story differently now:

Irit looked back to see if her two firstborn daughters were following, and she saw that they weren't and what had become of them.

In such a moment of grief one knows only one desire: to follow after one's child, to experience what she's experienced, to be one with her in every aspect of suffering. Only to be one with her.

And it was for this desire that Irit was turned into a pillar of salt. She was turned into salt either because God couldn't forgive her this desire . . . or because he could.

The Medicine Woman's Daughter
A Charm to Keep You Part of the Whole

Anita Endrezze

May the white bark be nine times your mother
May my burnished cheeks be twice sun-daughters
May the apple that divides seeds into simple stars be the multiple of
    your life
May my breasts be the marigolds in your night garden
May the dark broom that is your shadow be a memorial to your father
May you live between my thighs and in my heart
May lapwings rise at your feet from every crossroad
May I be in between your two hands the way sky is the center of
    beech dreams
May our love be the mystery of wind and the soul's duration
May your life be as charmed, as strong, as the single white rose
    blooming in snowy circles

Shoplifting for Jesus

Marlene Blessing

I first met God in the trenches. Norris Halverson, our Lutheran minister, was still an army chaplain in spirit, and he filled his sermons with recollections of souls lost and found in wartime. We huddled together in the church basement, children and grown-ups alike, through the zing of bullets and the explosive surprises of war, feeling as if we wore helmets from the Almighty. I wiggled in my folding chair, caught between the rustle of my petticoats and Halverson's rich baritone. He was all bassoon and cymbal and drum, a human storm in a black collar, who shook the heavens before he reassured us with New Testament love and forgiveness. As a small girl, I could only piece together the fragments of religion in a crazy-quilt way: God was with the angels and the bombs. But I liked Halverson's Sturm und Drang approach to God, for the dramatic appealed to me. And although I dreaded the obligatory Saturday night hair washing and pin curls, I looked forward to the Sunday school stories, especially the ones with wild miracles. Daniel and the lion was my favorite. Samson ran a close second. The crimes of Eve and Jezebel and other doomed women perplexed me. Just what had they done that was so bad? And was it God who cursed them?

Outside, my father waited in our '53 Mercury sedan, where he spread the Sunday paper over the steering wheel, smoking Camels and catching up on sports scores. When my mother emerged from the service, genuinely refreshed, he seemed to have the urge to break the mood. His favorite method was to drive us all in our Sunday finery to the home of his friends Joe and Fran. Mother's lips grew thinner when we did this. She said drop-in visits were rude, but I suspected she just didn't want to have to look at all the naked women on the ceramics Fran made for Joe—on the handles of mugs and beer steins, twined around lamps, Fran's eye for detail at its very best on their perfect nipples and round, red lips. These scantily clad women had a kind of iconic power that eclipsed gentle images of Jesus the lamb.

After Dad had spent a couple of hours with Joe in the basement, admiring his latest projects and pinup calendars, we headed home to observe the day of rest. My mother would busy herself in the kitchen, lost in the rituals of Sunday dinner. My sister and I tried to sit still and be quiet, to wait patiently, but it was hard for us. As in a Bergman film, we could hear the clock ticking on the mantel, signaling slow time, heavy time, Sunday time. I used to wonder about eternity. Would it pass like this? Would you just be stuck forever with the wholesome aroma of fried chicken or pot roast, and nothing to do until the table was set?

God as a big production made sense to me when Pastor Halverson was recounting the hallelujah moments during bombing raids and field maneuvers. Once home, however, He seemed to slip in glory. The domestic realm was booby-trapped with sighs and guilt and insincerity. My dad got to the point where he simply said "grace" to my mother's request that he perform the duty of a proper, God-fearing head of household at the table. My mother really didn't have a prayer with any of us.

The more I learned about Dorothy in Oz and Huckleberry Finn and all the other fabulous truants of literature, the less weight Bible stories carried with me, with their pointed references to my inadequacies and sinful nature. In my mother's eyes, I spent entirely too much

time playing on the shores of Puget Sound and climbing trees in the
woods across the street and picking fruit from the overhanging
branches of our neighbor's trees. To her, this made me a pagan, restless—"just like your father," she said. I knew this meant I made her
feel lonely, just like he did. She didn't seem to know any way to draw
me to her except through recrimination. She never told me she cared
to spend time with me. She only invoked the Lord, trying to convince
me that he shared her disappointment in a wayward child who didn't
have an ounce of piety in her bones.

I recall thinking even then that belief ought to be a private matter,
not something that became real only if you could attest to it before
your mother. To me, my mother had things all stirred together in the
oddest religious brew: Take one starched petticoat and add small
white gloves, then stir in a big dash of Bible stories and the ability
flawlessly to recite the Lord's Prayer and the Twenty-third Psalm. Season with a sprinkling of humility and a pinch of pure duty, and voilà, a
Norwegian Lutheran mother's ideal child.

By my teens, I was spending half of every Saturday studying for
my confirmation. Mother drew even closer to God as her estrange-
ment from my father grew. They were well on their way to the divorce
that would hit when I graduated from high school. It was as though
God had gone from being her once-a-week bridge partner to her daily
confidant. I came to see God as the obstacle, a holier-than-thou presence who stood between my mother and me, impossible to please.
Those days of confirmation study only confirmed my certainty that
once I left home I would never feel obliged to attend another church
service, or to believe in the God of my mother. As I memorized the
Nicene Creed and all things Lutheran, resentment for all my lost Sat-
urdays built steadily. The tales of triumph and child sacrifice, of giants
overcome and walls blown down—all seemed to recede into a distant
time, a time of stories. Gone was Pastor Halverson, with his battle
scenes and power pulpit. He'd been so effective in building our congregation that, brick by brick, our church had become stately, with
Gothic towers rising above the old church basement. We sat on elegantly carved pews now, and I allowed myself to be proclaimed one
of the faithful in the huge stone maw that was our place of worship,

with its grand stained-glass windows and the concrete columns that blocked our vision.

Pastor Halverson had been called to a ministry in the Bronx by now, and we all pictured him catching bullets by hand in the midst of gang warfare. Our new minister was a learned man who had studied at Yale and could translate from the ancient Greek and Hebrew. He even sang in our new call-and-response service, his mild tenor straining for passion, and missing. His delivery was flawless and edifying, and for the first time, I fell asleep during sermons. The Sturm und Drang had disappeared. Sins seemed forgiven before they were committed. It was probably not this man's fault that he could not stir me (or many others). But if I was going to go home to a quiet Sunday with the monstrous clock ticking and supper taking an eternity to arrive, I wanted an operatic experience at church to see me through.

On one such bloodless Sunday, my mother and I took the bus to church. By now, the only good thing about religion as far as I was concerned was that it was the occasion for two-inch heels and nylons. As we sat through the service, I drifted off into a pleasant fantasy. I was traveling by train, with a perfect vanity case crammed with forbidden cosmetics, prickly hair rollers, and a perfect set of baby-doll pajamas. I was on my way to San Francisco, where I would begin my stunning new life by the bay. "Young lady, you are so bright, you can have any job you'd like," said the perfectly coiffed woman at the employment agency.

"Ouch!" I said too loudly. My mother had pinched me when she noticed that I was not joining in the lugubrious strains of "Lord, have mercy upon us."

"What do you think you're doing?" she whispered harshly.

"I was just trying out direct communication with God," I responded. This whopper should have earned me damnation on the spot, but Mother only sniffed her disapproval and looked straight ahead, undoubtedly making plans for dressing me down at home.

• • •

The walk back to the bus stop was a staccato of high heels, *click, click, clickety-click*. My mother didn't say a word, although occasionally she grabbed my arm for balance. Her multiple sclerosis was beginning to make it difficult for her to walk. Her physical neediness frightened me. Would it swallow me and my dreams of independence? Would she turn to me one day and command, "God requires you to be a faithful daughter, just like in the Bible—stay and take care of me"? Next to the bus stop was a jewelry store. Even though it was Sunday, the store was open for business. "They're Jewish, you know," she said. I knew she disapproved. All the same, I could tell she wanted to go inside. "C'mon," I urged. "The bus won't be here for at least fifteen minutes. Let's look."

Mother's face relaxed into almost a smile. Maybe after the fried chicken or the pot roast, she would forget my lapse, and I wouldn't have to hear one more time, "You're just like your father. You only think of yourself." We went in.

Jade was Mother's favorite stone, and the store had a whole case of it. It made her think of spring, she said, and solid things. Before she could stop herself, she was asking to see—really, to touch—a beautiful carved brooch. "This is an estate piece," said the saleslady, "a very old, valuable piece."

Behind Mother, I was looking over a sale table strewn with cheap costume jewelry—rhinestone bracelets, fake gold earrings, poodle pins. A tiny pillbox caught my eye. It had four playing cards enameled on the cover, the aces of each suit. I had to have it. If I didn't have religion, I had to have luck. I fingered it just as my mother fingered the old brooch.

There were rumors at school about a girl, a "cheap" girl, who was supposed to be shoplifting her way through life. Every new ruffled blouse or charm bracelet or purse she wore was suspect. I looked up at the round mirrors suspended from the ceiling at each corner of the store and contemplated joining the ranks of the criminal. I understood how a person could reach beyond reason and just grab a thing. Gingerly, I wrapped the fingers of my left hand around the box while my right hand continued to touch, sift, sort. The mirrors revealed no sign of anyone watching. If I plunged my hand into my coat pocket and dropped the tiny box into its silk lining, my little sin would be as buried as a teacup on the ocean's bottom. Here in the jewelry store, my response was faithful.

Mother turned to me. "Time to go." My left hand seemed permanently stuck inside my silky pocket, cupped around my crime.

. . .

I had no pills to put in my lucky enameled box, and it seemed too small for any other contents, except maybe grains of sand. And so it remained empty, empty as I felt with my booty. Whatever satisfaction I had taken in the act of stealing the box dissipated almost as soon as I dug it out of my pocket. I couldn't even look at it except in the privacy of my closet, because I was sure my mother would catch me. There was only one thing to do. I had to release this treasure, to bury it.

There was nobody at the beach. For some time, I sat on a salty, beached log while sand fleas jumped on my feet and legs. I hardly noticed them. Across the water, I could see Vashon Island and the ferry heading toward downtown Seattle. Seagulls careened in the gray-blue sky and squawked in their familiar way. I was grateful for this company. And I was grateful for the water.

It wasn't a conscious thought, I know, but somehow I understood that I needed the water. I had enough faith to believe that God, with his X-ray vision, was going to know where the box was, no matter how far I tossed it or how deep it sank. My fingerprints would be all over it forever, but I would be cleansed. I needed a clean slate, forgiveness, and my mother couldn't give it to me. I had to find my own path. I would be unworthy, imperfect, human. And I'd need a faith that would wash back and forth, carrying me home and carrying me to distant shores.

The sea rushed out as it foamed and gushed. I tossed the pillbox into the waves and imagined it tumbling to China. To complete the ceremony, I rolled up my jeans and waded into the water. I took a deep, salty breath and blew it out, then another. I inhaled and exhaled relief. Waves eased the pillbox away, then swirled back to my feet. With me or without me, life would flow in its moon-driven, starstruck way, carrying my sins and dreams as if they were no more than small fish swimming free.

Songline of Dawn

Joy Harjo

We are ascending through the dawn
the sky blushed with the fever
                        of attraction.
I don't want to leave my daughter,
                        or the babies.
I can see their house, a refuge in the dark near the university.
Protect them, oh gods of the scarlet light
who love us fiercely despite our acts of stupidity
our utter failings.
May this morning light be food for their bones,
for their spirits dressed
                        in manes of beautiful black hair
in skins the color of the earth as it meets the sky.
Higher we fly over the valley of monster bones
left scattered in the dirt to remind us that breathing
is rooted somewhere other than the lungs.
                        My spirit approaches with reverence

because it harbors the story, of how these beloveds appeared to fail
then climbed into the sky to stars of indigo.
                         And we keep going past the laughter and tears
of the babies who will grow up to become a light field
just beyond us.
And then the sun breaks over the yawning mountain.
And the plane shivers as we dip toward
                         an old volcanic field.

It is still smoldering
motivated by the love of one deity for another.
It's an old story and we're in it so deep we have become them.
The sun leans on one elbow after making love,
                         savoring the wetlands just off the freeway.
We are closer to the gods than we ever thought possible.

Native Origin

FROM *Mohawk Trail*

Beth Brant

The old women are gathered in the Longhouse. First, the ritual kissing on the cheeks, the eyes, the lips, the top of the head; that spot where the hair parts in the middle like a wild river through a canyon. On either side, white hair flows unchecked, unbound.

One Grandmother sets the pot over the fire that has never gone out. To let the flames die is a taboo, a breaking of trust. The acorn shells have been roasted the night before. Grandmother pours the boiling water over the shells. An aroma rises and combines with the smell of wood smoke, sweat, and the sharp, sweet odor of blood.

The acorn coffee steeps and grows dark and strong. The old women sit patiently in a circle, not speaking. Each set of eyes stares sharply into the air, or into the fire. Occasionally, a sigh escapes from an open mouth. A Grandmother has a twitch in the corner of her eye. She rubs her nose, then smooths her hair.

The coffee is ready. Cups are brought out of a wooden cupboard. Each woman is given the steaming brew. They blow on the swirling liquid, then slurp the drink into their hungry mouths. It tastes good. Hot, strong, dark. A little bitter, but that is all to the good.

The women begin talking among themselves. They are together to perform a ceremony. Rituals of women take time. There is no hurry.

The magic things are brought out from pockets and pouches.

A turtle rattle made from a she-turtle who was a companion of the woman's mother. It died the night she died, both of them ancient and tough. Now, the daughter shakes the rattle, and mother and she-turtle live again. Another Grandmother pulls out a bundle that contains a feather from a hermit thrush. This is a holy feather. Of all the birds in the sky, hermit thrush is the only one who flew to the Spirit World. It was there she learned her beautiful song. She is clever and hides from sight. To have her feather is great magic. The women pass around the feather. They tickle each other's chins and ears. Giggles and laughs erupt in the dwelling.

From that same bundle of the hermit thrush come kernels of corn, yellow, red, black. They rest in her wrinkled, dry palm. These are also passed around. Each woman holds the corn in her hand for a while before giving it to her sister. Next come the leaves of Witch Hazel and Jewelweed. Dandelion roots for chewing, Pearly Everlasting for smoking. These things are given careful consideration, and much talk is generated over the old ways of preparing the concoctions.

A woman gives a smile and brings out a cradleboard from behind her back. There is nodding of heads and smiling and long drawn-out ahhhhs. The cradleboard has a beaded back that a mother made in her ninth month. An old woman starts a song; the rest join in:

> Little baby
> Little baby
> Ride on Mother's back
> Laugh, laugh
> Life is good
> Mother shields you

A Grandmother wipes her eyes, another holds her hands and kisses the lifelines. Inside the cradleboard are bunches of moss taken from a menstrual house. This moss has stanched rivers of blood that generations of young girls have squeezed from their wombs.

The acorn drink is reheated and passed around again. A woman adds wood to the fire. She holds her hands out to the flames. It takes a lot of heat to warm her creaky body. Another woman comes behind her with a warm blanket. She wraps it around her friend and hugs her shoulders. They stand quietly before the fire.

A pelt of fur is brought forth. It once belonged to a beaver. She was found one morning, frozen in the ice, her lodge unfinished. The beaver was thawed and skinned. The women worked the hide until it was soft and pliant. It was the right size to wrap a newborn baby in, or to comfort old women on cold nights.

A piece of flint, an eagle bone whistle, a hank of black hair, cut in mourning; these are examined with reverent vibrations.

The oldest Grandmother removes her pouch from around her neck. She opens it with rusty fingers. She spreads the contents in her lap. A fistful of black earth. It smells clean, fecund. The women inhale the odor, the metallic taste of iron is on their tongues, like sting.

The oldest Grandmother scoops the earth back into her pouch. She tugs at the strings, it closes. The pouch lies between her breasts, warming her skin. Her breasts are supple and soft for one so old. Not long ago, she nursed a sister back to health. A child drank from her breast and was healed of evil spirits that entered her while she lay innocent and dreaming.

The ceremony is over. The magic things are put in their places. The old women kiss and touch each other's faces. They go out in the night. The moon and stars are parts of the body of Sky Woman. She glows on, never dimming. Never receding.

The Grandmothers go inside the Longhouse. They tend the fire, and wait.

Resurrection

Suzanne Edison

Resurrection I: An Invitation

In the aging ripeness
of autumn's bounty
I am the sweet air dripping
vanilla scented Katsura leaves.
Search for me
among earth's cool carpet,
where delicate chanterelles fan out
around their hosts.
Pluck my burnishing apples
eyes one step ahead of hands,
fill your woven baskets to brimming,
squeeze the purple-nectared grape
the golden-syruped pear
and feast.

Resurrection II: A Longing

Teach me how
a leaf curls inward
releasing its hold on the branch
or a raindrop's silken skin
bursts when it joins
another.
When I burn
like the star bright eyes of my daughter
reaching her hand
toward wind washed bamboo,
then in holiness
will I be made anew.

Have You Forgotten? I Am Your Mother
La Nuestra Señora de Guadalupe

Clarissa Pinkola Estés

The Mother I know is not clean and not demure. She is called La Conquista, meaning The One Who Conquers All, and also Mother of the Conquered. She is a high-spirited Jewess and a force majeure Azteca. She is an unwed mother, betrothed to a reluctant groom, turned away from door after door while pregnant, and even more pathetically, spurned while in the final wall-clutching stages of labor. In the corner of some stinking mucked-out stall, homeless, she gave birth alone, a *prima gravida*, first-time mother, without midwife or sister or mother to soothe her back or to comfort her cries. She stayed awake and stayed awake to feed her child, and when her child's life was threatened by the ruling military junta of her time, she fled across the desert while still bleeding from childbirth. Across the cold, cold desert, poised on a spine-jolting wooden saddle tied to the back of a little donkey, mi Madre, my Mother and yours, bound the little Child of Light tightly to the one place on her body that kept its warmth—to her naked breasts. Those beautiful breasts, leaking like the stars of the Milky Way, nourished the precious baby. Our Lady thought of only one thing: that she, the mother upon whom this child's very life depended, and that He, this tiny child of perpetual light, should live.

La Nuestra Señora, this Miryam, Maria, Mary, Madre Guadalupe, is no *la niña pura,* no nice, pure, obedient girl. She is instead pure woman, obedient only to the wildest Force imaginable: that Source without source, La Voz, The Voice so much larger than her own voice, the One who asked that she lend her blood, her bones, and her spirit to create a Life that would forever after be named Eternal Love.

There have been thousands of sightings and experiences of Blessed Mother this very day as we speak. They are not rare as some suggest. Millions have been visited by Our Lady of Guadalupe since the beginning, and not just in Mexico or Spain, but worldwide. Some in the church want to verify or disprove appearances, advisories, and miracles of Mary in all her many manifestations. Speculation continues about whether Don Diego existed. But meanwhile Our Lady, Seat of Wisdom, pays no attention. She keeps appearing to those in need without anyone's permission, without any institution's sanction. Thus, she bypasses all gatekeepers—appointed or self-appointed—to intervene, lift spirits, direct, to liberate souls throughout the world.

What did Our Lady of Guadalupe say to Don Diego, that smooth-faced, beautiful, dark-skinned man? Did she say, "I am purity personified, and you must behave yourself, for God is watching"? No. She infused courage, tenaciousness—her very own attributes. In essence she said:

> Have you forgotten, my dear child?
> I am your Mother.
> Do not be afraid.
> Do not be concerned about anything.
> Am I not here with you?
> You are under my protection . . .

The meaning of these words cannot be interpreted by the cosseted or by those who are secure. They must be interpreted by one who has been conquered. To such they command: Get up off your knees. You are not meant to be a subjugated people in subservience to a ruling power. You were not born to beg for your life, to be happy with crumbs. Guadalupe reminds them, Proclaim that I am with you; that you move under aegis; that you are mine and I am yours. She makes clear, You belong to no ruler other than the greatest Source imaginable. You are not abandoned, for I am here; and I leave no one stranded.

Undoubtedly the "investigating and deposing" of ordinary people's experiences with Our Lady were begun by persons in love with the endless beauty of God. They wanted no chicanery with regard to the Sacred, no exploiting of naïve persons. But these valid concerns gradually turned to politicized pronouncements, becoming more strident over time. Thus, the church has built up a language of legalisms that attempt to "verify" such "alleged" visitations in order to "deliver a verdict"—even though visitations cry out to be described in the language of the soul who embraces the mystical nature of all—even though numinous experience, by definition, is nonquantifiable by outside sources. What was meant to protect from harm seems to have too often become intrusive effect poised to negate revelation.

When I was at university years ago, my grandmothers and aunts were among my *conciliares*. Even though "uneducated," they were old believers and smart. When I learned something that might interest them, I would sit in the kitchen and tell them all about it—and they would thoughtfully and thoroughly "correct it" for me and tell me how it all really went together.

When I told them about diocesan commissions that voted on the authenticity of private visitations and revelations by Blessed Mother, they listened carefully. Such commissions are capable of making one of three "rulings": *constat de supernaturalitate*—an apparition, a visitation, a revelation, or a miracle displays "all evidences" and therefore is judged to be an authentic intervention from heaven. (Some required "evidences" are that the person receiving the visitation/revelation be "mentally sound . . . of upright conduct, obedient to ecclesiastical authorities, able to return to normal practices of the faith," meaning communal worship, receiving sacraments, and so on.)

"Ruling" number two: *constat de non supernaturalitate*—the "alleged" experience is clearly not miraculous, found to have no supernatural basis. (Such a ruling may be based on the commission's opinion that the person "claiming" visitation is either "mentally ill" or else possessed "by Satan.")

The third "ruling" is *non constat de supernaturalitate*—meaning it is not evident whether or not the alleged apparition is authentic. In other words, to use trial lawyers' jargon, "win, lose, or hung jury."

After listening quietly to this précis and consulting among themselves, my grandmother Caterin spoke for all. She averred that new visionaries and prophets were needed in each generation. She said they all agreed that visionaries and prophets were like geraniums. (You have to remember, my elders were from the old country.) As the plant grew sturdy new branches, the mother plant needed to be transferred into larger and larger containers so her roots could continue to grow deep and well. By limiting who is and who is not sanctioned or sanctified enough to have experiences with Our Lady, the church, the elders thought, had instead willfully transplanted her into increasingly smaller pots.

One of the "smallest containers" I can think of is the idea that the Holy Mother appears only to persons of "upright conduct" and so forth. One would have to infer that Our Lady would never think to appear to a person who is distressed or disturbed in any way. I must say that mi Madre, the Mother I know, is no such relative idea but rather our relative, our blood clan, and She is in no way elitist. I know this from talking to thousands worldwide who have face-to-face relationships with her. She does not qualify or screen those she visits. She appears to every heart regardless of its owner's status, authority, dishevelment, or saint potential. In fact, Our Mother appears in striking ways and far more often to people who will never be saints but who are Blessed Mother's dearest daughters and dearest sons, beloved in her giant flower-perfumed heart forever. It is clear that the souls she appears to most are the ones who need her most. I have met her many grateful witnesses: the lonely—all who have been abandoned; the despairing—she reminds them that God and despair cannot exist in the same place at the same time. She has reunited people and creatures who have lost each other. She visits those imprisoned, whether in a rhetoric, or whether in paper, golden, or iron cages. She carries souls across the cold deserts of cultural pollutions and harming constraints; she infuses strength into many who are threatened with physical and spiritual deaths; she is intercessor in their hardships—the privations as a result of deceptions, thefts, the death cults of our times. She is drawn to those who have experienced any travail, any challenge that she herself faced—to be believed, to be accepted, to be found worthy, to shelter the Truth and the Light. This is why she is called La Nuestra Señora, because she is mother of all. No qualifiers, no proofs required.

She has been called adviser, helper, intervenor, mediatrix. Yet to reduce Our Lady to a mere coping mechanism, saying she has no rational function, grit, or imagination, as some have ventured, is to say that Yahweh must have been a weekend hobbyist who took seven days off to make some "stuff." La Madre, La Nuestra Señora, Our Mother, continues regardless of those who say she did or did not appear, did or did not enter a house, did or did not lay hands on, did or did not heal, did or did not speak love to everything and everyone. As vast intercessor, she is essential to *tikkun olam*, the Hebrew words meaning repair of the soul of the world. She is essential to the concept of *ometeotl*, the Aztec word that means the one who enters the world from highest heaven to sweep clear "the two-way path" between the great earthly and heavenly hearts once again.

She has granted me liaison so many times. I fully admit: Her fingerprints are all over me. Perhaps they are all over you, too. I hope so. Her palm prints are on my shoulders from trying to steer me in various proper and difficult directions—such as the path of a long and hard-won education for which I, as a welfare mother, had little means. Mi Guadalupe was there always during those "decades of nights" it took to earn degrees. She whispered, "I crossed a long desert with little means, so can you." I have the literal experience of the strength of her great arms holding me up when I thought I would die; Her arms held me tight as I struggled to hold my fainting daughter up as she miscarried her beloved child. I have lain against mi Madre's breasts sucking, for strength to go on. During my recent struggle with a misdiagnosis of terminal illness for which I was given but four months left to live, she took off her piscus of rayos and bid me to pass through her fiery corona, burning away my terror and grief time and again. She has warmed me, and warmed me in prescient ways, allowed me to put my hands inside her hands, responded forcefully to healing petitions for family members, friends, and strangers. She has answered petitions for recovery and abatement of threats, harms, wounds, *las luchas*, struggles of many kinds. And even so I am still terribly deficient in many ways, and even so I still struggle to learn to love more every day. But as my drollest grandmother used to say, "Just think of how much worse we would have turned out without Her." Perhaps most powerful of all, I pray to Our Lady daily along with thousands of other old women throughout the world. I do not have all the answers about how Our Lady goes, but I carry the essential conviction that Our Lady cannot resist listening to a gaggle of such comic, imperfect, devout and lively souls.

La Conquista, who raised up Don Diego in more ways than one, is no simple, compliant girl, no matter who tries to make her so. She is on the side of life and she is for the world—all of it. So, come all those who feel or fear they have been broken, those who have been conquered in any way. Rise up, come forward, for there is a Lady waiting, a Lady who knows you by name, and by heart:

> Have you forgotten, my dear child?
> I am your Mother.
> Do not be afraid.
> Do not be concerned about anything.
> Am I not here with you?
> I am your mother, and
> You are under my protection . . .

Holy Land

Naomi Shihab Nye

Over beds wearing thick homespun cotton
   Sitti the Ageless floated
poking straight pins into sheets
   to line our fevered forms,
"the magic," we called it,
   her crumpling of syllables,
pitching them up and out,
   petals parched by sun,
the names of grace, hope,
   in her graveled grandmother tongue.
She stretched a single sound
   till it became two—
perhaps she could have said
   anything,
the word for peanuts,
   or waterfalls,
and made a prayer.

After telling the doctor "Go home,"
   she rubbed our legs,
pressing into my hand
   someone's lost basketball medal,
"Look at this man reaching for God."
   She who could not leave town
while her lemon tree held fruit,
   nor while it dreamed of fruit.
In a land of priests,
   patriarchs, muezzins,
a woman who couldn't read
   drew lines between our pain
and earth,
   stroked our skins
to make them cool,
   our limbs which had already
traveled far beyond her world,
   carrying the click of distances
in the smooth, untroubled soles
   of their shoes.

At One with the World

The Possible Suffering of a God During Creation

Pattiann Rogers

It might be continuous—the despair he experiences
Over the imperfection of the unfinished, the weaving
Body of the imprisoned moonfish, for instance,
Whose invisible arms in the mid-waters of the deep sea
Are not yet free, or the velvet-blue vervain
Whose grainy tongue will not move to speak, or the ear
Of the spitting spider still oblivious to sound.

It might be pervasive—the anguish he feels
Over the falling away of everything that the duration
Of the creation must, of necessity, demand, maybe feeling
The break of each and every russet-headed grass
Collapsing under winter ice or feeling the split
Of each dried and brittle yellow wing of the sycamore
As it falls from the branch. Maybe he winces

At each particle-by-particle disintegration of the limestone
Ledge into the crevasse and the resulting compulsion
Of the crevasse to rise grain by grain, obliterating itself.

And maybe he suffers from the suffering
Inherent to the transitory, feeling grief himself
For the grief of shattered beaches, disembodied bones
And claws, twisted squid, piles of ripped and tangled,
Uprooted turtles and rock crabs and Jonah crabs,
Sand bugs, seaweed and kelp.

How can he stand to comprehend the hard, pitiful
Unrelenting cycles of coitus, ovipositors, sperm and zygotes,
The repeated unions and dissolutions over and over,
The constant tenacious burying and covering and hiding
And nesting, the furious nurturing of eggs, the bright
Breaking-forth and the inevitable cold blowing-away?

Think of the million million dried stems of decaying
Dragonflies, the thousand thousand leathery cavities
Of old toads, the mounds of cows' teeth, the tufts
Of torn fur, the contorted eyes, the broken feet, the rank
Bloated odors, the fecund brown-haired mildews
That are the residue of his process. How can he tolerate
    knowing
There is nothing else here on earth as bright and salty
As blood spilled in the open?

Maybe he wakes periodically at night,
Wiping away the tears he doesn't know
He has cried in his sleep, not having had time yet to tell
Himself precisely how it is he must mourn, not having had
    time yet
To elicit from his creation its invention
Of his own solace.

Shamans

FROM *Walking with the Great Apes*

Sy Montgomery

The concept of beings part animal, part human is an ancient one, as old and intimate as our human lineage, reflecting beliefs of paleolithic antiquity. For millennia it was not only desirable for a person to become an animal, it was necessary. In totemistically conceived cultures, not only are animals great shamans and teachers, wrote [Joseph] Campbell, they are also "co-descendants of the totem ancestors." The various clans or groups are regarded as "having semi-animal, semi-human ancestors." To become an animal is to be one with the ancestors, to return to the source of our lineage, to join in the mystery of the original creations of the gods.

This insight was precisely what Louis Leakey, the son of an Anglican missionary, had in mind in his search for the ancestors of Adam. He, too, looked to animals—our closest living relatives, the great apes—to tell us about ourselves. In the great apes rested the story of our creation, our lineage, our place in the world. Sending forth Jane Goodall, Dian Fossey, and Biruté Galdikas not only to watch but to live among these apes must have been, to this deeply religious man, more than a scientific exploration; it must have been a sort of vision quest. Theirs was a profoundly sacred journey to the brink of the chasm that modern man has carved between himself and the animals; and once there, to peer over its edge and perhaps, if they dared, to cross.

At first, of course, the three young women approached their task as a great adventure, not a sacred quest. There were logistics to be worked out, goals to be named and achieved; it was an exercise in problem solving, which is, after all, what scientists do.

But it didn't work out that neatly. Each woman's first few months in the field were marked by despair, as the study subjects either could not be located at all or fled at first sight. The women couldn't *make* it work—not by extra stealth, not by better equipment, not by new techniques. One can manipulate an experiment to hasten it, but one cannot force or hurry a revelation.

The people of cultures older than ours know this well. On any vision quest the seeker must first achieve a purification, an altered state. The Yanomamo court the spirits by imbibing mind-altering drugs; the Oglala fast for many days, as did the Jew Jesus during His forty days in the wilderness; in other cultures sacrifices must be prepared, pilgrimages made. Only after such ritual purification is the seeker prepared to see what ordinary people cannot normally see.

For Jane, Dian, and Biruté, purification was achieved through loneliness and despair and, particularly in Dian's and Biruté's cases, deprivation. Their waiting, their despair was their sacrifice. Only afterward were they permitted to see, to understand, what ordinary people could not: the individuality of the apes, each animal as clearly unique as is each person.

The women learned to approach the animals' world with the reverence of a priestess approaching an altar. Biruté thinks of the forest at Tanjung Puting as "a great cathedral" . . . When Biruté walks in the forest, she bends down to gather up the tiniest scrap of cigarette paper, any trace of human litter; this is desecration, she considers, of a sacred place that must be kept pure. She often compares the tropical rain forest to a holy place, calling it "the original Garden of Eden"— the place of creation, where once man walked with the gods and spoke with the animals.

At Gombe, too, Jane feels a holiness; for her it is a place of spiritual transformation. "At Gombe, I could wander in the timeless forest and touch the bark of ancient trees," she wrote in a chapter contributed to the inspirational book *The Courage of Conviction*. "I could sit on the beach and watch the moonlight glinting as the waves tumbled, one after the other, onto the sands. There I felt part of the harmony of all life, and that, for me, was to know God again."

In these holy places the women walked in the apes' footsteps or under their aerial pathways. They sampled the foods the apes ate. Sometimes they slept in the forests with the animals, Jane at the Peak, Dian in her tent, Biruté in her hammock hung under the treetop nest of a sleeping orangutan. Daily they made the pilgrimage into the animals' universe, not only to probe and record, but to enter, to join.

Whether it was voiced or subconscious, sustained or abandoned, each woman had to have felt the ancient longing to become one with the animals.

• • •

To become one with another. It is the promise of marriage: that the two shall become one. It is the glory of pregnancy: to carry another life within you. It is the goal of religion: to become one with God. So deep is our spiritual and emotional need to join with another, to become part of another, that it remains a centerpiece of modern Western religious practice. In the sacrament of Holy Communion, Christians reiterate what we once played out in the ancient ritual of cannibalism: in drinking the blood and eating the flesh, we take in the power and spirit of another. We achieve, in this way, oneness with the dead, oneness with the sacrificed Christ.

But to modern Western notions, the chasm between man and animal yawns wider than the gulf between male and female, between man and deity, between living and dead. We have largely lost the knowledge possessed by the shamans. We have created a God in our own image; our priests have rejected the animal gods, and our scientists deny that animals have souls. In the Garden of Eden man knew how to speak with the animals. But today we have mostly forgotten—or perhaps unlearned—how to do this.

There may be another reason why Louis Leakey selected women as the shamans to reapproach the world of animals. Traditionally men have been aligned with the world of culture; women, "coded dark," as Donna Harraway puts it, implicit and hidden, are aligned with the world of nature, with the wild, the ethereal. It is no coincidence that in much of the modern Western world, we worship a male god and that our priests are men; but most of our modern shamans, whom we call mediums, who slip between the worlds of the living and the dead, are women.

Until recently women have largely shared the status of animals in male-dominated culture: like animals, women were considered unpredictable creatures who responded to hidden impulses and required taming by a possessing male "master," as in "master of the house." In psychology, Carol Gilligan has pointed out, the human archetype has been the male. Women, so mysterious that Freud couldn't figure them out (even though most of his patients were women), were the exception to the human "norm"; like wild animals, they did not adhere to man's civilizing rules.

In many cultures a female deity presides over the world of wild animals. Among the Caribou Eskimo, this deity is named Pinga, and to her realm the shamans must go to request a successful hunt; Pinga alone looks after and understands the souls of animals, and it is said that she does not like to see too many of them killed. Somewhere in the collective human psyche we seem to know that women are best equipped to approach the world of the animals.

For millennia there have been legends of women who turn into animals, and animals that turn into women. In the Fox Woman tale of the Labrador Eskimo, a man follows the tracks of a fox to his house and inside discovers a beautiful woman who has hung a fox cloak up on his wall. They live together happily until he complains of a musky odor in the lodge. Thereupon she throws off her clothes, resumes her fox skin, and slips away, never to be seen again.

The story is similar to the Crane Wife tale of the Japanese, the Buffalo Woman myth of the Plains Indians, and the Wild Goose Woman legend common from Greenland to Asia. These tales bespeak old knowledge: a woman's talent for transformation. And indeed, Louis Leakey's three primates—a religious term in his Anglican church—transformed our views of man and ape, human and animal . . .

· · ·

One is struck, when talking with people who have known Jane or Dian or Biruté, at the frequency with which, unprompted, the analogies arise: Jane, the most socially poised of the three, is often compared to the social chimpanzee. Biruté, serene, quiet, and auburn-haired like the solitary orange apes she studies, is likened to the orangutan. And towering, dark-haired Dian, so often blustering with threat, intensely loyal to her group, is often described in the same terms as the mountain gorilla.

Jane used to joke about this once in a while. "I'm becoming increasingly arboreal," she once quipped to a reporter. She and Hugo used to kid each other about Grub "keeping up with the chimpanzees." In a recent magazine article on Jane, the lead illustration portrayed her thus: the left half of the face was her image, the right half that of a chimpanzee.

Yet Jane does not consider that she has actually crossed the line from man to ape. She refers instead to having seen "Through a Window"—as she titled her most recent book. We have many windows through which to view the world, she points out; some are "opened up by science, their panes polished by a succession of brilliant penetrating minds." There are windows "unshuttered by the logic of philosophers; windows through which the mystics seek their visions of truth; windows from which the leaders of the great religions have peered." Too often, she argues, these windows are "misted over by the breath of our finite humanity." Jane's was a window from which she wiped away that mist, a window opened through the power of her relationships with individual chimps like Flo, David Graybeard, Mr. McGregor, and Fifi.

Once Jane called this relationship friendship. She titled one book *My Friends the Wild Chimpanzees*. But since then she has changed her mind. She considers "friendship" inaccurate, for her relationship with the chimpanzees is not predicated upon the usual bonds between humans or even the usual bonds between people and animals.

Friendship, says Jane, "is different from what I have with the chimpanzees. Friendship is shared goals, aims, helping one another through life, depending on one another—and that's what I don't have with the chimps."

To David Graybeard Jane owes the first two major discoveries of her career, tool use and meat eating by the chimpanzees. To Flo, from whom she learned the joy and wonder and skills of mothering, she owes the debt of an initiate to her wisewoman. She owes much to the chimpanzees, but they do not participate in her debt.

Jane made offerings to the chimps. She left out piles of bananas for them, she administered medicines to those who were sick. Her first offering to a chimp—the palm nut she held out to David Graybeard—was rejected. He did not want or need the fruit from her hand. And this was the nature of the chimpanzees' relationship with her: they might choose her company, they might sometimes accept her offerings, but they never *needed* her. They refused to participate in the debts that tie humans together. "There's no way the chimps depend on me for anything. What I feel with the chimps is something rather different. It's a closeness, an awareness, an empathy with, a respect for, love of," says Jane today. "But to me that isn't friendship. Friendship must be reciprocal."

Jane has carefully nurtured her relationships with the chimps: she has kept her promises to them, to remain harmless, waiting, receptive. She has codified the knowledge they have handed over to her, less a scientist than an initiate, a scribe at the oracle. She has become a warrior in the cause.

Yet Jane is not one with these animals; the chimpanzees have never considered her one of their own. "Perhaps they think of me as another inferior creature like a baboon," she muses. She cannot cloak her Otherness from them. She is permitted to travel in their nation as a visitor, not a citizen; she lives only at the edge of their world. "They know they can get away from me if they want to," Jane told me, "be-cause I, as a human, can't keep up with them. They would have more trouble getting away from another chimp."

And perhaps, suggests Geza Teleki, this is why a chimp may some-times choose to keep company with a human for a while instead of another chimp: "He knows he can get away from you whenever he wants." A chimpanzee's relationship with another chimpanzee is re-ciprocal. But a chimpanzee's relationship with a human is always on the chimpanzee's terms.

• • •

"For the first ten years I was here," Biruté told me at Camp Leakey, "I wanted to be an orangutan."

Biruté had always been drawn to orangutans, more so than to any other being. When her departure for Indonesia was delayed again and again, Louis Leakey offered her the opportunity to study other ani-mals in other places—pygmy chimps, for example. But she held out for orangutans. Even before she saw a wild orangutan, she felt both awed by and connected to them. It was as if the orangutan—serene, solitary, self-contained—was her personal totem, an animal whose power and knowledge she wished, like the Oglala Indians, to gather into her personal *waken*.

"We Westerners," she says in her thoughtful, quiet voice, "aspire to be orangutans. If you look at the end goal of our culture, it's to be an orangutan, to be totally independent of everybody—spouses, par-ents, children."

And indeed, during the first ten years of her study, Biruté ques-tioned her own independence. She loved her husband Rod, but she did not depend on him. She loved her child Binti, but she did not need him with her to make her life worthwhile. But she was not, she realized, totally independent. She needed the orangutans. She wanted them to need her. "For the first ten years, I was totally immersed in them. You can get sucked in, if you want to be sucked in. I got sucked in. But they don't need that. If you want to get sucked in, you have to do it yourself. They don't do it to you.

"The difference is, if you're honest with yourself, orangutans never let you hold the delusion that they need you. They can just walk by you and never look back. They're very engaging animals. But you have to push yourself on them. The relationship is like seventy percent you, thirty percent them, not fifty-fifty. And what that means is, you have to push harder.

"Watching them, I realized I could never be an orangutan. Maybe you can be a chimpanzee; maybe you can be a gorilla. But you can't be an orangutan. If you step back you realize you're fooling yourself. But that's what gives them their majesty, their nobility—they don't need anybody."

Biruté, so thoughtful and seemingly self-contained, has realized her human needs: to raise a family, to love and depend upon a husband. Yet at times Gary Shapiro catches her staring into space with a peculiar expression. It is a gaze he has seen on the faces of the orangutans. He calls it "the fruit stare," the slow-motion gaze used by a slow-moving, intelligent ape to search the canopy for fruit. It is unlike the expression found on the face of any other animal. In this, he says, Biruté is "very much orangutan."

Biruté draws on a clove-flavored cigarette and says thoughtfully: "I am probably more of an orangutan than a lot of other things."

• • •

By the time I began work on this, Dian Fossey had been murdered. To learn about her findings and methods, I could consult her book, her scientific and popular articles, her Ph.D. thesis. But scientists are often loath to write about their feelings for the animals they study or about what they consider to be their place among them. I would not have a chance to talk with the living Dian about these things.

A friend of mine who is a medium—a sort of modern shaman—offered to try to contact Dian for me. Gretchen Vogel Poisson farms near our house. She had never read Dian's book and had not read anything about her recently in the popular media. Nearly two years after Dian's death, alone in her home on a Saturday in March 1987, Gretchen narrated her vision into a tape recorder. This is what she saw:

"My impression is of Dian in a cavelike structure. She has on light-colored clothes, and she is still surrounded by some gorillas, not very numerous. But she's in a place of so little light that the only way I can even perceive her is because of her clothing. And this seems very odd. I ask for my angels to take me right up to her."

Here Gretchen pauses. On the tape you can hear her suck in her breath: "She is actually a gorilla in the suit of clothes."

. . .

"When I look at a gorilla," Dian once told a reporter, "I feel like I'm looking at the better part of myself."

"I talk to the gorillas in their language," she said during an appearance on "The Johnny Carson Show." She leaned forward on her left forearm on Carson's wood-grained desk, lifted her chin, and stated: "Naoom, m-nwowm, manauum-naoumm, naooum?" And then she turned toward another guest and repeated: "Naoom, m-nwowm, manauum-naoumm, naooum?" At this point she was more relaxed than at any other time on the show.

Dian often stated to reporters that she would rather answer their questions in this way—to answer as a gorilla would. When Robinson McIlvaine last visited Dian at Karisoke, he said, "she was talking nothing but gorilla. Grunting and making all sorts of noises, for an hour. It was a little off-putting."

She was affected more deeply by the death of Digit than most people are by the death of a sibling or a spouse. Friends recall that after Digit's death, Dian could not so much as speak his name without a catch in her husky voice. "In reality," Biruté said after the murder, "this was Dian's second death. In reality, Dian died the first time with Digit."

To Dian, Digit was no "baby-releaser" stimulus. Digit "was the son she never had, the sibling she never had, the father she never had," said Diana McMeekin. "But the gorillas were far more than her children. They were her surrogate race."

It was during a visit with her in Sacramento a decade before Dian's death that Biruté first realized that "in some ways, Dian had become a gorilla." Dian was doing the comforting "naoom, m-nwowm, manauum-naoumm, naooum?" gorilla vocalizations. Biruté spoke about this at a memorial benefit for Dian's Digit Fund at National Geographic in March 1986: "I realized then," she said, "that Dian's soul was already tinged and had already merged with the gorillas'."

Some say that Dian's relationship with the gorillas, her feeling of oneness with them, bespoke a kind of psychological sickness. "A lot, I think, of her inexplicable sourness and unhappiness was accelerated [by the fact that] all the touchy-feely stuff with the gorillas was a need to substitute gorillas for the people in her life," said one American conservation official who knew her. Again the voice of the skeptic: Dian had lost touch with *reality*, the world of people, rather than attaining a new reality, the world of nonhuman minds. "I think she entertained the thought that gorillas cared for her and were more worth her love than human beings were," this person said. "The gorillas certainly tolerated her, but they certainly had no positive emotions with her. They were complete in their gorillahood, they had their own relationships. They had no need for her. They *didn't need* her."

Another scientist, one of Dian's former students, said, "Some of the gorillas may have real affection for us; nonetheless they don't like us as much as we like them, and they don't understand us as well as we understand them."

But perhaps, in a world "older and more complete" than ours, there is a love that does not demand a reciprocal debt of need. Certainly Dian needed the gorillas. But perhaps the gorillas understood Dian better than any human ever did.

Ian Redmond told a story at the National Geographic memorial benefit to Dian. He hadn't planned to tell it; it was prompted by a question: how did the gorillas react to Dian's death?

"This goes beyond the bounds of strict science," Ian said. "Just after Dian's death, three gorilla groups who had been at some distance from Visoke suddenly homed in on the mountain. One group traveled almost continually for two days to arrive in the vicinity." Ian is a scientist and would not want to volunteer the interpretation implicit in the gorillas' sudden, purposeful movement toward the mountain that was Dian's home: that they had come, in her hour of death, to be near to her.

•   •   •

In all of the ancient legends about women who become animals—the Fox Woman tale, the Buffalo Woman legend, the Crane Wife story— the women all return to their animal form in the end. And there is yet another common thread: the men they leave become angry. In many of the tales, after the woman's final transformation into an animal, she is hunted down and killed by men.

This is what happened to Dian Fossey. And perhaps this names the unease some people feel about Biruté and Jane as well: that these women—and women are our most domesticated beings—would become transformed and then leave us to go wild.

Both Biruté and Jane are firmly rooted in the world of human endeavor. Jane has not become a chimp; Biruté has not become an orangutan. Yet the lives of all three women have been transformed by their visions; they are inexorably linked to the other nations through which they have traveled. In a sense they are, in the words of Henry Beston, living by voices we shall never hear; they are gifted with extensions of the senses we have lost or never attained. You need only listen to Jane's excitement at seeing "a tree laden with *luscious* fruit"—fruit that to human senses is so tart it prompts a grimace. You need only remember how Dian would sing to the gorillas a gorilla song—praising the taste of rotting wood. You need only imagine what goes through Biruté's mind when she does the "fruit stare" of the orangutan.

Western scientists do not like to talk about these things, for to do so is to voice what for so long has been considered unspeakable. The bonds between human and animal and the psychic tools of empathy and intuition have been "coded dark" by Western science—labeled as hidden, implicit, unspoken. The truths through which we once explained our world, the truths spoken by the ancient myths, have been hushed by the louder voice of passionless scientific objectivity.

But perhaps we are rediscovering the ancient truths. In his book *Life of the Japanese Monkeys*, the renowned Japanese primate researcher Kawai Masao outlines a new concept, upon which his research is built: he calls it *kyokan*, which translates as "feel-one." He struck upon the concept after observing a female researcher on his team interacting with female Japanese macaques. "We [males] had always found it more difficult to distinguish among female [macaques]," he wrote.

"However, a female researcher who joined our study could recognize individual females easily and understood their behavior, personality and emotional life better. . . . I had never before thought that female monkeys and women could immediately understand each other," he wrote. "This revelation made me feel I had touched upon the essence of the feel-one method."

Masao's book, unavailable to Western readers until translated into English by Pamela Asquith in 1981, explains that *kyokan* means "becoming fused with the monkeys' lives where, through an intuitive channel, feelings are mutually exchanged." Embodied in the *kyokan* approach is the idea that it is not only desirable to establish a feeling of shared life and mutual attachment with the study animals—to "feel one" with them—but that this feeling is *necessary* for proper science, for discovering truth. "It is our view that by positively entering the group, by making contact at some level, objectivity can be established," Masao wrote.

Masao is making a call for the scientist to return to the role of the ancient shaman: to "feel one" with the animals, to travel within their nations, to allow oneself to become transformed, to see what ordinary people cannot normally see. And this, far more than the tables of data, far more than the publications and awards, is the pioneering achievement of Jane Goodall, Biruté Galdikas, and Dian Fossey: they have dared to reapproach the Other and to sanctify the unity we share with those other nations that are, in Beston's words, "caught with ourselves in the net of life and time, fellow prisoners of the splendor and travail of the earth."

Poamoho

FROM *Writing the Sacred into the Real*

Alison Hawthorne Deming

*I*n the Hawaiian Islands, the spiritual and terrestrial are never far apart. Traditional Hawaiians call spiritual energy "mana," and for them it is present in people, animals, plants, and rocks. It demands respect. The old beliefs came with way-finders who sailed here in great outrigger canoes, navigating by stars and wave patterns, from the Marquesas and Society Islands. Their culture was guided by a complex hierarchy of gods and ancestral spirits who entered into all aspects of daily life. Sacred stories, some taking more than a year to tell, conveyed the history of ancestors to the community, and chants carried prayers and offerings to gods and guardian spirits, among them the *'aumākua* (guardian god) of a family into which a divine offspring was born, providing the family with special protection and requiring special reverence. According to scholar Martha Beckwith, the *'aumākua* could take the form of an animal or plant or other natural object and could grant more-than-natural powers to family members because of their sacred descent. As contemporary as much of Hawaiian life has become in recent years, the echoes of old beliefs can be heard everywhere in the islands. During my months of living there, I sought out those echoes. At times it seemed they sought out me . . .

In Hawai'i the question that began to form is this: How can I authentically speak about my experience of the sacred in nature when I do not feel connected spiritually or intellectually with a tradition, such as that of native Hawaiians, that grounds its beliefs in nature? My faith lineage begins with childhood in an agnostic family—my mother a lapsed Christian Scientist who enjoyed reading about such religious exotica as the Hunzas of Kashmir, and my father a man who found the ritual of Communion too cannibalistic to inspire his faith and refused at age fifteen to return to any church. As a teenager I developed a weak alliance with the West Avon Congregational Church (I joined so that I could sing duets in the choir with my best friend). I practiced meditation for five years so that I could walk in step with a contemplative boyfriend. I dabbled in churchgoing, various liberal denominations, but never felt a deeply shared sense of spiritual hunger in those congregations. More often I felt a constraining sense of propriety when what I longed for was to give myself to joyful lamentation in the presence of—the mere invitation to—the divine. I've read broadly (if not as deeply as disciplined spiritual practice may require)— Hinduism, Taoism, Confucianism, Native Americanism, Teilhard de Chardin, Thomas Berry, Annie Dillard, Carl Jung, Simone Weil, Saint Augustine. The most auspicious evidence I can offer for the seriousness of my spiritual quest is a thirty-year relationship with the *I Ching*, the ancient Chinese *Book of Changes*, lauded by Jung as "the right book" for "lovers of wisdom," though "like a part of nature, it waits until it is discovered." The book offers neither facts nor power nor causal explanation, but rather teaches an abiding relationship with the forces of change and chance that govern nature and the human spirit.

I take comfort in knowing that I'm not alone in this feeling of being a spiritual orphan. I take comfort in the words of Karen Armstrong, who left the Catholic convent after seven years because she found the church's definition of God too arrogant for her faith. People are turning away from God, she reports. In the United Kingdom only thirty-five percent of people say they believe in God. She thinks that number is optimistic. Churches have stood empty and now are becoming restaurants, theaters, warehouses, and private homes. The god who once presided there, she says, died in Auschwitz. If God existed, how could he remain unmoved and powerless over such atrocities? But God is not a being. To say that God does not "exist" violates nothing, because "existence" refers to the dimension we are able to perceive, and "God" refers to a whole other level. Jews and Christians were once called atheists by their pagan contemporaries because their concept of the divine was so new. The Sufi mystics said that each one of us is an unrepeatable expression of the divine, therefore each one of us will know God in an entirely different manner.

"We are not," Armstrong says, "like dogs. We cannot just relax into existence. Dogs do not worry what happens after death or what is happening now to dogs in other parts of the world." Ever since our ancestors climbed out of the trees, we have needed art and religion to get to the gut level of our being. Even lacking a definition, we know the terror and wonder of what stirs in us below the rational, beyond our control, what wounds us into prayer and compassion. One may catch glimpses, moments of insight may flicker against moments of doubt, one may feel the dimension of the sacred in one's life, but "God" lies beyond our human conception.

What is God? I do not know. I am deeply religious and deeply skeptical of religion. "You are a pagan," a friend once told me, "because you see deity not just *in* things, but *as* things."

· · ·

So, when I got the call from Steve about the hike, I put on my shorts and bright white new sneakers, slipped my lunch, rainslicker, and pocket notebook into my daypack, and drove up to Kamehameha High School to meet the *Hui Lama* (hiking club). The school is dedicated to educating children of native Hawaiian descent. I was almost the last to arrive. The others were assembled in the parking lot, a dozen or so teenagers, a few teachers and parents, all dressed in long pants and the rugged gear one wears knowing one's going to get dirty.

Two ROTC boys dressed in camouflage fatigues with loops of climbing rope strung to their belts looked me over. I must have been a sorry sight, a *haole* (the Hawaiian equivalent to "gringo") dressed for a stroll in the park. Biology teacher Chuck Burrows—a muscular man who'd been leading student hikes for something like fifty years, giving new vigor to anyone's notion of the elderly, a loved man, one could tell, from the way people spoke his name—handed me a permission slip so cautionary it seemed more appropriate for bungee jumping than a hike in the woods. Details emerged bit by bit, pebbles in the flow of conversation. Our destination was Poamoho, a region in the Koolau Range northwest of Honolulu. A fourteen-mile hike to the summit and back. To get to the trailhead we needed permits from Dole Pineapple and the United States Army, both of which control a surprisingly large amount of land on Oahu. I signed my name, dismissing the climbing ropes as macho excess, though I began to realize that the idea of a "moderate hike" for a man who has searched the wilderness throughout the Pacific Islands for undiscovered bugs might lean a bit closer to "rigorous" in my guidebook of this day.

I was assigned to ride with the only other person wearing shorts, Keawe, a young man teaching Hawaiian language and culture at the university. I may have been *haole* and he *kama'aina*, but we were clearly the items to circle in the drawing titled "What doesn't fit in this picture?" So we climbed into his little pickup truck and joined the caravan heading for the hills.

"Are you named after the tree?" I ask, thinking *kiawe*, the acacia.

He laughed, then frowned.

"That's what everyone says. No, after an important man in my ancestry, a chief on the Big Island."

He did not belong to the hiking club, but was a graduate of Kamehameha High School and had asked if he could come along because he had a special quest. He was happily engaged to be married. But he had dreamed of finding a white lehua flower. The red lehua blooms on the ohia tree, but a white blossom on that tree would be very rare indeed. He had sought out two interpretations of the dream, one from his grandmother, and one from another respected elder. One reading of the dream said that he had already found his white lehua in his fiancée; but the other said that he must go and find the flower in order to win her.

We compared notes on the upcoming hike. He too had expected an easy go of it.

"Fourteen miles?" he asked, blanching at the prospect. "Did you see those ropes?"

"Someone said it's the same route up and back, so we can stop and wait, if we wear out." I said this to console myself as much as him.

We compared notes on the ROTC boys and our shorts, admitting we hadn't prepared for paramilitary action. And we drove on to reconvene with the caravan at the Dole Pineapple Visitor's Center. Some other kids and a father, head of the local fire department, joined us. The father too carried ropes. Keawe and I exchanged glances, and we climbed back into the cars, trucks, and vans to wind along dirt roads through pineapple fields at the base of the finned green mountains. The dirt was slick from the previous night's rain. We fishtailed and skittered, took wrong turns then right ones, until we came to a rutted red dirt turnout just into the woods. It was too wet to go on, so we unloaded and prepared to hike the last mile of road to the trailhead.

Chuck convened the group into a circle where we stood and introduced ourselves one at a time. The students said where they lived and what grade they were in. Steve said, "I'm in grade fifty-one," and everyone laughed. Chuck asked Keawe to tell the special reason why he had joined us for the day. Then Chuck said we should listen to the sounds of the birds and winds when we entered the forest, and we would be with our ancestors. He asked Keawe to give us a chant, and the visceral music of it bound us. He asked him to tell us what it meant. Keawe said that he had asked permission for us to go into the forest and for us to go safely.

Steve led us on the way up the Poamoho Trail, and we followed in single file into the woods, stopping to learn things he knew along the way. Prehistoric banana tree. *Pinao*, the largest dragonfly in America (though I wondered later had I confused this in my notes with *Pinao ula*, the endemic red damselfly?). *Hame* (welcome), orange berries. *Loulu*, the fan palm, the only palm native to Hawai'i. He pointed across the steep valley to the opposite ridge—the royal palm, which has no dispersal agent here so had to be planted, a native of the Florida Everglades. Then Steve ran on ahead, slipping and sliding in the mud, eager to get to the next fascination. He wore Japanese reef slippers—better than sneakers or hiking boots, he said, on rain-slicked jungle trails—and green combat pants with big pockets. The trail rose into the green folding cliffs, ridges bending and rippling into one another, rising to one side of us and falling to the other, and we hiked along the edges or over the tops of the cliffs, everything softened with lush foliage so that it was easy to forget the height and steepness always at our sides. When we approached a fallen rotting tree downslope of the trail, Steve stumbled willingly down through the scrub into the composting mulch. We learned that this was the characteristic behavior of the creature, the denser the scrub the more likely he'd slither and clamber and tuck his way into it, disappearing for pregnant minutes, then reemerging with a grin and a clear plastic pill bottle boasting his find. This time it was a tiny spider carrying a pearly white egg case on her back. He handed me the vial.

"You want to carry this for me?" And I nestled the treasure in my pack.

Back on the trail, he led us on. There were ferns clustered in the crotch of a tree—their name meaning "Woman who sits on the mountain." There was *aha kea*, in the coffee family, its yellowish wood the traditional material for the gunwales of canoes. When a boat builder uses another wood, he paints the gunwales yellow. There was *Clidemia* and more *Clidemia* (Koster's curse), the South American weed that wages chemical warfare with other plants by stopping them from germinating. In some places there was nothing else growing, though insects had been brought in to control it. In others, strawberry guava from Brazil spilled its fruit all over the trail. The Chinese leafhopper sucked sap from one hundred different kinds of plants, its saliva toxic to many of them. Researchers were looking for a wasp to attack the invader and restore the balance. There was the *olapa* tree (Chuck looked over my shoulder to help with the spelling of Hawaiian words); and the *akia* plant producing a neurotoxin used for catching fish, the weed thrown into a tidepool and fish gathered up with a scoop net; and *uluhe* ferns, spreading over the island for the past two and a half million years and covering the steep cliffsides, the first plant to grow after a landslide and called with affection the "forest Band-Aid."

The higher in altitude we climbed, the more dispersed became our group and the thinner the vegetation. The square-stemmed mintless mint and New Zealand tea and *uki* grass. The higher we got, the wetter and stonier the trail became. The mountain we climbed was a shield volcano, its summit in the altitude most favored by Oahu's daily rain clouds. Gullies had been eroded in the trail, and narrow slot canyons were filled with soupy red-brown water. We were all soaked to the knees already when the rains and winds came, pelting us as we puffed up the last stretch to the summit. The ROTC boys joked, "If the Viet Cong don't get you, the leptospirosis will." Steve had long since left us in favor of bugs.

As we neared the summit, I was in the lead, breaking out of the last passage of thin forest into the rolling grassy, wind-whipped meadow. Ahead I spotted a plant that stood as tall as a cornstalk, a single spiky magenta blossom capping it like a crown.

"There's a really strange looking plant up here," I called back to the group.

"Show Chuck," someone answered.

I stepped aside, so that he could be the first to get close to it.

"Oh, that's the lobelia. *Koliʻi.* That's what we come up here to see."

We saw it. Then went on, the wind and the rain now so fierce no one wanted to linger. From the summit we could see the Pacific to the north and far below. We could see that sunlight was meeting the beach, though here the tempest made us each seek a leeward shelter. How could it be so cold and harsh at a mere three thousand feet in the tropics? The kids whirled and raced in the wind. Those of us who were older shuddered and leaned into ourselves for warmth. I turned my back on the lookout and found the sheltered backside of a hillock, joining two teachers who sat and pried their way with icy fingers into the sandwiches and cookies they'd brought for lunch. Everyone was soaked from head to foot, and after sitting for ten minutes in the wind no one looked happy, and the group began to disperse by twos and threes and fours heading back down the trail to warmth. I was sitting with Debbie, and we'd been telling our stories—she'd come to

Hawai'i as a Navy wife, had kids, then divorced, now was a science teacher at the high school and trying hard to make her life work out. I did not know her, but I knew she was not really *in* her life, the way one is when it feels that one's choices fit. I knew she was still trying on her fate, that she did not yet love it. How could I know such a thing about a stranger? Forgive me if I am mistaken—so many ways it is possible to get the world wrong.

She was quiet, staring at the knee of her wet jeans where a dopey bee staggered along. She set her palm beside it like a little boat, and the bee walked on board. She held it close to her face and admired it, then showed it closely to me.

"It doesn't belong up here," she said. "It's way too cold. I wish I had some way to take it down with us."

I remembered the plastic eyeglass case in my backpack and pulled it out. We popped the bee inside, and I tucked the case into my pack.

Debbie and I made the descent together, the others dispersed ahead or behind, and occasionally we'd intersect with some of them but seemed to keep ending up alone. We talked about work and marriage and mothering—our disappointments and our hopes. We helped each other over the gullies and savored guavas when our water ran out. Our legs were sore, muscles wasted and tense, our clothes and hair soaked; one or the other of us kept slipping and falling on slick mud or stone, and there was ridiculous joy in being so dirty and sweaty and exhausted together as we hiked farther from the stormy summit and deeper into sun-mottled forest. I might have preferred to hear more of the wind and birdsong in those last miles of wilderness, but our talking went on, and I gave myself to it.

We were within a quarter mile of the trailhead when she fell, though we didn't know where we were at the time. For miles we'd been encouraging each other, "We're almost there now." We were long past the most perilous passages of the trail—here was level ground, an easy curve, a wide pathway. A relaxed weedy cliff rose to our right, and to our left a steep fern-covered cliff descended out of sight. One minute she was walking a few feet ahead of me, and the next she was falling head first over the edge.

"It was the strangest thing," I later told Keawe, "as if some force came along and threw her over the cliff."

"There are powers in the mountains," he'd said. "We call them the home of the gods."

Even more strange to me was my response to Debbie's falling. I stepped up to the edge and looked down. I could see her, just barely, through the ferns and scrub, clinging to the nubby cliffside, maybe twenty feet below.

"Are you all right?" I called down.

"I think so," she said, though her breath was shallow and fast with panic. *No problem*, I thought, though I wasn't really thinking this, because clearly this really *was* a problem. I was feeling it—a calm washing through my body that made me certain everything was all right. Whether I say that the calm was a physiologic response—endorphins perhaps pumped up by the danger—or whether I say that the calm was holy spirit—a more-than-human power—flowing into my body does not matter. The fact is that a woman clung for her life to a cliffside, and I was certain and calm, and both of these facts were beyond my control. I leaned over the edge to hear her whispering Hail Marys between hyperventilating gasps. Below her the cliff fell another fifty feet or so, then met a seam where another cliff joined it, and the crease between the two ferny basaltic walls fell far below toward the tiny stream that laced through the distant valley floor.

"We'll get you up, don't worry," I said. "Try to breathe slowly. Try to hold on." And I looked around me for anything that would tell me what to do. And when I looked, I found a tree limb that had fallen in the trail, and I thought I could reach her with it, knowing she could not hold on long to wet rock and ferns. I lowered the limb to her.

"Brace as much of your weight as you can against the rock," I said, thinking, How can I hold her? What if I feel myself starting to fall? I kneeled on the trail, braced a knee against the slight mound of a protruding rock—surely not enough resistance to hold me, but it did, as I centered my body's gravity over the earth rather than the chasm.

For how long did we struggle there, reaching and grasping and praying and calling for help? Maybe twenty minutes. Maybe thirty. Maybe forever. I was fearless and I have no idea why. I thought calmly—after she'd said, I can't hold on anymore, after I'd felt the weight of her pulling me closer to falling, after I'd said, I'm not going to leave you, after we'd gotten her close enough to let the limb fall and grip each other's wrists, after we'd each said, Wait, I don't think I can hold on anymore, after we'd both called out, Dear Jesus help us—I thought calmly, What will I do if I feel myself going over? Will I let her go? And I thought calmly, Yes, I will let her go.

What horrifies me is the calmness with which I decided to let her life go out of my hands if saving her meant giving my own. But that was only thinking. I did not let her go. I was stronger than it was possible for me to be, and so was she. The thought of making the other choice gave me strength I did not know I had. At the last moment of our strength, her elbows now braced over the lip of the cliff, one of the ROTC boys came running, finally hearing our cries. He bristled with energy, leaned over the edge, grabbed her by the belt and heaved her body up onto the ground. She wept there for a while, lying on her stomach. I stroked her back, and then we walked down to the trailhead.

The others who had preceded us were standing around eating snacks and drinking sodas, wiping mud off their boots and putting on dry T-shirts, if they had them. Debbie tried to tell them what had happened, but no one seemed sufficiently impressed for her to feel they understood.

"She won't be happy," one of her colleagues joked, "unless we say it's the biggest thing that's happened since Princess Di was killed."

But one of the Hawaiian kids heard her, a quiet boy who stood with us to listen and talk.

"Were there any animals around when this happened?" he asked.

"No, I don't think so," I said. Then I remembered the bee I still carried in my eyeglass case. Debbie and I stared at each other, as if we'd seen something invisible. She leaned over and pulled her jeans up over her calf to reveal her bee tattoo.

"Bees have always been very special to me," she said.

"That's amazing," I said, though I wasn't sure what I meant.

"Not really," the kid said. "That kind of thing happens all the time."

I knew then he was thinking that the bee was her '*aumākua*—a fact as apparent to him as life-saving endorphins had been to me and the Holy Mother of Jesus had been to Debbie. Maybe it was not our belief that an animal or bug could give a person special protection, but it seemed as plausible as anything we could imagine. Maybe we didn't really believe that, but the bee was so integral a part to the pattern that was the day, we could not dismiss it, any more than we could dismiss the tree limb or the grip of our own hands. Meaning, like the sacred, is present if you look for it, but absent if you do not.

I dug the eyeglass case from my backpack and released the sleepy passenger. It wasn't until the next day when I woke up with my back and arms aching that I remembered the spider carrying her egg case, which I also had brought down from the mountain. I called Steve and asked him what to do with her, and he told me where to find the research lab on campus. I went there and handed the pill bottle over to a woman in a lab coat.

"I'm sorry it took so long for me to get her here. I hope she's okay," I said.

"Oh, she looks just fine," said the woman admiringly, and I handed over my charge.

I went to the library to research Hawaiian legends, to see if historical texture would add anything to my understanding of the remarkable events on Poamoho. I read some ancient stories, complex genealogies, and myths. But they did not help, because as rich as they were, they were not my story.

I'd been looking for a way to talk about the sacred that was authentically mine. What had I learned on that day? What was the ground note of its music? Bugs, I thought. Steve's more-than-twenty discoveries and my one apprenticeship to monarchs that had brought us together, the insects collaborating with scientists to restore balance within a besieged botanical system, Debbie's real and tattooed bees, and the spider carrying her egg case into the lab—all parts of the pattern that was the day, parts of the whole that is not perceivable because, as John Steinbeck wrote, "the pattern goes everywhere and is everything and cannot be encompassed by finite mind or by anything short of life—which it is." Bugs, I thought, on whose backs the world rides, unlike human beings who ride so heavily on Earth's back. Bugs, the smallest perceivable part of the biological whole. The world would be fine if people became extinct, but without bugs, the basic work they do of pollination, decomposition, stirring up the soil, and cleaning up everyone's mess with their fastidious appetites, Earth would become a barren dirty rock.

In my story I may not know how to define the sacred, but I have felt its presence in nature and in the coming-into-form that is language and art. I have felt it in the space inside the body and in the space between the stars. What holds the Creation together? Not emptiness. Without the health of the smallest among us, we could not exist.

Healing

FROM *Reasons for Hope: A Spiritual Journey*

Jane Goodall

with Phillip Berman

ne day, among all the days, I remember most of all. It was May 1981 and I had finally made it to Gombe after a six-week tour in America—six weeks of nonstop lectures, fund-raising dinners, conferences, meetings, and lobbying for various chimpanzee issues. Six weeks in and out of hotels, living out of a suitcase, packing and unpacking. I was exhausted and I longed for the peace of the forest. I wanted nothing more than to be with the chimpanzees, renewing my acquaintance with my old friends, getting my climbing legs back, relishing the sights, sounds, and smells of the forest! . . .

Back in Gombe. It was early in the morning and I sat on the steps of my house by the lakeshore. It was very still. Suspended over the horizon, where the mountains of the Congo fringed Lake Tanganyika, was the last quarter of the waning moon and her path danced and sparkled toward me across the gently moving water. After enjoying a banana and a cup of coffee, I was off, climbing up the steep slopes behind my house, carrying only my little binoculars, a notebook, a pencil, and a handful of raisins for lunch. I never feel the need for food, and seldom for water, when I am roaming the forests. How good it felt to be alone at last, reveling in the simple life that had nourished my spirit for so long.

In the faint light from the moon reflected by the dew-laden grass, it was not difficult to find my way up the mountain. All around, the trees were shrouded with the last mysteries of the night's dreaming. It was quiet, utterly peaceful. The only sounds were the occasional chirp of a cricket, and the soft murmur where the waves caressed the stones on the beach below. Suddenly there was a burst of song, the duet of a pair of robin chats, hauntingly beautiful. I realized that the intensity of the light had changed; dawn had crept upon me unawares. The coming brightness of the sun had all but vanquished the silvery, indefinite illumination of its own radiance reflected by the moon.

Five minutes later I heard the rustlings of leaves overhead. I looked up and saw the branches moving against the lightening sky. The chimps had awakened. It was Fifi and her offspring, Freud, Frodo, and little Fanni. I followed when they moved off up the slope, Fanni riding on her mother's back like a diminutive jockey. Presently they climbed into a tall fig tree and began to feed. I heard the occasional soft thuds as skins and seeds of figs fell to the ground.

For several hours we moved leisurely from one food tree to the next, gradually climbing higher and higher. On an open grassy ridge the chimps climbed into a massive mbula tree, where Fifi, replete from the morning's feasting, made a large comfortable nest high above me. She dozed through a midday siesta, little Fanni asleep in her arms, Frodo and Freud playing nearby. How healing it was to be back at Gombe again, and by myself with the chimpanzees and their forest. I had left the busy, materialistic world so full of greed and selfishness and, for a little while, could feel myself, as in the early days, a part of nature. I felt very much in tune with the chimpanzees, for I was spending time with them not to observe, but simply because I needed their company, undemanding and free of pity. From where I sat I could look out over the Kasakela Valley. Just below me to the west was the Peak. A surge of memories flooded through me: from that vantage point I had learned so much in the early days, sitting and watching while, gradually, the chimpanzees had lost their fear of the strange white ape who had invaded their world. I recaptured some of my long-ago feelings as I sat there, reflecting. The old excitement of discovery, of seeing things quite unknown to Western eyes. And the serenity that had come from living, day after day, as a part of the natural world. A world that dwarfs yet somehow enhances human emotions.

As I reflected on these things I had been only partly conscious of the approach of a storm. Suddenly, I realized that it was no longer growling in the distance but was right above. The sky was dark, almost black, and the rain clouds had obliterated the higher peaks. With the growing darkness came the stillness, the hush, that so often precedes a tropical downpour. Only the rumbling of the thunder, moving closer and closer, broke this stillness; the thunder and the rustling movements of the chimpanzees. All at once came a blinding flash of lightning, followed, a split second later, by an incredibly loud clap of thunder, that seemed almost to shake the solid rock before it rumbled on, bouncing from peak to peak. Then the dark and heavy clouds let loose such torrential rain that sky and earth seemed joined by moving water. I sat under a palm whose fronds, for a while, provided some shelter. Fifi sat hunched over, protecting her infant; Frodo pressed close against them in the nest; Freud sat with rounded back on a nearby branch. As the rain poured endlessly down, my palm fronds no longer provided shelter and I got wetter and wetter. I began to feel first chilly and then, as a cold wind sprang up, freezing; soon, turned in on myself, I lost all track of time. I and the chimpanzees formed a unit of silent, patient, and uncomplaining endurance.

It must have been an hour or more before the rain began to ease as the heart of the storm swept away to the south. At four-thirty the chimps climbed down, and we moved off through the soaked, dripping vegetation, back down the mountainside. Presently we arrived on a grassy ridge overlooking the lake. A pale, watery sun had appeared and its light caught the raindrops so that the world seemed hung with diamonds, sparkling on every leaf, every blade of grass. I crouched low to avoid destroying a jeweled spider's web that stretched, exquisite and fragile, across the trail.

I heard sounds of greeting as Fifi and her family joined Melissa and hers. They all climbed into a low tree to feed on fresh young leaves. I moved to a place where I could stand and watch as they enjoyed their last meal of the day. Down below, the lake was still dark and angry with white flecks where the waves broke, and rain clouds remained black in the south. To the north the sky was clear with only wisps of gray clouds still lingering. The scene was breathtaking in its beauty. In the soft sunlight, the chimpanzees' black coats were shot with coppery brown, the branches on which they sat were wet and dark as ebony, the young leaves a pale but brilliant green. And behind was the dramatic backcloth of the indigo sky where lightning flickered and distant thunder growled and rumbled.

Lost in awe at the beauty around me, I must have slipped into a state of heightened awareness. It is hard—impossible, really—to put into words the moment of truth that suddenly came upon me then. Even the mystics are unable to describe their brief flashes of spiritual ecstasy. It seemed to me, as I struggled afterward to recall the experience, that *self* was utterly absent: I and the chimpanzees, the earth and trees and air, seemed to merge, to become one with the spirit power of life itself. The air was filled with a feathered symphony, the evensong of birds. I heard new frequencies in their music and also in the singing insects' voices—notes so high and sweet I was amazed. Never had I been so intensely aware of the shape, the color of the individual leaves, the varied patterns of the veins that made each one unique. Scents were clear as well, easily identifiable: fermenting, overripe fruit; waterlogged earth; cold, wet bark; the damp odor of chimpanzee hair and, yes, my own too. And the aromatic scent of young, crushed leaves was almost overpowering. I sensed a new presence, then saw a bushbuck, quietly browsing upwind, his spiraled horns gleaming and his chestnut coat dark with rain.

Suddenly a distant chorus of pant-hoots elicited a reply from Fifi. As though wakening from some vivid dream I was back in the everyday world, cold, yet intensely alive. When the chimpanzees left, I stayed in that place—it seemed a most sacred place—scribbling some notes, trying to describe what, so briefly, I had experienced. I had not been visited by the angels or other heavenly beings that characterize the visions of the great mystics or the saints, yet for all that I believe it truly was a mystical experience.

Time passed. Eventually I wandered back along the forest trail and scrambled down behind my house to the beach. The sun was a huge red orb just vanishing behind the Congo hills and I sat on the beach watching the ever-changing sunset as it painted the sky red and gold and dark purple. The surface of the lake, calm after the storm, glinted with gold and violet and red ripples below the flaming sky.

Later, as I sat by my little fire, cooking my dinner of beans, tomatoes, and an egg, I was still lost in the wonder of my experience. Yes, I thought, there are many windows through which we humans, searching for meaning, can look out into the world around us. There are those carved out by Western science, their panes polished by a succession of brilliant minds. Through them we can see ever farther, ever more clearly, into areas which until recently were beyond human knowledge. Through such a scientific window I had been taught to observe the chimpanzees. For more than twenty-five years I had sought, through careful recording and critical analysis, to piece together their complex social behavior, to understand the workings of their minds. And this had not only helped us to better understand their place in nature but also helped us to understand a little better some aspects of our own human behavior, our own place in the natural world.

Yet there are other windows through which we humans can look out into the world around us, windows through which the mystics and the holy men of the East, and the founders of the great world religions, have gazed as they searched for the meaning and purpose of our life on earth, not only in the wondrous beauty of the world, but also in its darkness and ugliness. And those Masters contemplated the truths that they saw, not with their minds only but with their hearts and souls too. From those revelations came the spiritual essence of the great scriptures, the holy books, and the most beautiful mystic poems and writings. That afternoon, it had been as though an unseen hand had drawn back a curtain and, for the briefest moment, I had seen through such a window. In a flash of "outsight" I had known timelessness and quiet ecstasy, sensed a truth of which mainstream science is merely a small fraction. And I knew that the revelation would be with me for the rest of my life, imperfectly remembered yet always within. A source of strength on which I could draw when life seemed harsh or cruel or desperate.

How sad that so many people seem to think that science and religion are mutually exclusive. Science has used modern technology and modern techniques to uncover so much about the formation and the development of life-forms on Planet Earth and about the solar system of which our little world is but a minute part. In recent times astronomers have charted the atmosphere of planets and identified new solar systems; neurologists have learned astounding truths about the workings of our brains; physicists have divided the atom into smaller and smaller particles; a sheep has been cloned; a little robot has been sent to wander about on the surface of Mars; the whole miraculous world of cyberspace has been opened up. Truly the human intellect is awesome. Alas, all of these amazing discoveries have led to a belief that every wonder of the natural world and of the universe—indeed, of infinity and time—can, in the end, be understood through the logic and the reasoning of a finite mind. And so, for many, science has taken the place of religion. It was not some intangible God who created the universe, they argue, it was the Big Bang. Physics, chemistry, and evolutionary biology can explain the start of the universe and the appearance and progress of life on earth, they say. To believe in God, in the human soul, and in life after death is simply a desperate and foolish attempt to give meaning to our lives.

But not all scientists believe thus. There are quantum physicists who have concluded that the concept of God is not, after all, merely wishful thinking. Physicist John C. Eccles, although he felt that questions regarding the human soul were matters beyond science, warned scientists that they should not give definite negative answers when asked about the continuity of the conscious self after death. There are those exploring the human brain who feel that no matter how much they discover about this extraordinary structure it will never add up to a complete understanding of the human mind—that the whole is, after all, greater than the sum of the parts. The Big Bang theory is yet another example of the incredible, the awe-inspiring ability of the human mind to learn about seemingly unknowable phenomena in the beginning of time. Time as we know it, or think we know it. But what about before time? And what about beyond space? I remembered so well how those questions had driven me to distraction when I was a child.

I lay flat on my back and looked up into the darkening sky. How sad it would be, I thought, if we humans ultimately were to lose all sense of mystery, all sense of awe. If our left brains were utterly to dominate the right so that logic and reason triumphed over intuition and alienated us absolutely from our innermost being, from our hearts, our souls. I watched as, one by one, the stars appeared, the brightest first and then, as the sun's light faded, more and more until the sky was studded with brilliant, flashing points of light. Albert Einstein, undeniably one of the greatest scientists and thinkers of our time, had sustained a mystical outlook on life that was, he said, constantly renewed from the wonder and humility that filled him when he gazed at the stars . . .

And so I have reached the end of my story. I have tried to answer the questions that people ask me, about my religious and spiritual beliefs, about my philosophy of life, about why I have hope for the future. I have answered as honestly and candidly as I can. Indeed, I have laid bare a lot of my mind, heart, and soul. But there is one story as yet untold. To me, with my love of symbolism (surely inherited from my superstitious Welsh forebears!), it seems that this story may explain why I have done much of what I have done, lived as I have lived. And why I must continue to the bitter—or perhaps glorious—end.

It happened when I was less than a year old—before I could talk. I was in my pram outside the grocery store, guarded by Peggy, our white bull terrier. Nanny was shopping inside. A dragonfly began swooping around me, and I screamed—so a well-intentioned passerby hit the dragonfly to the ground with his newspaper, and crushed it with his foot. I continued to scream all the way home. In fact I became so hysterical that they called the doctor, who prescribed a sedative to calm me down. I heard this story for the first time about five years ago. Vanne was writing about my early life and asked if I could remember the incident at all—why had I been so terrified?

As I read what she had written, the sixty intervening years fell away and I was transported back in time. I remembered lying in my nursery. There was a lot of green, I thought—and Vanne said yes, green curtains and green linoleum. And I remember watching a big blue dragonfly which had come in through the window. I protested when Nanny chased it out, but she said it might sting me, and that it had a sting as long as its "tail" (meaning, of course, its abdomen). That is a *long* sting! No wonder I was scared when a dragonfly zoomed around my pram. But being afraid of something did not mean I wanted it killed. If I close my eyes I can see, with almost unbearable clarity, the glorious shimmering and still quivering wings, the blue "tail" gleaming in the sunlight, the head crushed on the sidewalk. Because of me it had died, perhaps in pain. I screamed in helpless outrage. And from a terrible sense of guilt.

Perhaps I have subconsciously lived my whole life trying to assuage that guilt. Perhaps the dragonfly was part of some plan, to bring a message to a little child, all those years ago. If so, all I can say, to my God, is: "Message received and understood." I have tried to assuage some of the guilt we all must feel, for our inhumanity to man and beast alike. And, with the support of all people of compassionate and loving heart, I shall go on trying until the end. And the end . . . will be the beginning?

Imagining the Divine

Diane Ackerman

On cold days, the divine haunts
the exhalations of squirrels
whose breath hovers
starch-white as tiny souls.

Like the sky, heaven begins
at one's feet. Look down.
When the here and now
becomes the there and then,
the red-winged blackbird's rasp
sounds angelic, summer croons
pontifications of light,
and, my god, life fancies trees.

Because I believe we become
a neverthriving of dreams,
all our senses leveled,

I imagine the divine
drawing on of evening,
belted at the waist,
the divine cloud-slung stars
burning black holes
into the fabric of night,

I divine the lusty sun
in each aching-green leaf,
and revere the silver
ceremonies of the moon
cradled in its own arms.

Just imagine the divine
hilltops padded with trees,
the bone-wings of a river basin
hipped in daylilies, Canada goose chicks:
fluff-budgets that waddle.

Before my one and only
three-pound universe, I stand
in judgment, alone with the world,
so long as we both shall live,
or vanish when eyelids close.

Because life will have been all
my days, I imagine the divine
face of my loving dear,
who shares the harsh and softer fate-falls
inside these garden walls
where the divine agency of love
will have mattered in the end
more than faith, call, reward,
or a vein of panting stars.

Like the planet, we seemed
to be traveling through space
but were always in a holding pattern
between the earth and sky,
waiting to unbecome, plural once more.

The divine I imagine
speaks to me through pleats
of perfect taffeta in my study,
between the wingbeats of hummingbirds,
when love smiles humbly
at sunrise and in evening rain.

The Great Without

FROM *Parabola*

Linda Hogan

*I*n European natural histories, human imagination was most often projected onto the outside world. Pliny's *Natural History*, for instance, was an errant map of a true world. There were dog-headed humans who could only bark, men with heads in their chests, and people with only one foot but with the ability to leap powerfully and to use the foot as a shade tree. There were mermaids, springs believed to grant eternal life, and islands where demons or angels lived. At one time the Egyptians thought that people on the other side of the world walked upside down. Bestiaries included the phoenix, griffins, and unicorns. Unshaped by fact, knowledge, or even observation, these fantasy worlds became the world as seen by the human mind.

Even in later times, the relationship between nature and humanity posed a dilemma. Once it was thought that the world entered the human eye, and that only through our seeing of it did it exist. There was much discussion about how a mountain could fit into the human eye. This difficulty with perspective pushed humans toward other conclusions just as erroneous as believing foremost in the eye of the beholder. Euclid thought the eye was the point of origin for all things. Plato believed the world emanated from the eye, while others thought that there was something given off from objects by which we perceived them. In any case, most of the theories made nature smaller than it is and made the human larger. Vision was about the seer only, not the seen.

Nothing could be more different from how tribal people on all continents have seen the world. From the perspectives of those who have remained in their own terrain for thousands of years, there were—and are—other points of view. For tribal thinkers, the outside world creates the human: we are alive to processes within and without the self. It is a more humble way to view the world, and far more steady. Nature is the creator, not the created.

There exists, too, a geography of spirit that is tied to and comes from the larger geography of nature. It offers to humans the bounty and richness of the world. Father Berard Haile, a priest traveling among the Navajo in the 1930s, was in awe of the complexity of their knowledge, one that exists within the context of what we now call an ecosystem. In the Upward Moving Way, for example, the ceremony brings in all aspects of the growth of plants: the movement upward as the roots deepen, the insects beneath and above the ground, the species of birds which come to this plant. All aspects of the ceremony reveal a wide knowledge of the world. In order to heal, this outside life and world must be taken in and "seen" by the patient as being part of one working system.

Laurens van der Post, a writer, naturalist, and psychologist who grew up in Africa, wrote in his essay "The Great Uprooter" about how his son's illness was announced by a dream. In the dream, the young man stood on a beach, unable to move, watching a great tidal wave of water bearing down on him. From out of the swell of the wave, a large black elephant walked toward him. It was this dream, van der Post was certain, that announced his son's cancer, the first point of cellular change. Van der Post called the dream something that came from "the great without": such an experience seemed to encompass, he said, all the withouts and withins a human could experience.

Nature is now too often defined by people who are fragmented from the land. Such a world is seldom one that carries and creates the human spirit. Too rarely is it understood that the soul lies at all points of intersection between human consciousness and the rest of nature. Skin is hardly a container. Our boundaries are not solid; we are permeable, and even when we are solitary dreamers we are rooted in the soul outside. If we are open enough, strong enough to connect with the world, we become something greater than we are.

Turn-of-the-century Lakota writer Zitkala Sa (Gertrud Simmons Bonnin) wrote of the separation between humankind and the natural world as a great loss to her. In her autobiography, she said that nature was what would have helped her to survive her forced removal to Indian boarding school.

> I was ready to curse men of small capacity for being the dwarfs their God had made them. In the process of my education I had lost all consciousness of the nature world about me. Thus, when a hidden rage took me to the small, white-walled prison which I then called my room, I unknowingly turned away from my own salvation. For the white man's papers I had given up my faith in the Great Spirit. For these same papers I had forgotten the healing in trees and brooks. Like a slender tree, I had been uprooted from my mother, nature, and God.

Zitkala Sa might have agreed with Pliny that there were dog-headed, barking men, and men with heads, not hearts, in their chests.

· · ·

Soul loss is what happens as the world around us disappears. In contemporary North American Hispanic communities, soul loss is called *susto*. It is a common condition in the modern world. *Susto* probably began when the soul was banished from nature, when humanity withdrew from the world, when there became only two things—human and nature, animate and inanimate, sentient and not. This was when the soul first began to slip away and crumble.

In the reversal and healing of soul loss, Brazilian tribal members who tragically lost their land and place in the world visit or reimagine nature in order to become well again. Anthropologist Michael Harner wrote about healing methods among Indian people relocated to an urban slum of Peru. The healing takes place in the forest at night, as the person is returned for a while to the land he or she once knew. Such people are often cured through their renewed connections, their "visions of the river forest world, including visions of animals, snakes, and plants." Unfortunately, these places are now only ghosts of what they once were.

The cure for *susto*, soul sickness, is not in books. It is written in the bark of a tree, in the moonlit silence of night, in the bank of a river and the water's motion. The cure is outside ourselves.

In the 1500s, Paracelsus, considered by many to be a father of modern medicine, was greatly disliked by his contemporaries. For a while, though, he almost returned the practice of medicine to its wider place of relationships by emphasizing the importance of harmony between man and nature. His view of healing was in keeping with the one that tribal elders still hold, that a human being is a small model of the world and the universe. Vast spaces stretch inside us, he thought, an inner firmament, large as the outer world.

The world inside the mind is lovely sometimes, and large. Its existence is why a person can recall the mist of morning clouds on a hill, the fern forest, and the black skies of night that the Luiseno call their spirit, acknowledging that the soul of the world is great within the human soul. It is an enlarged and generous sense of self, life, and being, as if not only the body is a creation of the world elements, but air and light and night sky have created an inner vision that some have called a map of the cosmos. In Lakota astronomy, the stars are called the breath of the Great Spirit. It is as if the old Lakota foresaw physics and modern astronomy, sciences that now tell us we are the transformed matter of stars, that the human body is a kind of cosmology.

The inward may have been, all along, the wrong direction to seek. A person seems so little and small, and without is the river, the mountain, the forest of fern and tree, the desert with its lizards, the glacial meltings and freezings and movements of life. The cure for soul loss is in the mist of morning, the grass that grew a little through the night, the first warmth of sunlight, the waking human in a world infused with intelligence and spirit.

Cargo

Amy Schuring

The world is gone. I must carry you.
—PAUL CELAN

When my world was young I carried the first death,
my true friend, over miles of dunes to reach God,
weaving webs along pale trails of sand. *Please
take him from me.* Claim this adolescent, golden boy
you have stolen from the dawn too soon.

My staggering dance beneath the moonless night,
two billion heavy stars my only audience.
I've got nothing to hold on to, no belief
except for this ghost, the weight of the ocean,
locked in my arms.

Spin me something smooth and determined
with the instinct of hope. I am lost on these paths

surrounded by a quiet wilderness of birds, an atlas
of extinct animals long lost to my world.
They tell me nothing.

When my world was old I walked the same dune roads
to where God rests. Holding an armful of my dead,
light as birds, I walk the last shore in the world
carried by this wind, the slow centuries' breath.

If I find God, I would draw my grief and longing
in wide bands of iridescent blues—this painting
swirled with the songs of the dead, loves lost
flashing silver, like fish-light throughout.

Suddenly we walk by you God, and you say nothing,
your massive shoulders the size of a ship's hull
anchored gracefully in the beach. You turn your mossy
head away from us, slowly, like a rolling whale.
I set my dead into the surf, never imagining they could swim
    like that.

Initiation

Kim Chernin

I n 1971 I went to Israel to live on a kibbutz. I was longing for regeneration through humble work. I connected this desire with *eretz Isroel*. The earth, the soil. Since I had first walked into the valley of black sheep at the Powerscourt Estate, I had longed to kick back the dead leaf and uncover the true ground of myself. But with every step I took, the skeptic in me had something to say.

This skeptic, hard-edged, never innocent, born knowing, rather bitter, not likely to take the risk of believing in anything, narrowing its eyes, puffing out its chest, smiling scornfully at my "female exaggerations," had been driven against the wall and was fighting back for all it was worth. It directed its sharpest thrusts against my "mysticism, and related rot," trying to reason me out of my growing fascination with the subtle, extremely potent, as yet unnamed something I found in nature.

Every time I walked off the kibbutz, into the fields and hills that surrounded it, I responded to the landscape with a growing rapture, as if I were returning home after thousands of years of absence. The black goats grazing on the white rocks in a rust-red earth, the wild river valleys where dark-skinned women from neighboring villages tended their flocks, the purple mountains covered in mist, drawing away into the distance, all called to me from an old knowledge, demanding my surrender.

But how could I surrender?

The gossip. The woman raving. The witch. The woman who mutters beneath her breath. The woman who can't think without weeping. The woman who gathers herbs by moonlight and dries them in secret beneath her bed. The woman who claims to see what isn't there. The woman who knows the future before it happens. The woman who doesn't read the newspaper, hasn't a clue what is going on in the world, but insists that her daughter, ten thousand miles from her, is in danger. This creature, for whom we have been taught so much contempt—is she what I was becoming?

I had left my daughter in California with her father. It was painful to think of the time that would pass before I was settled enough to send for her. In fact, I never did get settled enough. I returned home ten months later. I was a different person when I got back. An arrow, spinning in circles all my life, had now pointed.

On the kibbutz I became an expert pruner of trees. I made a few friends. They came over to have tea with me in the late afternoons. But the nights were difficult; the wild mountain setting, a few yards from the Lebanese border, where the Israeli army was building a security road, did little to give me peace of mind. I was not frightened by the sound of shelling or the sudden arrival of Israeli soldiers on the track of terrorists hidden in the neighboring caves. It was, rather, the wildness of the place calling to the kindred wildness in me that unsettled my efforts to become a hardworking farmer, hands hardened by toil. In the early evenings I would climb up into the guard towers that looked down over the valley.

One day a bird swept out over the landscape. I watched it soaring and wheeling against the darkening sky. Then I noticed something remarkable. For that brief instant the world was suspended in a perfect balance. In everything there was an equal light and darkness. In the grass below me, in the purple mountains, in the piercing blue of the Mediterranean, in the taut wings of the bird. A poise. A stillness. All things divided equally between day and night, the light and the dark, the expectation and the fulfillment. It was a universe held in perfect balance, its opposites contained and reconciled. I sensed, in that image, the sudden, rapturous possibility of bringing about a state of accord between the warring parts of myself.

By the time I got back to my room I saw a lot in this idea. Reason had its place, without doubt, in what I was experiencing. Its categories had helped me give shape over the years to a highly irrational, often chaotic experience. But there were times when these categories had to be set aside so that a new perception of life could emerge. If this experience upset the neat labels that had been put upon things then it would be the work of reason to reorder its ordering principles and make them serve the exposition of intuitive truth. I would never cease to think about my experience. But I could not use reason as a way of warding off the power of rapture. That was like being forced to choose between day and night, light and darkness, the known and the unknown, as if only one of these polar opposites were real.

I lit the heater and got under the covers. That was it? As simple as that? Here, finally, was the next step I had been trying to take? Where I had previously perceived irreconcilable opposition between reason and worship, I now grasped the possibility of bringing them together. This was the lesson I had been trying to learn. . . . I was capable of logic, discipline, and self-control. I was capable of wild, exuberant, visionary dreaming.

A few days later I was in my room after a day of strenuous labor in the orchards. Lying in bed, I heard a voice. It said: "For it is possible to rise by joy, through those same stages of initiation suffering required."

I sat up and folded my arms around my knees. "Voices? Now she's hearing voices?" the undying skeptic in me immediately brought out. But this time instead of mocking and dismissing the voice, why not listen to it?

I went to look out the window; I opened it wide and leaned over the valley. Later, if I wanted to, I could work out some theory about subvocal mental voices. For now, this voice had named what until then had been nameless. From the moment I had knelt down before the tree in the mountains above Dublin, I had been involved in a process of initiation.

What could I say about this experience? To begin with, it was not separate from my body. Usually it arose as my menstrual blood dropped down. Although spiritual, it did not require a mortification of the body. Furthermore, it made me capable of a particular type of thought. Since that day in Dublin I had been fascinated by questions about the nature of reality, which had not really interested me before that time. Evidently, this type of initiation asked me to overcome the conflict I had always perceived between thinking and feeling.

And then there was nature: In my early twenties I had felt myself to be outside of nature. Now I participated in it. The flow of my blood was connected to the cycles of moons and tides; a bird in flight called me into its flying. Working in the orchards I felt in need of strong roots, seasons of change. When the afternoons were hot we lay down under the apple trees to rest and I grew back into the earth, into a second body.

Moreover, over the years the initiation process had irreversibly changed my mode of perception. Now, every stone and tree I looked at seemed to have a soul, to feel and bleed, rejoice and suffer. All this I had come to understand not through reading holy books that instructed me in religious doctrine, but through my own immediate, intensely felt relationship to the universe, which I had come to know not by taking it as an object of study but through a process of identification and participation that overcame all sense of separation between what I looked at and what I became in the process of looking.

Consequently, the organizational categories I had always taken for granted had also changed over the years. One day, observing the tiny blue star-shaped flower that grew from a weed out of the cracked earth on the path behind the kibbutz, I had wondered why people categorized some plants as desirable and some as weeds—everything I looked at seemed to have, in that moment, the same quality of a majestic beauty. It must have been that day I first noticed the exquisite purple color of cow dung drying on the path. It, too, although it em-

barrassed me to think it, seemed to hold the same quality of a revealed divinity, a sense that the deepest possible meaningfulness and
presence were woven into the humblest, most insignificant bits of
matter. Cow dung and weeds, apple trees and black goats, the Arab
boys wandering after their flocks in the dry river valley, the hawks
soaring overhead, the woman crouched down on the ruins in a state of
ecstatic observation—all told the same story of a divinity embedded in
the human body, rising from the earth, dropping down from the sky,
weaving together thinking and feeling, perceiving and being in a
linked participation that gave order, meaning, and direction of life. If
this experience shattered the idea of the divine as male and unknowable, if it called into question the idea of spirit as an elusive essence
that hovered unattainably outside of human reach, then it was time to
give up these ideas and place myself at risk in a new relationship to
the universe. Whatever I might someday become, for now this is what
it meant to be a woman.

The value of such thinking was immediately apparent. It shifted
the focus of my preoccupation from theories about experience to the
experience itself. It brought to mind an event that had occurred almost two months earlier, a few days after I had arrived in Israel.

I had been wandering about by myself in a small village of Moroc-
can Jews visible, below in the valley, from our kibbutz. We had driven
down in the late afternoon and parked the truck discreetly out of
sight, knowing that we should not be driving. It was the evening of
Yom Kippur. Most of us had eaten a small meal in the dining room and
would not eat again until nightfall of the next day. When we reached
the village on foot the others went ahead, walking in a purposeful
stride toward the synagogue. I came along more slowly. The village
was interesting to me. It reminded me of the small town in Russia
where my mother had been born. The same dusty streets, dilapidated
houses, dogs and chickens wandering in and out. A sense, too, of
something ancient and enduring that had managed to survive the
poverty and dirt.

I lost track of my companions. The village girls, who had not gone
to temple on the holiest night of the year, came to walk with me. At
first there were only a few of them. We walked on, the little girls trail-

ing after me. Soon we were joined by others, who came running toward us, delighted by this opportunity for diversion. I provided plenty. There I was, in a long, brightly colored dress, a shawl over my shoulders. I looked as if I belonged somewhere ethnic but I was unable to speak a word to them. My only Hebrew was the absurd phrase that I could not speak Hebrew. This set them off into wild laughter; after all, there I was, speaking it.

They tried again and again, chattering at me, pointing to themselves, pointing to the kibbutz on the mountain, running around me in circles. I would listen intently to what they were saying, hesitate for a moment when they had finished talking. Then, as they waited with great anticipation, standing up on their tiptoes, their eyes wide, mouths open, sucking in their breath, I did it again. No, nothing had changed: I still had only my one phrase. I could not speak Hebrew.

Eventually they must have decided that I was not playing a game. They began to look at me with a serious compassion. Finally, overcoming their shyness, they drew close and took charge of me. They crowded around me, grabbed my skirt; they went on chattering at me in Hebrew and kept right on laughing when I couldn't chatter back. Then I had an inspiration. I knelt down in the dust. I put my arms around them and told them my name. That much at least I had learned in Hebrew class. *"Ani Kim,"* I whispered. "I am Kim."

It exhausted my eloquence, but they no longer cared. They grabbed me by the hand, pushed each other aside, threw their arms around my neck, kissed me, dragged me to my feet. I had a fleeting thought about my companions in the synagogue. Would I have learned more about God if I had joined them there? And then I heard, as we walked on together about the village, echoing from the whitewashed buildings and the dirt streets, at nightfall in this ancient homeland that did not cherish its girls, "Keem, Keem, Keem, Keem." My name had become an incantation.

I thought of those girls while I stood at my window, looking down past the village all the way to the Mediterranean—the sea that had carried those of my people who survived away from their homeland after Bar Kochba, the great legendary hero, had failed in his uprising against the Roman legions during the first century of the Christian

Era. I thought about those girls and wondered when I would see them again, with their dark eyes of old knowledge. I told myself it had been no commonplace event, that wandering in the dusty streets while my companions sat indoors, the women excluded from the service upstairs behind the scene in the synagogue. Initiation, was it?

Through the doorway of a crumbling house I had seen an old woman, wrapped in a fraying shawl, crouch down to place cow dung on a fire. She beckoned me in when she saw me looking, hobbled over on bare feet, drew me inside. The little room was filled with smoke; it smelled of too many lives and too much poverty. I drew back when she placed in my hand a cup of mint tea. The little girls, who had trooped in after me, were watching my face apprehensively, afraid I might refuse this hospitality. I wanted to. There were circles of grease floating in the pale green liquid, the glass was smudged, and I knew, nevertheless, I was going to drink it. The old lady watched me as I sipped. Sweet, hot, fresh as the night sky. I had to wonder whether wine sipped from a ceremonial goblet on Shabbos was any more holy than this smudged glass offered, from the fullness of poverty, to a stranger.

I held the glass between my hands when I had finished, bowed my head over it to thank the old woman, pressed the glass to my chest. That pleased her; she came up close to me, took me by the elbow, shook me lightly. Then she began to talk and chatter with the same urgency the little girls had shown when they began to love me. She pointed to her heart, to each of her breasts, and then drew me to the threshold and pointed to the mountains, just then taking on their purple shadow beneath the sky. I strained toward her with my entire attention, but I could not figure out what she was trying to say. Finally she gave up, took me by the shoulders, drew me down, fixed me with a penetrating gaze, released me.

A short time later I caught sight of my companions from the kibbutz winding back toward the truck parked on the outskirts of the village. It was dark by then; the moon was not yet up. The girls came along with me, looking pleased with themselves, very secretive. They wouldn't let me join my companions, a few streets ahead. They pressed close against me, led me on a route of their own so that I arrived at the truck a good while before the others. And then, in twos and threes, they took themselves off, waving good-bye to me. A tall girl remained with me, holding my hand until everyone else had climbed into the truck. Then she pressed my hand against her heart, whispered my name to me in a meaningful way, and said: "You don forghet uz . . ."

I had thought back to the night of Yom Kippur before now. But always I had been involved in my usual conflict, insisting the event had been "more than ordinary, very significant, guided by some nonrational force," while at the same time I hollered with derision. Distracted by this inability to determine "the true nature of the event," I had not paid attention to my desire to return to the village to see the girls again, or to the fantasy set loose in me when I wondered what the old woman had told me. Could she have asked me why that night was more holy than any other? For the first time, at my window looking down over the valley, I asked myself whether the girls had led me to her deliberately.

The answer to these questions did not come to me for many years. When it arrived finally I did not link it to the little girls, the old woman, the mint tea, the waking rapture at the window. But I had decided to write a story about a sect of women that secretly worshipped the Goddess within traditional Judaism and had done so for the thousands of years since the Hebrew conquest of Canaan, handing the tradition down from mother to daughter.

The idea for this novel, *The Flame Bearers*, came to me in 1978, seven years after I left Israel and returned to California. But I no longer doubt that fiery seed was cast deep into my imagination during that night walk through the small village in the darkening valley. Not a single man had been visible in the streets. For those hours of sunset we walked and wandered in a women's world, making up incantations, finding ceremonial forms and our own sense of the sacred in the dusty streets, outside the synagogue.

The Goddess was with us that night, even if the little girls knew nothing of her. She was there when the small fire was kindled from cow droppings by an old crone stooping over the flames. It was she who helped me put the dirty glass of tea to my lips. I had no need to think of her as an objective reality hidden somewhere in the universe keeping an eye on the world as God is said to do. She was fully present long before I learned to name her. Already then, she had risen from the dark soil, to lend a more than ordinary significance to my encounter with the girls. In darkness she had been born to my imagination, in darkness over the next seven years she continued to ask me questions.

I had gone far when I walked away from my companions and went out wandering with the girls. But I continued to fuss about whether one should trust to irrational events and what their true nature might be and whether the girls' coming upon me in the streets was simply coincidence or some other kind of guidance. And if guidance, on what authority? And if authority, from what source? I had glimpsed the possibility of bringing peace between the skeptic and believer who continued to war within me, but that brief glimpse was all I could achieve.

I stayed awake with these thoughts. I woke wrestling with them as if they were a mighty angel that surely would bless me if only I could get the upper hand. And meanwhile I did not go back to the village, although I lived in Israel for many months. I did not go back although I continued to gaze down longingly at it from my window. Within a few months I no longer thought about the old woman and what she had been trying to tell me. Even today I do not know.

But I had touched the hem of the long skirts of the Goddess, there in the streets on the holiest night of the year. I had tasted her in the cup of tea, looked into her eyes, failed to understand her. To figure out what she had told me I would have to unearth the reasons I fought so militantly against my imagination. Why is this night more holy than any other night? To answer that question I would have to go on following the little girls.

God in the Art of
the Everyday

The Sound of Grace

Catherine Johnson

Because inside human beings is where God learns.
—RAINER MARIA RILKE

I live in two worlds: one which is bright and sharp, bursting
with amplified sound; the other muted, whispering, and soft.
Hearing aids give me days that are like oil paintings, rich in
detail and definite in line, while my own unaided hearing
presents me with watercolor landscapes, scenes more abstract and
fluid. Most of the time, I prefer the quieter world. Released from the
effort of accurate understanding, I feel free to simply listen. My other
senses open like windows bringing in light, textures, and smells to ac-
complish what my ears alone cannot. And every once in a while, out of
that softer wash of sound around me, a clear and perfect voice
emerges, the voice of the divine.

On a recent trip to Paris, I paused at the top of a steep concrete
stairwell that led from the street to the underground world of the city's
métro. I removed my hearing aids, anticipating the overwhelming

sounds that lay ahead. Instantly, the traffic and the conversations around me blurred and receded. The iron handrail I grasped felt hot where the sun rested on it. A little breath of breeze brushed through my hair, and something savory drifted by from a café next door. Because it was my last afternoon in that enchanting and beautiful city, I wanted to remember everything—even the pull of people: young, old, tourist, Parisian, flowing around me, descending the steps and vanishing into the shadows below. I stood there, at the top of the stairs, listening for a few more moments, taking it all in. Then I, too, headed down to the trains.

While the tunnels of the métro provided instant relief from the city's summer heat, they assaulted the senses in other ways. Fluorescent light glared against white-tiled walls only to be swallowed by winding miles of concrete and darkness. The place was both too bright and depressingly dim. A deep breath uncovered the fruity smell and acrid taste of axle grease, perspiration, and old urine. And every few minutes, the air swelled with the roar and vibration of an arriving train.

Shuffling forward with my ticket, I could hear the *thunk, thunk* of turnstiles ahead, but there was something else as well. A few errant notes of music filtered through the chatter and hum of the moving crowd. As I passed through the turnstile and headed for the train that would carry me to the Louvre, the crowd thinned but the music remained, growing louder and more pure. Long and soulful tones, rising and falling, reminded me of someone crying out in pure pleasure, then weeping gratefully in such pleasure's fading wake. The voice of a single violin was filling that tunnel with grace.

I do not remember walking the rest of the way to the platform that day, only how the music inhabited me. Each draw of the bow made me large, each return across the strings, small. A distance that could have taken only seconds to cover became a pilgrimage. Deep sorrow and deep gladness moved through me, as if I had been away from one I loved and had returned home at last. Finally, I reached the source of the beautiful music: a middle-aged man sitting on a folding aluminum campstool with an open violin case at his feet.

He was heavy in the belly but sat on his stool with a straight back, as if occupying a principal chair with the symphony. His hair was pulled into a scraggly gray ponytail and his dark flannel trousers were worn, frayed at the cuffs and along the seams. The sweat stains that darkened his light blue shirt belied the otherwise invisible effort with which he played. I stared, unable to look away. Not only was I hearing the music, but it poured in through my eyes. Each line shimmered brighter, the pitch building and straining, like the cries of a lover well loved. The music was so pure that the fibrous strings of my own heart began to vibrate and break. And in that moment, standing on the platform slightly apart from the crowd, I knew something of God, and God knew again the incandescent instant when suffering ceases, could feel the breaking of a grateful heart.

With tears streaming down my cheeks, I searched the musician's pale round face hoping for his gaze. In the presence of such grace, I could not bear to be alone. Surely, he will understand I thought. But when my eyes finally found his, they were half closed and empty—the wandering white oceans of the blind. I have thought many times since how the voice of God spoke that afternoon to a woman hard of hearing through the hands of a man without sight.

Rapture

Rita Kiefer

Still the woman from Ávila,
how light her body drifting from its chapel
stall, the other nuns flinging themselves like
affectionate harpies to hold it down.
Teresa with her actual grace
hair after hair bristling, almost sizzling
from the heat her body carried. *Divine*
she called that Light.

That light. We all want it.
Is anything worth saying without it?

Yet suppose it was longing for the almond she loved
or the pepper that took her
off the ground or the river spasms in April
not any Lord at all, but
the world and words like God
kept rushing.

"Under My Napkin? In Sky? In Trees?"

A *Child's* Questions About
Death and Sex, God and Life

Susan Biskeborn

he first time our daughter Mary ever stumped us with a metaphysical question she was three years old, sitting in her high chair and eating dinner. My husband's great-aunt Neva had recently died at the venerable age of ninety-three, and although there would be no memorial service, we planned to drive from our home in Seattle to Portland, Oregon, to visit Neva's son.

Would we see Aunt Neva, too, our little girl wondered. My husband Tom and I were prepared for this question. We had read some books about discussing death with children and we were determined to do it right, kindly but without any sugarcoating. Talk concretely, the experts advised. If you were not religious (we aren't) and did not believe in an afterlife (we don't), the books counseled against abstractions like heaven. Give children examples, the book recommended, of what it means to be dead.

No, we would not see Neva, we answered. She had died a peaceful death after a long, long life and we would never see her again. She was dead and that meant that she couldn't see or smell or taste or touch or feel or hear or talk or move anymore. That was what being dead meant, and it was sad, but it was a part of life, too. All living things, all plants and animals and people, eventually died.

Mary didn't look sad but rather bewildered. Glancing at the pink paper napkin on her high-chair tray, she burst out, her baby syntax belying the complexity of the question, "Where she go? Under my napkin?" Looking out the window, she continued, "In sky? In trees?"

Tom and I glanced at each other, dumbfounded at Mary's mystical leap from mundane napkin to sublime sky. Unprompted, she had gone straight for the metaphysical gold: after all that living, what happened to our I-ness after death? Where did it go?

It was a question I had often pondered myself, for example, when Tom's mother had died years before. Where had she gone, my skinny, cerebral mother-in-law, I wondered, as my homebound plane ascended through Oregon's clouds after her funeral. Where indeed had our irreverent and brilliant friend Andy gone after dying at age forty from cancer? Although Tom and I had watched him waste away during years of futile experimental treatments, I sometimes caught myself imagining things: there he went, loping down that dark city street. Or maybe he was over there, his shoulders characteristically hunched, waiting for a late-night bus in a hooded sweatshirt.

"Oh, honey," I haltingly answered my daughter, trying to keep it simple. "After dying, people's bodies are buried, but we don't know what happens to their minds or spirits. Some people say those die with them, others think that spirits go to heaven. But everything's just a guess—nobody knows for sure."

At this, Mary's face wore a puzzled look. You're joking, it seemed to say—nobody, not even any adult, knows the answer? Her bafflement reminded me of the time, not long before, when she had asked to see photos of her birth parents.

"We don't have any," we had replied then.

"Just look in the book," she offered, meaning the fat album of snapshots my husband had taken in her orphanage in China.

"We wish we did have photos of your China mom and dad," we said, "but we don't." Saved for later were the difficult explanations.

If Mary had any dissatisfaction with our careful, qualified answers to her important questions about her birth parents or Aunt Neva, she persisted nonetheless.

"Why do people die?" she asked not long after we returned from our trip to Portland.

"People get very badly sick or they die from accidents or from old age, like Neva," said my husband.

"But you won't get old," Mary countered with a tone of either hopefulness or anxiety.

"But we will," I said quietly, and our daughter reached out from her high chair with her chubby hands for ours. There was an eloquent moment of silence then, as our young daughter registered the sorrowful realization that we, too—her parents, her protectors, those seemingly invincible grown-ups—would die one day.

Despite their small size, children ask very big questions about life and death. At age three, Mary already sought answers to two essential questions about life: where did I come from, and where am I going?

As Robert Coles writes, children are "seekers," "young pilgrims well aware that life is a finite journey and as anxious to make sense of it as those of us who are farther along in the time allotted us."

Unlike me as a child, Mary is not being raised in a religious household and does not go to church regularly, but nonetheless she is a seeker.

Dorothy Day, the visionary founder of the Catholic Worker movement who was nominated for sainthood in 1997, wrote, "How much did I hear of religion as a young child? Very little, and yet my heart leaped when I heard the name of God. I do believe every soul has a tendency toward God."

"Do you believe in God?" my daughter asked from her car seat when she was about five. As usual, she saved all her most crucial questions for when I was behind the wheel, preferably when Seattle's relentless rain had snarled traffic.

"Well," I began, "I was raised to believe in God, and we know plenty of people who believe in God, but I'm just not sure if I do."

"Then I don't either," she declared.

"Wait a minute, honey," I said, a bit exasperated. "Whether or not there is a God is a big question. It can take a whole lifetime to answer it. You don't have to make up your mind at age five."

"Was Jesus a real person?" came the next salvo.

"Yes, he was. He lived a long time ago and he was a holy person. Some people believe that Jesus Christ was God, and they're called Christians."

Then, in one of those sudden detours that are a specialty of children, Mary said, "Why can't men have babies? Did God make it that way?"

I couldn't help it—I laughed as hard as she had the previous week when I had forthrightly addressed her question, delivered in the middle of a crowded mall, about how babies come out of the mother's body.

"The *vagina*?" she kept repeating amid gales of hilarity, obviously amazed at the very thought. To a child, vaginas and God and Jesus and death and sex are all brand-new concepts and all equally exotic and idiotic and enigmatic.

In essence, Mary's theological and metaphysical questions are of a piece with her inquiries about fairies and ghosts and monsters, and all her many questions could be summarized thus: Are there wonders in the world?

Clearly, the answer is yes. Even if we are not religious, all of us teach our children about the ineffable in mundane ways, for example, when we tell them stories about Santa Claus and the Tooth Fairy and the Easter Bunny. How else are we to communicate that life is mysterious, more than just the sum of its parts? How else to say that the world is a lovely and terrible and perplexing place, full of both marvels and terrors?

No, Lord Voldemort does not exist, we say, but Osama bin Laden does, and he is a true monster, a devil.

No, Saint Nicholas is make-believe, but there are sainted people among us, such as those who minister to the poor, like Dorothy Day. In their kindness and compassion, these people are goodness incarnate, gods indeed.

"Human beings are full of love" read the Chinese characters on a banner in Mary's orphanage. As a mother, it's my job to pass on that crucial message to my daughter and also to teach her its opposite: human beings are full of hate. People are capable of everything imaginable, I tell her, both good and bad.

Are there such things as fairy godmothers, Mary wanted to know when she read *Cinderella*. No and yes, I said. You have plenty of fairy godmothers, I answered, although they don't have magic wands and wings: they are my good women friends who love you and look after you.

"How was the world made?" is yet another big question Mary asked me when she was seven or so.

I explained that roughly fifteen billion years ago there was nothingness and then came the Big Bang, the birth of the universe, and after that the stars and then the sun and finally the Earth formed.

"The big boom?" Mary repeated incredulously. "Nothingness? No dirt, no sky?"

"I know it's hard to imagine, honey," I said lamely. How much easier, I thought, just to repeat the first sentence in Genesis and be done with it: "In the beginning God created the heavens and the earth."

I didn't even mention one of the finer points of the Big Bang theory: that scientists now believe that the universe is not only expanding, still flying apart after the initial cataclysm that formed it, but that its expansion is actually accelerating. In five billion years, astronomers estimate, the sun will swell up and die, burning up the Earth in the process. And after that the galaxies will fly apart, black holes will gobble galaxies and stars, and even black holes themselves will eventually explode. The universe might last forever, cosmologists theorize, but it will be as it was in the beginning—a dark and cold and silent entity, a Genesis-like "darkness . . . upon the face of the deep."

In other words, the future of life as we know it is hopelessly bleak.

As astrophysicist Dr. Lawrence M. Krauss has said, "All our knowledge, civilization and culture are destined to be forgotten. There's no long-term future."

In the face of such an apocalypse, what does life itself matter? If our ultimate fate as both individuals and a species is oblivion, what does goodness or evil matter, or love or death or books or laughter or a child's questions about God and the meaning of life?

But to me, a middle-aged mother, life—the right here, the right now of it—does matter, in no small part because it matters to my daughter, who has blossomed into an open-hearted and curious ten-year-old.

And do I believe in God? At age fifty-two, I still don't know, but here is my koan of an answer: I believe that God is a child, asking, "Is there a God?"

The Soul House

Molly Peacock

To the soul house no guests can be asked
though it is calm as a lake, its shore so prepared
anyone who stops by wants to build there.
But no. Who lives here lives unmasked.
Across the waxed floors slips only a soul
in a soul's bathrobe, tattered of course.
This is what spirits at home wear. That bowl
receives real plums, the vases real flowers.
Soul breath is quite real, too, its naked powers
insisting it be housed exclusively
for its air alone—pure being. And no
secrets in the soul house, only privacy.
A place to grow in, but not outgrow.
Not emptiness, but emptiedness. A source.

Spirit Matters

Demetria Martinez

riters are contemplatives. Daily we give ourselves over to silence, only to find the world at its worst marching across the snowy horizon of the page. The characters one had such hope for turn out to be, well, human. They hate, manipulate, seduce other people's spouses. They love money, worry about their looks, and fume about the state of the nation while making no effort to change things.

This is not to say that grace does not happen in their lives; instances of beauty and truth, wee epiphanies that unleash desire to live for . . . something more, something the world's religions have named variously as compassion, agape, wakefulness, tikkun, the call to repair the earth. But all it takes is a traffic jam, a bad-hair day, and my characters—those mirrors of my own heart—forget, entering once again into what Buddhism calls maya, illusion, or what Christians call sin.

Still, the novelist hopes. We watch our characters without judgment, embracing equally what is lovely and sinister. We hope that in the end they will learn something about life and love—that is, if the darkness they court does not swallow them up first.

At times we try to push our creations toward safety and right action. But souls, even fictional ones, are not so easily manipulated. Like a parent, the novelist must eventually get out of the way so that characters can become their own persons, enter into their own pacts with God and the Devil. Chapter by chapter, our characters teach us that few people are wholly good or wholly evil. The writer who cannot love the color gray, who cannot embrace a world that is less than black and white, will not last long. Our creations will die for lack of compassion if we replace truth telling with moralizing.

I'm not sure what any of this has to do with God or spirituality. Those words, bandied about so readily, frighten me even as they draw me like a moth to fire. I'm always amazed by the number of artists I know who once dreamed of becoming priests or nuns, myself included. It seems, however, that in reaching for heaven we fell all the harder back to earth.

The novelist is condemned to earth. We are called to be faithful not to abstract doctrine, so vaunted by organized religion, but to what our five senses tell us about the world around us. We may be affiliated with religions that preach a loving, all-powerful, and just God, but we are not God's public relations flacks. In our writing we must be willing to indict God, to tell the other side of the story. We tell stories as we find them—of the war veteran, the refugee, the diseased, the lonely, the insane. The novelist raises the question, "Where were you, O God?" We leave it to theologians to formulate answers. Our work is to stand in solidarity with those who have no answers.

And when our characters experience what seems to be the presence of the sacred in a moment of healing, heroism, cleansing anger, or bliss, we tell that story, too. For who is not to say that the world as a whole is not struggling to realize a greater experience of the sacred? The writer's imagination must be roomy and supple enough for hope and joy as well as gloom and doom.

Our imaginations must be on call at all times, open to any possibility. So we fight sloth and fear and struggle to show up each day, before the blank page. If a writer can be said to have a spiritual practice, this is it: to stay awake until the imagination stirs and characters come alive in our hands. My hope is that by writing well I will help keep you, the reader, awake—and in love with the human project despite the dark times in which we live.

Light

Linda Hogan

In the first morning of the world created,
on the skin of water reflected,
is the spread of a sun,
and the sun, like god, is a power
you cannot see.
Only what it lights on,
only what it touches with warmth,
and yet it always has a shadow at its feet.

Then there is the sea, the sheer weight of it,
but the lightness of its creatures,
some silver as they leap above it,
and those at the bottom
making their own light
in what would have been
night infinite, as if the sea carries no
shadows at its feet.

Then there is the light of wood decaying
out by the stagnant pond,
where the eyes of the prey nearby
shine in the dark, betrayed
when the deer stares one last time
to see if the hunter still follows
out in the shadows of living trees.

And bodies of men at war, they say,
give off light.
One I knew fished the sea
and told me of the silver fishes falling
from the mouth of the netted one.
As if in the last breath
perhaps we give back all the swallowed,
all the taken in, and it is light, after all,
first and last, we live for, die for.
We fly toward it
like those who return from it say.

But for now, for here, we fly without will
toward it, drink a glass of it,
see it through green leaves.
There, walk toward it.
Lift it, it has no weight.
Carry it, breathe it, cherish it.

You want to know why god is far away
and we are only shadows at his feet?
Tell me, how long does it take a moth
to reach the moon?

The Feminine and the Tao: A Dialogue with Ursula K. Le Guin

Brenda Peterson

BRENDA: Your new rendition of the *Tao Te Ching* strikes me as a very direct, pragmatic, and poetic classic. It is scrupulously fair and embracing, not addressed, as are previous translations, to rulers or sages or masters. In your introduction you write, "I wanted a Book of the Way accessible to a present-day, unwise, unpowerful, perhaps unmale reader, not seeking esoteric secrets, but listening for a voice that speaks to the soul." With that intent, how did you work on your *Tao*?

URSULA: Since my twenties, I've been working on these poems. Every decade or so I'd do another chapter. I don't know Chinese, but I drew upon the Paul Carus translation of 1898, which has the Chinese characters followed by a transliteration and a translation. This was my touchstone for comparing the other translations. The *Tao Te Ching*, though very old, is accessible because the Chinese characters haven't changed. One Chinese character can mean so many different things, and as you know, the meanings have changed. Every reader has to start anew with such an ancient text.

BRENDA: In his book *Immortal Sisters: Secret Teachings of Taoist Women*, Thomas Cleary notes that Lao Tzu, if he ever existed, had a female teacher. You wrote that you wanted to make a version of the *Tao Te Ching* that doesn't limit wisdom to males. Given the centuries of male interpretation from which you drew your revision, was this a difficult task?

URSULA: When you gender the philosopher and when you talk only about kings and sages—though technically the word "sage" is nongender—I do believe that most readers immediately see an ancient person with a beard. A bit like God. And since I had taken this book to my heart as a teenage girl, it is obviously a book that speaks to women. Lao Tzu feminized mysteries in a different way from anybody else. These are not "feminine mysteries," but he makes mystery itself a woman. This is profound, this goes deep. And the most mystical passages in the book are the most feminine. This is something women need, I think, and long for, often without knowing it. That's undoubtedly one reason why all my life I've found the *Tao Te Ching* so refreshing and empowering.

BRENDA: Several times when reading your rendition I felt so moved by the feminine beauty of your *Tao*. For example, you interpret Number 61, "Lying low," as "The polity of greatness / runs downhill like a river to the sea, / joining with everything, / woman to everything." This is such a startling definition of greatness. And your vision of Lao Tzu's ideas of power defies the traditionally masculine definition, which is usually about status, conquest, or hierarchy. But your interpretation is "Power is goodness . . . Power is trust."

URSULA: You know, the words really come out that way. That's one of the less obscure passages. It's almost shocking. Sometimes, of course,

Lao Tzu really is talking about a person in power, a ruler, and I played that down because I didn't figure a whole lot of rulers would be reading it. On the other hand, people in positions of responsibility, such as mothers, might be. And if you want to read the book as a manual for rulers, there is the magnificent Arthur Waley translation.

BRENDA: Yes, a real classic. Another thing that came through very strongly in this rendition, was the humor—your humor, Lao Tzu's humor, a philosophy of nature and humor. I laughed out loud when I read your note on Number 53, "Insight": "People wearing ornaments and fancy clothes, / carrying weapons, / drinking a lot and eating a lot, / having a lot of things, a lot of money: / shameless thieves." And your comment was, "So much for capitalism."

URSULA: You know, in general, Lao Tzu seems to be pretty cagey, and a line can mean five or six different things, and then he just comes straight-out and says something, bang! Like that. It took me a bit by surprise.

BRENDA: And yet you also note that Lao Tzu was not a dualist or an ascetic like Henry David Thoreau. You say that Lao Tzu, though he often sounds like Thoreau in his philosophy of nature, was kinder. You wrote, "When Thoreau says to distrust any enterprise which requires new clothes, I distrust him. Lao Tzu knows that getting all entangled with the external keeps us from the eternal, but he also understands that sometimes people like to get dressed up."

URSULA: Americans have this tremendous Puritan streak, and it's about a mile wide in Thoreau. I love Thoreau, and Thoreau was a kind of Taoist, but then there's the puritanism. I'd been thinking for years about that line about new clothes. There's a difference. Lao Tzu does understand innocent vanity.

BRENDA: Doesn't that go along with Lao Tzu's three treasures, which you interpret as mercy, moderation, and modesty? Don't you think that humor requires a certain modesty?

URSULA: "Modesty" is a very unfashionable word, isn't it? Partly because it has been demanded of women and not of men, which is why a lot of women kind of flinch when you say "modesty." But when you degender it, it really is a lovely characteristic.

BRENDA: Given these Taoist definitions of power as trust and goodness, and the tenets of mercy, moderation, and modesty, have you ever imagined—perhaps in your novels—a Taoist society?

URSULA: All of my writing has been deeply influenced by the *Tao Te Ching*. And in *Always Coming Home* I did imagine a Taoist society in the Kesh people of a distant future, whose culture flourishes on the Pacific coast. But I'm not as antitechnological as Lao Tzu by a long shot.

BRENDA: One of my favorites of your renditions is Number 47, "Looking far": "The farther you go, / the less you know." You write that Lao Tzu's point was that "it's the inner eye that really sees the world." And your own inner eye has imagined the world so many times over in novels and poetry. Would you talk a little bit about this inner eye and how it discerns deeper than reality?

URSULA: As a novelist I was told you have to go out and get experience. And there's some truth to that. Most of us don't have a lot of fiction to write until we're heading on to thirty. You have to do some living. But it isn't wandering around and driving cattle and working on boats and all those manly jobs that authors always used to put on the back of their book covers. I think the get-experience rule made a lot of us women feel really crummy, because what have we got? Maybe college, a couple of kids, some stupid job, and a lot of women didn't even have jobs at that point. None of that counted as "experience" because it wasn't male experience. This is why I mention both Emily Brontë and Emily Dickinson in the note to that poem. It's what you do with what you've got. It's the eye that's seeing. It doesn't much matter what it sees, if the eye is a seeing eye. And if it isn't a seeing eye, then of course you can wander all over the world like some of those poor souls on tours, with eyes that have never learned to see at all.

BRENDA: Lao Tzu's insistence on the inner authority of this discerning eye is an antidote to those of us drowning in an Age of Information. His philosophy is also a balance to the media obsession today with the cult of personality, self-consciousness, and ego. Can you talk about this?

URSULA: Lao Tzu says things like, "Don't be controlled by love." He says that people who don't cherish their own bodies can't look after other people effectively. It's a bit shocking. Lao Tzu is antialtruist. That's pretty clear. Altruism and egoism are just two sides of one coin to Lao Tzu: either you look after yourself, or you turn away from yourself and look after others. Lao Tzu says no no no, that's not where it's at! That's the wrong choice! You have to do both.

BRENDA: Is this what you meant when you wrote that for Lao Tzu "Nature and its Way are not humane because they are not human" and that "Followers of the Way, like the forces of nature, act selflessly"?

URSULA: Nature is definitely not humane. And Lao Tzu says we should be like nature. We should not be humane, either, in the sense that we should not sacrifice ourselves for others. Now that's going to be very hard for Christian readers to accept, because they're taught that self-sacrifice is a good thing. Lao Tzu says it's a lousy thing. This is perhaps the most radical thing he says to a Western ear. Don't buy into self-sacrifice. Any more than you would ask somebody to sacrifice themselves for you. There's a sort of reciprocity—that's the only way I can understand it.

I've been thinking about this since Mother Teresa's recent death. I have never been comfortable with her or with any extreme altruism. It makes me feel inferior, like I ought to be like that, but I'm not. And if I tried to be, it would be the most horrible hypocrisy. But why, what is it that I'm uncomfortable with? And I think maybe Lao Tzu gives me a little handle on that. In a sense, this kind of self-sacrifice occurs only in a society that is so sick that only somebody going too far can make up for the cruelty of the society.

BRENDA: And it's not self-sacrifice without a reward, because the reward is in heaven.

URSULA: Yes, if you are Christian or Muslim, there's a reward. So I find it morally puzzling and a little suspect. Whereas Lao Tzu is kind of scary for us. On the other hand, I think that's why he talks about how to govern and what society should be like. Because if society weren't so incredibly rotten, with so many poor people, you wouldn't have the kind of misery that calls for a saint. I'm not faulting Mother Teresa. Yet I'd be happier with her if she'd somehow gotten to the root of things, the causes of wealth and poverty, where the heart of the problem is.

You know, Gandhi was certainly not a Taoist. Yet in some respects— despite his enormous activism and his probably enormous ego—I can fit him into Lao Tzu's world. Because Gandhi struck at the root. He struck at inequality. He wanted the society to make itself better. And he did it by the most modest means, because he refused violence.

BRENDA: So who do you think would be in the true spirit of the Taoist way? Someone like Mother Teresa who consciously does noble deeds that have a heavenly reward? Or someone in battle who in an unselfconscious moment of mercy falls on a hand grenade and saves everyone around him?

URSULA: Well, that's the kind of thing that soldiers in battle and workmen at work [and firemen in the World Trade Center—ed.] are always doing. They do the next thing because that's the next thing to be done. It's simply a sense of duty and responsibility—two more unfashionable words!

BRENDA: Do you think that Lao Tzu, along with being subversive to politics, power structures, and dogma, is also subversive to mainstream religions?

URSULA, *laughing*: Well, Lao Tzu didn't have a god. The *Tao* is really an action rather than a person. And it's an action in which everyone can share. The more you share, the more you approach what a theist or deist is going to call "union with the godhead"—although this is not in Lao Tzu's vocabulary. He is a godless mystic. However, there's also the practical bit in Lao Tzu for the nonmystic. He does offer a good, wide range.

BRENDA: I think your version of the *Tao Te Ching* is, as you say, the most demystified mysticism that I've ever read, and that's why I think it's comforting and accessible.

URSULA: I certainly didn't want it to be mystifying. I don't think Lao Tzu did, either, except occasionally where he's deliberately hiding things. But he wanted his teachings to be a followable Way—while stating firmly from the beginning that you can't follow the Way. Paradox is essential to his thought.

BRENDA: During your long study of the *Tao*, how has it helped you in your own life and work?

URSULA: It's become so deep in me, so much a part of my fiber and my work, that it's certainly influenced some of my life choices. I'm not Taoistic enough, but I try to let things happen and then if they happen to say, "Yeah, that's the way it was supposed to be." It has been a guide. But always a guide toward not trying to be in control, toward trying to accept the fact that one is not in control. If you go along with things they'll probably go in the right way in the deepest sense, in a way you can't understand at the time. And since I'm always trying to take control, I need Taoism to prevent me from trying to control everything.

BRENDA: Another of your interpretations I admired was from Number 58, "Living with change": "the wise . . . they are the light that does not shine." In the Stephen Mitchell translation, he reads this line as "radiant but easy on the eyes."

URSULA: A phrase like "easy on the eyes" sounds wrong to me. It's got exactly the wrong aura or implication about it.

BRENDA, *laughing*: Can you imagine a Taoist advertising agency? "Buy this if you feel like it. If it's right. You may not need it."

URSULA: There was an old cartoon in *The New Yorker* with a guy from an advertising agency showing his ad, and the boss is saying, "I think you need a little more enthusiasm, Jones," and his ad is saying, "Try our product, it really isn't bad."

BRENDA: As a product of two thousand years, the *Tao* has certainly proved itself an enduring spiritual text.

URSULA: It is impressive and touching, isn't it? That this weird book has just gone on so sturdily. All through Chinese history. It was written during a really bad period in China's history, the Warring States period. Society then was much less reliable even than our own. And in the middle of it, here comes this book that seems not very comforting, that seems to put everything at risk—and yet it does give comfort in a bad time. Even now.

BRENDA: And that bad time in Chinese history had to do with the orthodoxy of the state Confucianism?

URSULA: War was the problem—war, violence, injustice. But Confucianism did control Chinese society so strongly that I suppose this book was a necessary counterbalance. The orthodoxy had grown so rigid that you had to have this anarchist Lao Tzu setting off his little firecrackers.

BRENDA: Why, do you think, in any time or culture, are people so often comforted by orthodoxy?

URSULA: That's an interesting question. I'm thinking about McDonald's. It's very important, for one thing, that McDonald's, wherever it is, be exactly the same as it is everywhere else. So that people don't feel foreign, and they don't feel like fools—and they know how to order. All this is intensely comforting because the world is really very much more threatening than most of us want to admit. And going into a strange restaurant for most of us takes a certain amount of courage, if you don't know how to order, don't speak the language. But the thing is, if you do go into an unfamiliar restaurant and you do get something in a foreign language and like it, then you've enlarged your comfort zone. If you always go to McDonald's, your comfort zone is so narrow and pitiful.

You know, I think people are very brave and often are a lot more frightened than they're allowed to admit. Life is much harder to live for most people than we want to admit. And so many things take a summoning up of courage. It makes one's own life a little bit easier when you can acknowledge that. I love the poem Number 76, which talks about dead things that are still and rigid, so strong and invulnerable—whereas live things are very tender and easy to break. As I said in that note, "To be alive is to be vulnerable."

BRENDA: I think my favorite is still Number 43, "Water and stone." You read this famous passage as, "What's softest in the world / rushes and runs / over what's hardest in the world." Isn't this what we've been talking about with the feminine—that ability to be vulnerable and slowly to work away at something, like water abrading and shaping stone over time?

URSULA: I would add one little footnote to what you just said. I agree that for those of us who feel ourselves to be vulnerable, soft, and feminine, it can be very cheering to be told that "the stiff tree is felled." If we just hang in here and wait them out, the big boss men will eventually wear themselves away. I think small people need to be told that.

BRENDA: You've written elsewhere that the rise and fall of society is not usually told in battles and heroes but simply by portraying the enduring life of family, creating, and nature. Isn't Lao Tzu offering a very different and perhaps more authentic way of looking at human history?

URSULA: Yes, it's the continuity in which the real life is.

BRENDA: Can you think of an example of this, that what is softest in the world rushes and runs over the hardest—an example from everyday life or one of your books?

URSULA: One of my recent books is called *Four Ways to Forgiveness*. It's a science fiction book. It's about a pair of worlds in which slavery has been a major element of society. We come on these worlds just as they're beginning to emerge from slavery. There is a revolution on one of the planets where the slaves actually overthrow the mastery. We never see the revolution taking place in these stories; the people that I chose to write about are all essentially powerless. One of the stories is called "A Man of the People." He joins the women, they sing, and they lie down on the railroad tracks. They use essentially nonviolent Gandhian methods. They do by not doing. What I was trying to show was that the gentle people wear out the hard ones.

BRENDA: How does knowing this particular Taoist tenet help us in our own lives?

URSULA: Lao Tzu is very relevant at a time like ours. We're in one of those big yin-yang movements, and the yang is so extreme. But then it will do what all extremes do: it will suddenly begin turning into the opposite. There's another part of Taoism that we haven't discussed that is part of my view of the world—extremes always do implode and begin to turn into the other thing.

BRENDA: Taoism's sense of paradox reminds me of the wonderful Rumi poem, "Out beyond ideas of wrongdoing and right doing, there is a field, I'll meet you there." Can you imagine Lao Tzu meeting Rumi in that field?

URSULA: Rumi certainly is out there talking with Lao Tzu—probably giggling wildly.

BRENDA: Flowers wouldn't even have to be planted to rise up in that field. Any last thing you might like to say about your lifelong work on the *Tao Te Ching*?

URSULA: This book has given me a great deal of happiness. And I hope some of that comes through.

Postscript. *The Taoists say there are great lessons to be learned from a calm and happy spirit. In one of her final notes on the text, Le Guin writes that Lao Tzu is saying, "Enjoy your life . . . live in your body, you are your body; where else is there to go? Heaven and Earth are one. As you walk the streets of your town you walk on the Way of Heaven."*

The Angels

Judith Roche

The Angels

are not like the Saints.

They do not discriminate
but come to everyone.

Their eyes burn green fire
but their kisses are icy.

They can play rough when we get caught
in the heavy crosswinds that swirl about their wings.

They are not above artifice
and sometimes appear in disguise:

a mask of smeared lipstick, gypsy
bangles, or an old man's coat.

Now and again they carelessly give us gifts:
an unexpected hobbyhorse, a day's free babysitting,

a poke in the eye with a stick,
or sudden slant of light on water.

And we are grateful, once we figure out how
to move within their state of complex blessings.

They work within great wheels and circles,
turning light to dark and back again.

They do not obey the laws of gravity
but laugh a lot and arise at will

to hover like vast hummingbirds
when we require attention.

What they want of us is the mysterious secret
we unravel and reweave

down to dark and back again.

Practicing

Treatise on Narcissism, Evil, Good, Free Will and the Persistence of the Idea of the Self

Marilyn Krysl

If I could choose
I would say
  let me be the one on the arctic ice with an axe,
  the one who chops a hole in the ice,
  the one who is present when the whale rushes upward,
  thrusts into the air:

  let me not be the one who slips the halter
  over the head of the mother camel, leads the mother
  away from her baby, coaxes her up into the lorry,
  the one who drives the lorry across the border,

the one who secures the mother at the head
of a caravan of camels loaded with heroin
and lets her go
because she will go and not stop
until she reaches her baby.

But since I have already
chosen, since I am
    both this one and that one,
    and have been this one and that one
    all my life on earth,

it doesn't matter
    if I tear my hair my clothing, scour
    my face breasts belly with ashes
    and bang my forehead against the ground
    which will not let me in.

And if I beg the baby camel
    which will not drink, or drinks only
    a little, and then turns its body away, head
    down—if I whisper *forgive me,*

this is only my own
    dithering, my own need to imagine
    I'm the center of everything.
    The whale will leap and not think of me,
    the camel will walk and not think of me,
    walk and make of herself an arc
    toward that place in the universe

where she knows there is solace.
    Though I pray beside the deep waters
    to whom do I give my body?
    Though I thank the trout offering to be eaten,
    whom do I feed?

When I walk lightly through the forest,
my footsteps leave holes in the sea.

And if I am sometimes solace
        for this one, at other times
        I am terror for that one.
        Meanwhile my ravenous relatives
        take only what they need: hawk, shrike,
        anteater, ant. And

if I say I forgive myself, this is merely
        more dithering, more whining, more
        wandering in blindness, feeling the wall
        with my fingers: I, with my good intentions,
        my grand resolve not to do harm:

crying out and devouring with the same mouth
        and going on,
        a basket of light on one shoulder,
        backpack of darkness slung over the other.

When—when?—will I let it all fall away?
When will I rise up
and really pray?

Taking Vows

Kate Wheeler

ecently, stuck in traffic near my home in Boston, gazing in frustration at the sidewalk where passersby were moving faster than the cars, I had a transcendent experience. My mind's eye spontaneously transformed a few pedestrians into Buddhist monks and nuns, figures in robes with shaven heads.

I was a nun myself twelve years ago in Burma. Yet in that moment in traffic, I wasn't merely transported back to the monastery in Rangoon; I also reentered the mental training I'd practiced there. So I was stuck behind a long line of cars. Did I want to stay caught in desperate boredom, the misery that comes from wishing to be somewhere else? No! I took a slow breath and released my useless hatred of the car ahead.

My old teacher, the monk Sayadaw U Pandita, would have called the vision of nuns and monks a "sign of *samadhi*," an image arising from past meditation that allows the benefits of meditation practice to resurface.

Of course, the quiet, undramatic power to concentrate my mind and turn it toward freedom, the goal of meditation practice, results from twenty-four years of meditation and not just the eight months I spent as a nun. And irritation at bad traffic is a piece of cake compared to the tangled feelings I experience sometimes—say, listening to my partner tell me about his ex-wife's most recent e-mail about their daughter's boarding-school payments. At such times, my life as a nun can seem very long ago and far away; in fact, I don't remember it at all.

Yet after that experience in traffic, I began to notice how very frequently the imprints from being a nun actually do recur, seemingly independently of whatever is going on around me. Sometimes it is just a fleeting visual memory; or an easy straightening at the back of my neck, a remnant of the dignity I upheld when wearing robes; or a sense of cool stillness spreading under the surface of an event or conversation. Each is a reminder to wake up and reenter the practice I'd trained in so intensively. I resolved to take advantage of these moments when they came—and as a result, the sense of connection and openness in my life dramatically increased. Never once have I regretted opening my heart and mind toward the person I am speaking to, or recognizing my real emotions of feeling the sensations of my body.

There is an infinity of doorways that can open into this present moment. Yet I still wonder what it was that made nunhood so powerful. Was it just that it had been so intense, so focused, so exotic?

• • •

When I was ordained at thirty-three, I didn't know what else I was going to do with my life; I knew only that I needed to find out what was at the bottom of everything. This quest felt like an open wound— embarrassing, abnormal. Yet I could not get rid of it. Buddhist meditation, with its emphasis on paying direct attention to our everyday experience, seemed to point in the right direction. I'd been a meditator for eleven years and still "The Answer" eluded me. Gnawed from within, I couldn't settle down.

Friends spoke of a monastery in Rangoon so strict and so intense that you could hardly avoid getting enlightened there. In 1984 I'd met its head monk, Sayadaw U Pandita, when he was leading a retreat in the United States. He'd compared the monastery's method to a mathematical equation. "You are the number," he said. "You put yourself in, work the equation and come out as the answer." How cut-and-dried, I thought, how comforting! The notion of becoming a nun in this man's monastery held an appealing, truth-or-bust intensity for me. Even more alluring was the fact that in Southeast Asian Buddhism, it is legitimate to be ordained for a short time; even an hour in robes is considered better than nothing. I'd need more than an hour to resolve my burning questions, I realized. But I wanted to bring my suffering to an end, not to consign myself to an institution for the rest of my life. I'd do my utmost to become enlightened, but then I'd come home and be ordinary.

This was one of the first liberating paradoxes of being a nun. For me, you could almost say that ordination ended before it began. Knowing that my time in robes would one day come to a close is precisely what made total commitment possible for me. I applied for a special religious visa to stay in Burma for three months, renewable if needed. A year and a half elapsed; by the time the visa arrived, in the late fall of 1987, I was living with a boyfriend in Cambridge, Massachusetts. We'd met at a meditation center, we did long retreats together, but when I asked him for an indefinite hiatus while I went off to find truth as a nun, he broke up with me instead.

· · ·

It's odd that my mental image of the monastery is one of coolness and silence because the actual place was anything but—with cars revving, crows cawing, sermons in Burmese blasting over the loudspeakers. It was so noisy that most of us Western meditators wore earplugs during the day, and it was so hot that we sprinkled our skins with mentholated prickly-heat powder to prevent diaper rash from spreading all over our bodies.

Many things jarred my preconceptions. I'd expected serene gardens and instead found cement everywhere—on walkways, floors and walls. And the huge shiny white and gold Buddhas in the meditation halls looked tacky to me. The monastery complex was immense, twenty acres surrounded by a wall. It functioned not only as a monastery but as a laypeople's meditation center. Most Burmese meditators paid a nominal daily fee, but in reality anyone, regardless of ability to pay, could come for a retreat lasting a day or a lifetime. This place, called the Mahasi Sasana Yeiktha, depended entirely on donations— and such is the devotion of the Burmese that it was only one of many similar institutions in Rangoon, each centering on the meditation techniques of a particular master. Whole villages would sign up, years in advance, to cook enormous meals—meals large enough to feed the one thousand to four thousand people who were always there. About half were Burmese laypeople, plus eight hundred or so Burmese monks, one hundred Burmese nuns, and a few dozen Westerners, mostly from Europe, the Americas and Australia. We Westerners got the best food, our own dorms and meditation halls and a sermon from the head monk every night to keep our spirits up. Such treatment reflected standard Burmese hospitality to visitors; also we were considered a bit delicate, physically and philosophically.

Iron bells clanked on the hour, twenty-four hours a day, marking a rigorous schedule. Men and women meditated, in separate buildings, from 4 a.m. to 11 p.m. Beyond the official hours, someone was always awake, practicing. Teacher-monks gave interviews to every person every other day. Burmese meditators had interviews in groups; Westerners, individually, with assistance from a translator. We had to report our experiences according to a strict format, which allowed the teachers to pinpoint our stage of meditation, spot any problems we might be having and guide us onward. The instructions were usually terse, a word or two; yet when I applied them, such sweeping experiences often came to me that I gained great faith in U Pandita's promise that he could put us through a mathematical awakening process.

Other than at the interviews, we kept silent as much as possible, speaking only when strictly necessary. Among the Western yogis, we passed notes. Despite the monastery's formidable organization, Burma was a more complicated place in which to be on retreat than the United States. There were always visas to be renewed, a clothes-washing bucket to be borrowed or a health question to be asked of a fellow yogi. Our risks ran from life-threatening hepatitis and worms to the more ignominious but still painful hemorrhoids and varicose veins, the side effects of sitting so many hours in a cross-legged posture. I found I spent about half an hour each day in these small, necessary transactions. At the time, half an hour seemed a great deal of bother.

The dorms were mostly cement block with barred, glassless windows and forbidding padlocked grated doors. Our beds resembled low Ping-Pong tables, hard with only a thin straw mat, like a beach mat. There was no hot water. We ate fish soup for breakfast, every day, at sunrise. Lunch was at 10:30 a.m., and no dinner was served, because monks, nuns and most people on intensive retreat undertake a training precept not to eat solid food after noon. It's thought that this helps to increase energy while reducing sexual desire.

I relished the austerities for the sense of simplicity they provided. Besides, we had everything we really needed, and we lived at a standard obviously higher than most of our Burmese supporters. The only payment accepted from Westerners for a year of food, housing and instruction was a few bags of powdered cement for new construction. I managed to disapprove of this: Why were they so obsessed with cement? Mostly, though, I felt a commitment to practice hard, to deserve all the sacrifices others were clearly making in order to keep me there.

Anyone could see why this place deserved its Burmese name of Yeiktha ("refuge"). Inside, we were privileged to eliminate all responsibilities but one, paying attention to our lives in the present—moment by moment. Everything was organized around this practice, known as Vipassana (or Insight) meditation. Within days, I'd settled into the rhythms I knew so well from other retreats. Sit an hour, walk an hour, eat two meals a day, sleep as little as possible—four or five hours. I felt the sensations of the breath and body. I noticed when I was thinking and what emotions I was feeling, but I tried not to get caught up in what Buddhists call "the stories," all the ruminations, the analyses, the replays of ancient scenes.

Most of my stories had to do with how exciting, lovely or horrible everything was here; and I definitely got caught up in these musings and enthusiasms. We were expected to take notes of what happened in our meditations, but to forgo analysis and let go of all other thoughts. My own notebooks often contained descriptions of extraneous things, like the smell of a jasmine bush after a rain. Even with all my distractions, the silence of full attention always remained a mystery and a gift. Within it, any small event—even stretching my feet out after an hour of sitting meditation—might suddenly resound with unexpected beauty, like one of those slow-motion photographs of a water droplet falling into a pond.

This flavor of silence, its acute and fleeting richness, is one of the things I've treasured most in my life. It is really the flavor of an open mind, as sensitive to winter light slicing across a frozen garden in Massachusetts as to the lightness of my foot lifting from a cement walk in Rangoon. After I was in the monastery about two weeks, U Pandita agreed to ordain me as a nun. I'd shave my head, wear robes and maintain eight ethical precepts. I would vow not to kill any living being; not to steal. Nothing around us offered much temptation to break these first two precepts, especially since one of the Burmese nuns was good at gently sweeping away the scorpions. Next, we were supposed to use our speech wisely; on retreat this meant keeping silence. We were celibate. We didn't drink or take drugs, which took care of another precept. No solid food after noon was yet another. Avoiding movies, dances, personal adornments, high seats and luxurious beds? No problem!

All meditators, even laypeople, keep these same eight precepts while on retreat at the monastery. As for my hair, it has always been more bother than glory, so shaving it off didn't scare me. (Only convention keeps me from shaving it now.) Generally, I didn't think nunhood would pose any additional burden. And there was one particular way that I expected ordination to improve my life. Nuns wore pink; I couldn't wait to get rid of the brown skirt that all laywomen had to wear.

• • •

From the moment the rusty razor first scraped across my scalp, the experience of nunhood was surprising. I hadn't expected to look good bald, but I thought I did. Once I learned how to keep its skirt from slipping off, the carnation-pink nun's robe made me feel as glamorous as a ballerina.

My teacher gave me the name Khemanandi (pronounced K-hay-mah-nahn-dee), meaning "Bliss Without Fear." In my fabulous pink robes, with my beautiful new name, I believed that I would sink deeper and deeper into quietude and purity. Before being ordained, I'd thought of nunhood essentially as a personal commitment, almost a secret event—the ceremonial change of status mere window dressing for a profound change of heart within.

This was not to be. I lost all privacy immediately. For in a Burmese monastery, as I quickly learned, a nun's (or a monk's) special garb instantly converts a person into public property. As a Western nun, moreover, I was a sensation. Overnight, hordes (it seemed) of young women began appearing at the dormitory, eager to perform obeisances, feed and inspect me, beg for gifts and blessings and deluge me with questions. They stood at the windows of the meditation hall and stared in at us. I'd crack open my eyes and peek halfway through a sitting, and there they were, still staring.

I complained at the office that I was being distracted. So a sign was posted in Burmese, forbidding anyone to bother the Westerners, but it had no effect. Then U Pandita taught me a phrase in Burmese that I wrote down on a piece of paper. "I have come from far away to meditate. Please do not distract me." But I could never bring myself to say it. Instead, flustered, I'd try to wave the girls away. Besides not working, this seemed to hurt their feelings.

A fellow nun told me I was doing it all wrong. I must do what was expected of me: receive others' bows with dignity, uttering a brief formulaic blessing: "I share the merits of the ordination with you." Before letting my followers distract me completely and thus turn me into a bad example, I'd dismiss them by rearranging my robes, clearing my throat and saying, *"Hline . . ."* ("Well . . .").

The minute I tried this, my followers exchanged satisfied glances, made their three formal bows and exited with a speed that left me breathless with laughter.

I can reenter those days so easily. Like this: I am walking back from a midday bath, my shower shoes leaving damp prints on the cement. My enormous turquoise T-shirt, size XXXXL, flaps just above my white knees. If there were an opposite of nun's color, it is turquoise. Right now I'm not Khemanandi, Bliss Without Fear; I am just Kate Wheeler, or no one at all. I'm just enjoying the coolness of the air on my legs, not making any effort to meditate.

"Sayalay! Sayalay!" The girls are here, crying for me in Burmese. This word, the nun's title, means "Small Master." I freeze—how have they gotten through the grated door? My friend Katie Mitchell, the British laywoman meditator, smiles a compassionate, secret smile as she passes me with her bucket of laundry. She disappears into her room, leaving me with the girls. There are four of them, smiling at me. They show me a bowl of delicious milk custard they have brought. It is almost noon, the time when we have to stop eating. The girls don't seem to notice the hour, nor how dreadful my outfit is. I would like to grab the little bowl from them and vanish into my room to eat it as fast as possible. But I remember my dignity lesson, so I don't. They have not caught me at a bad time, since the present moment is always a good time for a real nun.

I smile as compassionately and as secretly as my friend Katie, raise one hand for them to wait, and go into my room. When I open the door again, my nun's robe is perfectly draped. As they enter, I retire to sit cross-legged on the bed. They take their positions on the floor, and their faces shine up at me as I take a bite of custard. One of the girls explains to me that the first half of the custard was eaten by a famous old monk and that I am being given this very special leftover.

"Thank you," I say in Burmese. Again I smile and put down the spoon. Rearranging my robes, I sit up straight and meditate for a few seconds. I actually feel almost as calm as I look. Funny how offering an appearance of dignity seems to unify the ups and downs of a nun's life, I think, while on the floor in front of me, I see the girls straightening their postures imperceptibly, too. They're waiting to see what I'll do next.

• • •

If anyone understood how entertaining, how exhilarating the robes were, would they think I hadn't been serious? Yet from my gaggle of giggling devotees I learned to bear the responsibility for my role, to mirror everybody's (including my own) deepest aspirations toward freedom, truth and all those other big ideas. I became more dignified and gentle. Even my posture improved. As people bowed to me, I felt I couldn't slump. I'd never believed in outward forms before; but even though I could see that this one wasn't perfect, I felt proud that I could live up to it.

This was the second great paradox of nunhood—and its most liberating surprise. Form was service. The superficial, public, distracting aspects of the robes turned out to go the deepest.

• • •

My existential questions are still being answered. I left Rangoon before I'd expected to, in August 1988, only days after the Burmese army gunned down unarmed demonstrators on the main road, a few blocks from the monastery gate. These were the first days of a military crackdown that still oppresses Burma. I often think about my fellow nuns. Their faces, glowing, almost swollen with quiet, were the only mirror in which to see myself, for there were no mirrors in our rooms or bathrooms. Older women, the stubble graying on their shaven heads, redefined beauty with expressions composed and relaxed from within. The younger ones looked fresh and clarified without their hair. Girls would be ordained during school vacations, to meditate until the next year started. Eight-year-olds were considered mature enough to understand the instructions, to practice and to become enlightened. In pink nun's robes, often holding hands as they practiced walking meditation, the little girls looked like pairs of flowers.

When I think of them, I wish my own culture had a form like this, some visible apparatus to remind us all to respect and cultivate our inner lives. I imagine lots of people would be interested, if they knew they could be ordained for a short time—and then return to their ordinary lives and families. I love to imagine what benefits this could bring to our culture, how by serving others we might help ourselves. If only all of us understood that meditation is not selfish, and that inwardness goes outward. Perhaps the robes, the demands made on us as nuns, only made it more obvious to me that what we cultivated in ourselves directly benefited other people. Where a form exists, this can even happen at a distance, just as knowing that nuns are still meditating in Rangoon supports me now.

. . .

In Rangoon, I could never have dreamed what my life would look like now, a bit more than a decade later. Whenever I can, I take time for retreats, and I try to make sure I do my daily exercise and meditation—but mostly life feels full, sometimes melodramatically active. I'm part of a stepfamily; I work as a travel and fiction writer. In all areas, I find fertile ground for practice. As an intimate partner and as a stepmother, my psychological buttons are often pushed. As a writer, I often feel self-doubt and pressure, worries about the quality of my work and a certainty that I have never worked sufficiently. I experience—like all of us—the pain of a closed heart and many other hurtful delusions.

But even the most powerful delusions cannot match the power of attention. Sometimes they vanish like morning dew under the gentle sunlight. When they don't vanish, they become more bearable, instead of simply overwhelming me. Awareness is always an improvement. All it takes is remembering to begin. That's why I regret scoffing at Burmese friends who'd said that being a nun would help me in future lifetimes. For what am I living now in Boston, if not my future life? I'm learning what seems to be nunhood's final and most important lesson: that it never really ended after all. Its imprints still pop up, proving that, for better or for worse, the potential for transformation is limitless. But I know I can't sit back and expect it to happen. Hence my next resolve: to give myself a lesson in how to uphold the dignity of a stepmother and a writer, here in the nunnery that is my life. I wonder what color robes I ought to wear!

Breathing the Ancestors

Georgiana Valoyce-Sanchez

W e have come to bury our dead. It is still dark. The dirt road leading down to Abalone Cove is rutted, and we bounce and sway in our seats as the van slowly winds its way down to the rocky shore. The people waiting below in the mist are like apparitions of the Ancestors we have come to return to the ocean. It is low tide, but the ghost-gray waves breaking along the dark shore leap high and wild, churning earth, rocks, and shells in their wake. Christ has arrived before me, shaking salt water from his hair, walking among the men in the darkness. He has walked these shores before, thousands of years before the first Christian missionaries ever arrived here. It is an old covenant, reflecting the light of Kakunupmawa, Mystery Behind the Sun.

The ashes of the Ancestors are close by. I cannot see them, but I know they are here. Several weeks before, I went with other Native Americans from different tribal cultures to the Arco Refinery in Carson, California, to discuss the reburial of the sixty or more Native people who had been found there. We walked in silence among the skeletal remains, the anthropologist hired by Arco making sure that we noted the evidence of violence on skulls and limbs. We are not sure who the people were, though some Chumash artifacts were also found with the bodies. The Chumash are my father's people, caretakers for thousands of years of a vast area of this land we now call Southern California. What we do know is that something terrible took place there.

We have been called to Abalone Cove by the Tongva/Gabrieleno people, the most likely descendants of the Ancestors. Because the remains of the Ancestors were found on acknowledged Tongva land, it is proper that the Tongva take responsibility for their reburial. The Tongva, particularly the Ti'at Society, have decided to cremate the remains and return the Ancestors to the ocean.

When the Catholic missionaries came to California, the Tongva people were given the name "Gabrieleno," for the Mission San Gabriel, just as my father's people were given the name "Barbareno," for the Mission Santa Barbara, our original names subjugated, lost. Diegeno, Luiseno, Gabrieleno, Ventureno, Barbareno, Purismeno, Obisbeno . . .

We are still veiled in darkness, but the ocean is silver-gray in Abalone Cove. Dawn is just beyond the cliffs. What is this sorrow I feel?

The night before my father died, I attended a women's sweat. The heat and steam inside the darkness of the sweat lodge seemed unbearable. I was in the womb of God, unable to be born. *Creator, mercy. Please help my father to have a good death.* I could not take the suffering one minute longer, until the woman next to me, in pain from sitting on the hard earth, asked me to rub her back. The next day, my father died with all his loved ones around him. A good death. Simple acts. And we are born.

I dance in a circle of new light. Dawn has come to Abalone Cove. We are holding hands, dancing in a circle, a Friendship Dance some tribal cultures call it. We pray and dance to the Sunrise Song, to the Water Song, to the Rock Song. Sun-splashed ocean, dark cliffs, shadows, rocky shore move past me as if I were standing still and they were dancing in the round. Circles, circles everywhere, from sun to galaxies, plants on the hillside, animals scurrying to their homes, ocean life, every living cell of our bodies, and seabirds flying overhead.

I cannot understand the words sung by the Western Shosone elder, but I understand their meaning—it is a great unknowing and it fills me with light. We offer Tongva and Chumash songs, Ancestor Songs and Healing Songs, songs with ancient words and meanings that we have remembered and reclaimed. I know these old songs—I have sung them before at other ceremonies—and I sing, respectful, serious. Inside, I am filled with joy, smiling.

The ashes of the Ancestors are carried to the beach in plastic bags by some of the Tongva people. Several small plastic bags from the crematorium, each containing the remains or partial remains of a person, are placed on the sand. I wonder if the mother, holding her baby, was cremated with her child.

My sister Susan and I are honored to be chosen to help prepare the Ancestors for their journey out to sea. We kneel on the beach and line two large boxes with cloth. My favorite sweat lodge towel is used to line one of the boxes. It is the same towel we draped over the steel bars of the rented hospital bed when my father was dying. A fine mist of ash rises as we empty the plastic bags. My sister and I glance at one another. "We are breathing the Ancestors," I say. "Yes," she says.

Chumash and Tongva men lift the *ti'at*, the traditional plank canoe of the Tongva so like our own *tomol*, carrying her to the ocean's edge on their shoulders. Her name is *Mo'omat 'Ahiko*, "Breath of the Ocean," and she is draped in a garland of sage. The boxes holding the Ancestors' ashes are covered in a beautiful purple cloth with black hibiscus blossoms printed on it. Susan has woven a wreath of sage for the Ancestors and it is placed on top.

The Tongva people carry the Ancestors' ashes to the *ti'at*, the rest of us walking in solemn procession behind them. Waves crash against the canoe, lifting her each time, tossing her against the rocks, and she reminds me of a wild mustang, straining to be free of the hands that try to hold her down. The captain enters the canoe and directs the people to place the boxes in the center of the *ti'at*. As always, the Ancestors are our ballast, the steadying point of our journey on Earth.

The paddlers and several other men begin to push the *ti'at* farther into the ocean, and she is bucking and heaving on the waves as the paddlers climb in and begin to paddle. Their long oars lift high into the air, circling down into the ocean and up again, like kayak paddlers, only with longer, larger paddles. They are beautiful to watch, and we pray earnestly for them to break beyond the pounding waves. Several of our men are still in the ocean, helping to push the *ti'at* into deeper water, and for a moment I am afraid she will not break free. *Creator, mercy.*

My brother John, who has followed the *ti'at* into the ocean, begins to sing the Dolphin Calling Song, praying for help for the paddlers. It is an old prayer, an old story: our people walking across a rainbow bridge, some falling into the depths of the ocean only to be saved, changed into dolphins by the compassion of Hutash, the Spirit of the Earth, and Kakunupmawa. " *'Alolk'oy! 'Alolk'oy!*" Dolphin! Dolphin! And the *ti'at* breaks free of the waves—*Mo'omat 'Ahiko* is out into the open sea, long oars rising and falling, and she is skimming over the water. We sing, we sing, and our tears mingle with our shouts of encouragement. Farewell, Ancestors! Good-bye! Welcome home.

• • •

The captain of the *ti'at* told us later that when the boxes containing the ashes of the Ancestors were lowered into the ocean they sank immediately, slowly descending into the depths. Bubbles, like a thousand little breaths, rose from below, whispering in some ancient language as they broke through the ocean's surface. I hear them sometimes.

I breathe the Ancestors and they breathe me. Because I breathe the Old Ones, because I love the Mystical Heart of Christianity, because I find goodness and truth in all the world's religions, I don't quite fit anywhere. I am an anomaly.

Sometimes, I am like the *Mo'omat 'Ahiko*, tossed between deep ocean and rocky shore. It is a difficult place to be, but I know this— God, Kakunupmawa, Mystery Behind the Sun, is good. Life with Hutash, the Spirit of the Earth, is good. I have been given teachers, ceremonies, stories, and songs; with the Ancestors, they are my ballast, my steadying point as I head out for the deep.

Ordinary Mysticism

Elizabeth Carothers Herron

At Nick's insistent barking as soon as I lifted his leash, we took off for the creek. The rain had stopped and the empty streets glowed like long slicks of silver under the emerging late sun. Layers of clouds shifted and regrouped and shifted again over the entire sky, limned with apricot, deepening to centers of lavender and blue, purple and gray. The shred of a rainbow between clouds—brilliant green and lush red-orange, linked by a shimmering yellow, luminous and transparent, for all the world a celestial divinity—hung briefly in the southeast, then vanished.

The sun sank behind the hills and patches of low gray fog flew across its final roar of tangerine and peach like smoke from a great fire, while a Tintoretto-blue sky opened here and there behind the restless clouds, to the east becoming greener, robin's-egg blue beside the cloud's dense gray.

I plucked one of the last wild apples from the tree behind the big coyote bush near the redwood grove. Polished and wet with rain, it glowed in my hand, scarlet on one side, blurring to pale yellow on the other. I took a bite—crisp, sweet, and chilled from the weather. Nick and I walked up the hill between the redwoods and I wished suddenly that one day I would see these trees grown tall, this grove old enough to be deep shade all summer, its fallen branchlets a burnished copper, littering the ground after rain.

The thought surprised me, and pleased me just as much. It was the first time I could remember a wish for the future of this place that was not associated with sadness. Mostly when I look ahead, I see ruin. More development, more loss. It was a hopeful thought, my wish to see the grove full-grown and shading the hill, spontaneous, as hope must be, I think, and it arose from joy, from a sense of belonging to this landscape where I have been so long, and been nourished, and been held and beheld.

How good to be here, how graced, how lucky, how alive I am too, I realized. And I went home to my warm house and built the first fire of the season, and listened to Bach violin concertos long after darkness fell.

. . .

The mystic moment of complete participation, giving rise to gratitude, is always available. This is the miracle of it. It is ever present. Rosario Costellanos wrote:

> The love that loves me
> does not turn its gaze from us
> even for a second.
>
> Beneath its gaze we are all gathered in
> like sheaves of wheat bound tight.

Within us is an old memory of a timeless peace. Cherokee/ Appalachian poet and essayist Marilou Awiatka says that Indian people call it the "Time Immemorial." When we enter there, outside time as we usually know it, we enter communion with creation. In that communion, we experience "the love that loves us" as the enlivening force in ourselves and the earth around us. We become aware of a larger awareness in which we are beheld and "gathered in." This is ordinary mysticism.

Such moments are less a loss of identity than a sweeping up of individuality in the quick of existence, which is always and everywhere arising but from which we have turned our gaze. In turning away from our sensate experience of the natural world, we live with the illusion of our separateness, while the earth loses its awareness of our presence. We no longer notice that the birds stop singing as we pass by the thicket, or that the fish disappear in the shadows as we lean out over the bridge.

The practice of ordinary mysticism begins with a recognition that the world is alive, and that it is aware of us. Sometimes we are filled with quiet joy, sometimes the sudden and overwhelming power is like being body-slammed by pure light. Sometimes we melt into it, sometimes we crumble before it. The farther our remove from it, the more powerful is our return from the distance.

One particularly forceful experience occurred a few years ago when I was away from home, visiting family. I had arrived weary from travel. Instead of the rest I had anticipated, a series of social gatherings filled the ensuing several days. On the afternoon of the fourth day, I came down with chills and a fever. In the solitude of my room, too ill to do anything but weep with exhaustion and relief, I lay in bed gazing blankly out the window, past the leafless branches of the trees into the clearing storm clouds of the winter sky. Gradually I became aware of the light caught in the drops of rain illuminated in the branches, as the afternoon sun found its way through the clouds. I noticed how the light pooled like milk, luminous with silent presence on the window sill, and shined off the window's frame. The stillness felt energized and alive, as if gathering an exhaustible power, invisible only at first, but soon apparent in everything I saw. The light on the sill seemed to flow into me, filling my being without diminishing as it did so.

Through the experience that was happening to me, which I did nothing to create (on the contrary, it was my *not* doing that made room for it), I realized that over the previous weeks I had lost my connection with the source of being. As soon as I was open to it, I resumed my place within its fold. This benevolent energy seemed to well around me from everywhere, intensified by my own stillness and the stillness of the objects from which it radiated—the vase of flowers on the dresser, the walls and shadowed corners of the room, the blanket, and my own hands resting on the coverlet. An energetic presence resided in all forms, and it had not *turned its gaze* from me. The sense of reunion with something that had never parted from me was no less powerful for its familiarity.

From this and other moments when time stopped and the busy struggling mind fell away like a husk, I have drawn a rudimentary map of conditions for the experience of ordinary mysticism. The first is a meandering state of being, a letting go of plans, allowing the moment to open to the senses. The not-me leads then, not the worrier or the planner or the social self, not the professor or the student, the mother or the manager, but an ambitionless, unhurried self, a liminal self, a know-nothing self, fluid and receptive.

Such a meandering requires the deliberate turning away from clock time. Time becomes the slant of light or shadow, the movement of the stars or clouds, the awareness of continual unfolding—leaves in the breeze, the passage of birds across the sky, or the drifting moon, the shifting scents of moisture or blossoms. No hurry. Letting oneself drift like a thistle on the wind, however briefly, can open the Time Immemorial, and even a fleeting rendezvous can put one back in touch with life . . .

Like the winter sunlight pooled on the sill of the window, the heart of existence is always waiting to receive us, to enfold us in an intimation of belonging . . . These are the moments when we come face to face with what is more enduring, more mysterious, more generous than anything we know. And while we may forget and stumble numbly forward, these awakenings are like the moss on the tree that dries and shrivels in summer. Already it glows, after a single early rain. Who would have thought it would take so little to restore that wet and brilliant green?

. . .

Late in the day, I sit under the willows by the creek. The sun slants sideways through the leaves. A breeze picks up to ease the summer heat and fans through the trees. The narrow slivers of silver-gray of the willows, like a thousand tiny scimitars, catch the sun in sporadic shimmers. The mother willow's many arms seem to spin from her gnarled and twisted trunk. She dances through the swirl of the seasons, while her roots hold fast and keep the creek bank stable through winter floods. One of her long arms wraps around behind me, low and into the ground so that if I did not follow its path I might imagine it to be a separate tree. Her sisters dance, too, up and down the creek.

In the center of a circle of movement, sun and shade, shiftings and changings, pattern not only the eye but the ear. I sit under a dome of green birdsong, as sparrows, titmice, finches, and birds whose names I don't know exchange their trills, whistles, chirrups, warbles.

In all this rising and falling, this sighing and sifting, this swimming singing in air, the constantly changing patterns move within something larger, an embrace of time, whole and unhurried, immediate and eternal, infinite and unrepeatable. The leaf that flutters past, the butterfly, the yellow-headed dandelions lifting from the meadow beyond the shelter of these trees, the narrow, hairlike grass that falls under my foot when it brushes the ground, the branch that creaks, the one that cracks and falls, the tiny flying insect crawling up my shirt, my own slightly sun-tanned hand, the small burn on the inside of my wrist from the oven rack—all of it ephemeral, never to be again, never this long moment, this time.

It is so pleasant, so complete. To live in time is what we hunger for, not to run to catch up with it, but to return to it. Thousands of years of life on earth made us capable of being here, in time. This is ordinary mysticism.

It isn't perfect . . .

Earlier today I watched salmon fry no more than a quarter the length of a willow leaf, no wider than the blades of grass. They swim facing into the current, and they go back and back and back in time, like we do, only further, through the Ice Ages, past the Pleistocene. And here they are.

You could find your way here, your own way. The paths are many and worn like deer trails. Come if you can. The world is waiting.

Silence

Sharman Apt Russell

"What do I do?" I ask my Quaker friend Ruth. "You are the Great Pooh-bah," she says. "You don't have to do anything."

As acting clerk of the Gila Religious Society of Friends, my main job is to open and close the hour of silence—to watch the clock. A clerk also runs the business meeting held once a month after silence. According to my copy of *Quaker Faith and Practice*, a six-hundred-page guide to being a Quaker, a clerk "needs to have a spiritual capacity for discernment and sensitivity to meeting."

Faith and Practice does not mention that the title of clerk instantly ages you twenty years. More often than not, this is exactly the age—as clerk—that you want to be.

In the Gila Friends Meeting, we are what is called "unprogrammed" Quakers. Meeting is our version of church, and a clerk is our version of a minister. Quakers believe that the Divine is right here, right now, and that the best way to find one's version of that is to sit quietly and wait. The idea of silence began more than three hundred years ago with George Fox, an Englishman who experienced a Light in his soul and who determined that this Light is in everyone, that there is "that of God" in every human being.

On time, then, at ten o'clock Sunday morning, I sit in my chair in a circle of chairs. If possible, clerks start the hour of silence by example. There is no shushing. I am not a librarian. I am here to wait for the Divine, and soon, nicely, all the other Quakers are sitting down and waiting, too. It's a big crowd for our small Meeting, with visiting Friends from other Meetings and with other friends just here to visit. Twenty of us (I count secretly) sit, breathe, get comfortable. Most of us close our eyes. Outside the door, a truck shifts into low gear.

In this circle, each time, I feel the same wonder. What makes a group of people at the beginning of the twenty-first century come together and sit silently in a room, as though we were doing something important? Do we really wait for a visiting God? Are we all thinking about peace and love? Do we believe in some kind of group vibration?

Are we trying to levitate?

I don't think so, although I can't say for sure. I think we are simply trying to be silent. We hope for the still mind. We notice our thoughts and let them go. We believe faithfully that in a moment of listening, we will hear something not our own voice. Then we won't be so lonely. We will feel a Presence. We will know what we have always suspected: eternal life is under the words.

I believe this in spite of myself, in spite of my experience and my education, so that it seems a Presence *has* been whispering to me, that I believe in something I do not yet know.

I think about these things more than I believe in them. Truthfully, my best thinking has been done in silence, where I have an agreement: this is not the place for work, relationships, children, sex, money, or vacation plans. There is not much left to do but be still or be thoughtful. The latter is so interesting that I often forget to concentrate on the present moment or on waiting for the Light.

As clerk, I keep looking at the big clock on the wall. Each time, another Quaker is looking, too.

Each time I look up and look around, I see other people. Quakers believe that corporate worship is more powerful than individual worship. This seems to be true. In any case, this circle of human beings is deeply reassuring. Both the familiar and the unfamiliar faces are all, somehow, familial. Their cheeks and brows look soft, relaxed in the struggle of letting go, going under the words.

Given the depth of this struggle, it seems odd that Quakers also endorse a "vocal ministry." Any Quaker at any time can interrupt the silence and say what is bursting in her heart, what she feels must be said. Very early Quakers got their name because the emotion of hearing God's voice and seeing the Light caused them literally to quake. Understandably, they might have imploded had they not been allowed to speak about the experience. Modern Quakers do not quake at all. Still, we continue to break silence. Some Meetings are quite talkative. My Meeting is not. Commonly, no one says anything.

Today, however, halfway through silence, a visiting Friend begins to sermonize. He goes on for at least five minutes. It seems much longer.

As clerk, with my spiritual discernment and sensitivity to meeting, I can actually see a wispy fog trailing in the air above the furniture. It is the physical manifestation of annoyance.

Finally the Friend stops. The room is quiet.

Another visitor tells a story about John Woolman.

Now a non-Quaker, seriously misled, lectures us about El Salvador.

"Oh, Jesus," someone says, and I start and try to hide it, looking into my lap. No one I know has ever addressed Jesus in this Meeting.

My judgments are rising, fish to bait. Vocal ministry is meant to be a ripple in the pool of silence. The pool is roiling. I feel surprisingly angry.

Shut up, please.

•   •   •

In Annie Dillard's essay "A Field of Silence," she writes of a holy and terrifying experience: "I have seen, from behind the barn, the long roadside pastures heaped with silence. Behind the rooster, suddenly, I saw the silence heaped on the fields like trays. That day the green hayfields supported silence evenly sown; the fields bent just so under the even pressure of silence, bearing it, palming it aloft: cleared fields, part of a land, a planet, that did not buckle beneath the heel of silence, nor split up scattered to bits, but instead lay secret, disguised as time and matter as though that were nothing, ordinary—disguised as fields like those which bear the silence only because they are spread, and the silence spreads over them, great in size.

"I do not want," Annie Dillard went on, "ever to see such a sight again."

But wait.

In a few paragraphs, she will change her mind. She will decide that the field of silence was a field of angels.

"If pressed I would say they were three or four feet from the ground. Only their motion was clear (clockwise, if you insist); that, and their beauty unspeakable."

Annie Dillard presumes now that there are angels everywhere, in all fields, just as there is silence everywhere.

This woman, I think, is working overtime.

We share many of the same concerns.

"Even if things are as bad as they could possibly be," she writes bravely, "and as meaningless, then matters of truth are themselves indifferent; we may as well please our sensibilities and, with as much spirit as we can muster, go out with a buck and wing."

It sounds so cheerful, a quality I admire. Quakers are also determinedly cheerful, even though many of them are social activists who spend their time actually thinking about places like El Salvador. After our hour of silence in the Gila Society of Friends Meeting, we will make announcements that include the most recent news about nuclear disarmament and children dying in Iraq. We will hand out clippings about massacres and injustice like some people hand out recipes. In that peculiar brand of Quaker sunshine, we will wait for the Light and talk incessantly about the dark.

In times of faithlessness, when things are as bad as they possibly can be, when there is nothing under the words and the silence is empty, I hope, at least, to go out with a buck and wing.

. . .

Lately, I have been researching Quaker humor. I started off with *Quakers Are Funny* by Chuck Fager, published in 1992. Hardly anything in the book made me laugh, except for the notice, "I am a Quaker. In case of emergency, please be quiet."

I also liked the joke:

"Why do liberal Quakers sing hymns so badly?"

"Because we're always reading ahead to see if we agree with the words."

In another anecdote, Herbert Hoover, a birthright Friend, typifies Quaker caution. Traveling on a train, he and a friend pass a flock of grazing sheep.

The other man remarks, "Look, those sheep have just been sheared."

"Yes," Hoover agrees and adds, "on this side, at any rate."

Me and Annie and Herbert in a circle. Something tells me to believe. Something tells me there are angels.

"Yes," I agree with caution. "On this side, at any rate."

. . .

Eternal life is under the words. What a strange thing to say. What do I seek under the words? Why do I seek wordless knowledge? In this hour of silence, am I simply trying to be more like a cat?

In a Quaker pamphlet on silence, I read, "When we drop our questions, paradoxically we find the answers, almost as if the answers had been waiting for us to discover them but had been drowned out by the noise of our questions. Out of such silence leaps the all-powerful word of God and we find ourselves seized with meaning."

I am here, of course, to be seized with meaning. Under my words I hope to find the word of God, not a word exactly, not a God exactly.

First I have to stop talking.

I look up at the clock. A restlessness has seized the meeting, a shifting of haunches, a cough, a sigh I interpret as a call for help: my back is killing me!

Some clerks end silence a few minutes before the hour, and some clerks end silence a few minutes after the hour, and some clerks end silence exactly on time.

I am a clerk who will end silence a few minutes before the hour.

Smiling, I extend my hands. We all join hands and clasp them tightly, looking at each other with gratitude, with happiness, and with relief.

Silence, for now, is over.

Witchcraft and Women's Culture

Starhawk

From earliest times, women have been witches, *wicce*, "wise ones"—priestesses, diviners, midwives, poets, healers, and singers of songs of power. Woman-centered culture, based on the worship of the Great Goddess, underlies the beginnings of all civilization. Mother Goddess was carved on the walls of paleolithic caves, and painted in the shrines of the earliest cities, those of the Anatolian plateau. For her were raised the giant stone circles, the henges of the British Isles, the dolmens and cromlechs of the later Celtic countries, and for her the great passage graves of Ireland were dug. In her honor, sacred dancers leaped the bulls in Crete and composed lyric hymns within the colleges of the holy isles of the Mediterranean. Her mysteries were celebrated in secret rites at Eleusis, and her initiates included some of the finest minds of Greece. Her priestesses discovered and tested the healing herbs and learned the secrets of the human mind and body that allowed them to ease the pain of childbirth, to heal wounds and cure diseases, and to explore the realm of dreams and the unconscious. Their knowledge of nature enabled them to tame sheep and cattle, to breed wheat and corn from grasses and weeds, to forge ceramics from mud and metal from rock, and to track the movements of moon, stars, and sun.

Witchcraft, "the craft of the wise," is the last remnant in the west of the time of women's strength and power. Through the dark ages of persecution, the covens of Europe preserved what is left of the mythology, rituals, and knowledge of the ancient matricentric (mother-centered) times. The great centers of worship in Anatolia, Malta, Iberia, Brittany, and Sumeria are now only silent stones and works of art we can but dimly understand. Of the mysteries of Eleusis, we have literary hints; the poems of Sappho survive only in fragments. The great collections of early literature and science were destroyed by patriarchal forces—the library of Alexandria burnt by Caesar, Charlemagne's collection of lore burnt by his son Louis "the Pious," who was offended at its "paganism." But the craft remains, in spite of all efforts to stamp it out, as a living tradition of Goddess-centered worship that traces its roots back to the time before the triumph of patriarchy.

The old religion of witchcraft before the advent of Christianity, was an earth-centered, nature-oriented worship that venerated the Goddess, the source of life, as well as her son-lover-consort, who was seen as the Horned God of the hunt and animal life. Earth, air, water, fire, streams, seas, wells, beasts, trees, grain, the planets, sun, and most of all, the moon, were seen as aspects of deity. On the great seasonal festivals—the solstices and equinoxes, and the eves of May, August, November, and February—all the countryside would gather to light huge bonfires, feast, dance, sing, and perform the rituals that assured abundance throughout the year.

When Christianity first began to spread, the country people held to the old ways, and for hundreds of years the two faiths coexisted quite peacefully. Many people followed both religions, and country priests in the twelfth and thirteenth centuries were frequently upbraided by church authorities for dressing in skins and leading the dance at the pagan festivals.

But in the thirteenth and fourteenth centuries, the church began persecution of witches, as well as Jews and "heretical" thinkers. Pope Innocent the VIII, with his Bull of 1484, intensified a campaign of torture and death that would take the lives of an estimated nine million people, perhaps 80 percent of whom were women.

The vast majority of victims were not coven members or even necessarily witches. They were old widows whose property was coveted by someone else, young children with "witch blood," midwives who furnished the major competition to the male-dominated medical profession, free-thinkers who asked the wrong questions.

An enormous campaign of propaganda accompanied the witch trials as well. Witches were said to have sold their souls to the devil, to practice obscene and disgusting rites, to blight crops and murder children. In many areas, the witches did worship a Horned God as the spirit of the hunt, of animal life and vitality, a concept far from the power of evil that was the Christian devil. Witches were free and open about sexuality—but their rites were "obscene" only to those who viewed the human body itself as filthy and evil. Questioning or disbelieving any of the slander was itself considered proof of witchcraft or heresy, and the falsehoods that for hundreds of years could not be openly challenged had their effect. Even today, the word *witch* is often automatically associated with "evil."

With the age of reason in the eighteenth century, belief in witches, as in all things psychic and supernatural, began to fade. The craft as a religion was forgotten; all that remained were the wild stories of broomstick flights, magic potions, and the summoning of spectral beings.

Memory of the true craft faded everywhere except within the hidden covens. With it, went the memory of women's heritage and history, of our ancient roles as leaders, teachers, healers, seers. Lost, also, was the conception of the Great Spirit, as manifest in nature, in life, in woman. Mother Goddess slept, leaving the world to the less than gentle rule of the God-Father.

The Goddess has at last stirred from sleep, and women are reawakening to our ancient power. The feminist movement, which began as a political, economic, and social struggle, is opening to a spiritual dimension. In the process, many women are discovering the old religion, reclaiming the word *witch* and, with it, some of our lost culture.

Witchcraft, today, is a kaleidoscope of diverse traditions, rituals, theologies, and structures. But underneath the varying forms is a basic orientation common to all the craft. The outer forms of religion—the particular words said, the signs made, the names used—are less important to us than the inner forms, which cannot be defined or described but must be felt and intuited.

The craft is earth religion, and our basic orientation is to the earth, to life, to nature. There is no dichotomy between spirit and flesh, no split between Godhead and the world. The Goddess is manifest in the world; she brings life into being, *is* nature, *is* flesh. Union is not sought outside the world in some heavenly sphere or through dissolution of the self into the void beyond the senses. Spiritual union is found in life, within nature, passion, sensuality—through being fully human, fully one's self.

Our great symbol for the Goddess is the moon, whose three aspects reflect the three stages in women's lives and whose cycles of waxing and waning coincide with women's menstrual cycles. As the new moon or crescent, she is the Maiden, the Virgin—not chaste, but belonging to herself alone, not bound to any man. She is the wild child, lady of the woods, the huntress, free and untamed—Artemis, Kore, Aradia, Nimue. White is her color. As the full moon, she is the mature woman, the sexual being, the mother and nurturer, giver of life, fertility, grain, offspring, potency, joy—Tana, Demeter, Diana, Ceres, Mari. Her colors are the red of blood and the green of growth. As waning or dark moon, she is the old woman, past menopause, the hag or crone that is ripe with wisdom, patroness of secrets, prophecy, divination, inspiration, power—Hecate, Ceridwen, Kali, Anna. Her color is the black of night.

The Goddess is also earth—Mother Earth, who sustains all growing things, who is the body, our bones and cells. She is air—the winds that move in the trees and over the waves, breath. She is the fire of the hearth, of the blazing bonfire and the fuming volcano; the power of transformation and change. And she is water—the sea, original source of life; the rivers, streams, lakes and wells; the blood that flows in the rivers of our veins. She is mare, cow, cat, owl, crane, flower, tree, apple, seed, lion, sow, stone, woman. She is found in the world around us, in the cycles and seasons of nature, and in mind, body, spirit, and emotions within each of us. Thou art Goddess. I am Goddess. All that lives (and all that is, lives), all that serves life, is Goddess.

Because witches are oriented to earth and to life, we value spiritual qualities that I feel are especially important to women, who have for so long been conditioned to be passive, submissive and weak. The craft values independence, personal strength, *self*—not petty selfishness but that deep core of strength within that makes us each a unique child of the Goddess. The craft has no dogma to stifle thought, no set of doctrines that have to be believed. Where authority exists, within covens, it is always coupled with the freedom every covener has, to leave at any time. When self is valued—in ourselves—we can see that self is everywhere.

Passion and emotion—that give depth and color and meaning to human life—are also valued. Witches strive to be in touch with feelings, even if they are sometimes painful, because the joy and pleasure and ecstasy available to a fully alive person make it worth occasional suffering. So-called negative emotion—anger—is valued as well, as a sign that something is wrong and that action needs to be taken. Witches prefer to handle anger by taking action and making changes rather than by detaching ourselves from our feelings in order to reach some nebulous, "higher" state.

Most of all, the craft values love. The Goddess's only law is "Love unto all beings." But the love we value is not the airy flower power of the hippies or the formless, abstracted *agape* of the early Christians. It is passionate, sensual, personal love, *eros*, falling in love, mother-child love, the love of one unique human being for other individuals, with all their personal traits and idiosyncrasies. Love is not something that can be radiated out in solitary meditation—it manifests itself in relationships and interactions with other people. It is often said "You cannot be a witch alone"—because to be a witch is to be a lover, a lover of the Goddess, and a lover of other human beings.

The coven is still the basic structure of the craft, and generally covens meet at the times of full moons and the major festivals, although some meet also on new moons and a few meet once a week. A coven is a small group, at most of thirteen members—for the thirteen full moons of the year. Its small size is important. Within the coven, a union, a merging of selves in a close bond of love and trust, takes place. A coven becomes an energy pool each member can draw on. But, because the group remains small, there is never the loss of identity and individuality that can happen in a mass. In a coven, each person's individuality is extremely important. Each personality colors and helps create the group identity, and each member's energy is vital to the working of the group.

Covens are separate and autonomous, and no one outside the coven has any authority over its functioning. Some covens may be linked in the same tradition—meaning they share the same rituals and symbology—but there is no hierarchy of rule. Elder witches can and do give advice, but only those within the coven may actually make decisions.

Covens are extremely diverse. There are covens of hereditary witches who have practiced rites unchanged for hundreds of years, and covens who prefer to make up their own rituals and may never do the same thing twice. There are covens of "perfect couples"—an even number of women and men permanently paired, and covens of lesbian feminists or of women who simply prefer to explore women's spirituality in a space removed from men. There are covens of gay men and covens that just don't worry about sexual polarities. A few covens are authoritarian—with a high priestess or high priest who makes most of the decisions. (Coveners, of course, always have the option of leaving.) Most are democratic, if not anarchic, but usually older or more experienced members—"elders"—assume leadership and responsibility. Actual roles in rituals are often rotated among qualified coveners.

Rituals also vary widely. A craft ritual might involve wild shouting and frenzied dancing, or silent meditation, or both. A carefully rehearsed drama might be enacted, or a spontaneous poetic chant carried on for an hour. Everyone may enter a deep trance and scry in a crystal ball—or they may pass around a bottle of wine and laugh uproariously at awful puns. The best rituals combine moments of intense ecstasy and spiritual union with moments of raucous humor and occasional silliness. The craft is serious without being dry or solemn.

Whether formal or informal, every craft ritual takes place within a circle—a space considered to be "between the worlds," the human world and the realm of the Goddess. A circle can be cast, or created, in any physical space, from a moonlit hillside to the living room of a modern apartment. It may be outlined in stones, drawn in chalk or paint, or drawn invisibly with the point of a sword or ceremonial wand. It may be consecrated with incense, salt water, and a formal invocation to each of the four quarters of the universe, or created simply by having everyone join hands. The casting of the circle begins the ritual and serves as a transition into an expanded state of consciousness. The power raised by the ritual is contained within the circle so that it can reach a higher peak instead of dissipating.

The Goddess, and if desired, the Horned God (not all traditions of the craft relate to the male force) can be invoked once the circle is cast. An invocation may be set beforehand, written out and memorized, but in our coven we find the most effective invocations are those that come to us spontaneously, out of the inspiration of the season, the phase of the moon, and the particular mood and energy of the moment. Often we invoke the Goddess by chanting together a line or phrase repeated over and over: "Moon mother bright light of all earth sky, we call you" is an example. As we chant, we find rhythms, notes, melodies, and words seem to flow through us and burst out in complex and beautiful patterns.

Chanting, dancing, breathing, and concentrated will, all contribute to the raising of power, which is the essential part of a craft ritual. Witches conceive of psychic energy as having form and substance that can be perceived and directed by those with a trained awareness. The power generated within the circle is built into a cone form, and at its peak is released—to the Goddess, to reenergize the members of the coven, or to do a specific work such as a healing.

When the cone is released, any scattered energy that is left is grounded, put back into the earth, by falling to the ground, breathing deeply, and relaxing. High-energy states cannot be maintained indefinitely without becoming a physical and emotional drain—any more than you could stay high on methedrine forever without destroying your body. After the peak of the cone, it is vital to let go of the power and return to a calm, relaxed state. Silent meditation, trance, or psychic work are often done in this part of the ritual.

Energy is also shared in tangible form—wine, cakes, fruit, cheesecake, brownies, or whatever people enjoy eating. The Goddess is invited to share with everyone, and a libation is poured to her first. This part of the ritual is relaxed and informally social, devoted to laughing, talking, sharing of news and any business that must be done.

At the end, the Goddess is thanked and bid farewell, and the circle is formally opened. Ending serves as a transition back into ordinary space and time. Rituals finish with a kiss and a greeting of "Merry meet, merry part, and merry meet again."

The underlying forms of craft rituals evolved out of thousands of years of experience and understanding of human needs and the potentials of human consciousness. That understanding, which is part of women's lost heritage, is invaluable, not just in the context of rituals and spiritual growth, but also for those working toward political and social change, because human needs and human energies behave the same in any context.

Witches understand that energy, whether it is psychic, emotional, or physical, always flows in cycles. It rises and falls, peaks and drops, and neither end of the cycle can be sustained indefinitely, any more than you could run forever without stopping. Intense levels of energy must be released and then brought down and grounded; otherwise the energy dissipates or even turns destructive. If, in a ritual, you tried to maintain a peak of frenzy for hours and hours, you would find that after a while the energy loses its joyful quality, and instead of feeling union and ecstasy, you begin to feel irritated and exhausted. Political groups that try to maintain an unremitting level of anger—a high-energy state—also run out of steam in precisely the same way. Releasing the energy and grounding out allows the power itself to work freely. It clears channels and allows you to rest and recharge and become ready for the next swing into an up cycle. Releasing energy does not mean losing momentum; rather, real movement, real change, happens in a rhythmic pattern of many beats, not in one unbroken blast of static.

Craft rituals also add an element of drama and fantasy to one's life. They allow us to act out myths and directly experience archetypes of symbolic transformation. They allow us, as adults, to recapture the joy of childhood make-believe, of dressing up, of pretending, of play. Magic, by Dion Fortune's definition, "the art of changing consciousness at will," is not so far removed from the creative fantasy states we enter so easily as children, when our dolls become alive, our bicycles become wild horses, ourselves arctic explorers or queens. Allowing ourselves, as adults, to play and fantasize with others, puts us in touch with the creative child within, with a deep and rich source of inspiration.

The craft also helps us open our intuitive and psychic abilities. Although witchcraft is commonly associated with magic and the use of extrasensory powers, not all covens put a great deal of stress on psychic training. Worship is more often the main focus of activity. However, any craft ritual involves some level of psychic awareness just in sensing the energy that is raised.

Ordinarily, the way into the craft is through initiation into an already established coven. However, because covens are limited in size and depend on some degree of harmony between personalities, it is often difficult to find one that is open to new members and that fits your preferences. In San Francisco, Los Angeles, and New York, covens often run open study groups and can be found through publications and open universities. In other areas of the country, it may be difficult to locate a practicing coven at all.

However, there is nothing to stop you from starting a coven or a *circle*—a term I use for a group whose members meet for rituals but are not formally initiated—on your own. Women, especially, are more and more joining together to explore a Goddess-oriented spirituality and to create rituals and symbols that are meaningful to us today. Starting your own circle requires imagination, creativity, and experimentation, but it is a tremendously exciting process. You will miss formal psychic training—but you may discover on your own more than anyone else could teach you. Much of what is written on the craft is biased in one way or another, so weed out what is useful to you and ignore the rest.

I see the next few years as being crucial in the transformation of our culture away from the patriarchal death cults and toward the love of life, of nature, of the female principle. The craft is only one path among the many opening up for women, and many of us will blaze new trails as we explore the uncharted country of our own interiors. The heritage, the culture, the knowledge of the ancient priestesses, healers, poets, singers, and seers were nearly lost, but a seed survived the flames that will blossom in a new age into thousands of flowers. The long sleep of Mother Goddess is ended. May She awaken in each of our hearts—Merry meet, merry part, and blessed be.

Re-Vamping the World
On the Return of the Holy Prostitute

Deena Metzger

nce upon a time, in Sumeria, in Mesopotamia, in Egypt, in Greece, there were no whorehouses, no brothels. In that time, in those countries, there were instead the Temples of the Sacred Prostitutes. In these temples, men were cleansed, not sullied; morality was restored, not desecrated; sexuality was not perverted, but divine.

The original whore was a priestess, the conduit to the divine, the one through whose body one entered the sacred arena and was restored. Warriors, soldiers, soiled by combat within the world of men, came to the Holy Prostitute, the *Quedishtu*, literally meaning "the undefiled one," in order to be cleansed and reunited with the gods. The *Quedishtu* or *Quadesh* is associated with a variety of goddesses, including Hathor, Ishtar, Anath, Astarte, and Asherah. It is interesting to note, according to Patricia Monaghan in *The Book of Goddesses and Heroines*, that Astarte originally meant "She of the Womb" but appears in the Old Testament as Ashtoreth, meaning "Shameful thing."

Despite scripture and orthodox thought, war was seen as separating men from the gods, and one had to be reconnected in order to be able to re-enter society. The body, the sexual act, was the means for re-entry. As the body was the means, so inevitably pleasure was an accompaniment, but the essential attribute of sexuality, in this context, was prayer.

In Pergamon, Turkey, I saw the remains of the Temple of the Holy Prostitutes on the Sacred Way, alongside the other temples, palaces, and public buildings. Whatever rites we imagine took place in these other buildings, it is common—whether we elevate them as do neo-pagans or condemn them as do Judeo-Christians—to associate the Holy Prostitutes with orgies and debauchery. But it is possible that neither view is correct, as each tends to inflate the physical activity and ignore or impugn the spiritual component. Our materialist preoccupation with form blinds us to the content.

But it is no wonder that from the beginning, the first patriarchs, the priests of Judea and Israel, the prophets of Jehovah, all condemned the Holy Prostitutes and the worship of Asherah, Astarte, Anath, and the other goddesses. Until the time of the priests, the women were one doorway to the divine. If the priests wished to insert themselves between the people and the divine, they had to remove women from that role. So it was not that sexuality was originally considered sinful per se, or that women's sexuality threatened property and progeny; it was that in order for the priests to have power, women had to be replaced as a road to the divine—this gate had to be closed. It was, we can speculate, to this end that the terrible misogyny that we all suffer was instituted.

Women had been the essential link to the three worlds. Through the mother one came into this world; through the Mysteries, the rites of Demeter or Isis, one entered the underworld; and through the Holy Prostitute one came to the divine. Access was personal and unconditional. It was not sufficient for a new priesthood to supplant the women. In the days of the *Quedishtu* every woman served the gods as Holy Prostitute, often for as long as a year. This was contradictory to the hegemony that a priesthood required.

For the sake of power, it is often necessary to set the world upside down. Therefore the priests asserted that the sacred was depraved, that the way to the divine was the way to perdition. Reversals such as this are not uncommon. Incoming religions often co-opt, then reverse, existing spiritual beliefs and practices. So Hades, the spiritual center of Greek paganism, became Hell. The descent into Hades, the core of the Eleusinian mysteries and a spiritually required initiation for anyone who was concerned with soul, was likened to suffering and perdition. Where once Pindar had written, "Thrice blessed are those who have seen these Mysteries for they know the end of life and the beginning," later Dante was to inscribe, "Abandon all hope, ye who enter here." Similarly, Dionysus, the life god, became Satan; Adonis, the consort of Aphrodite, became Christ. Mary Magdalene, the Holy Prostitute, was converted and transformed; Aphrodite became Eve became the Virgin Mary. The reversals were complete. Psyche's (soul's) journey toward individuation became almost impossible as Aphrodite, the mother of Eros, no longer existed to beckon the Self.

Three of the essential roads to the three worlds were blocked or debased. The gods did not die in Nietzsche's time, but centuries earlier with the subversion of the priestesses and the secularization and degradation of the holy body.

This essay is about seduction, about vamping, about eros; about an attempt to restore a tradition, to reinstitute a way of seeing the world. It is not only about restoring practices, it is first about restoring the consciousness from which those practices may derive.

What was the impact of the suppression of the Holy Prostitute on the world? We are not concerned here with the suppression of certain rites but rather with the deprivation of consciousness implicit in that suppression. All the practices that honored the way of the woman ceased. The Eleusinian mysteries, which had provided immortality, were suppressed; the mysteries of the Cabeiri, designed specifically to redeem those with blood on their hands, were suppressed; procreation was infused with anxiety and guilt; fertility festivals that had provided a link between earth and spirit were condemned. When the priests separated the body from the gods, they separated the divine from na-

ture and thereby created the mind-body split. The world was secular-
ized. We can only speculate as to the consequences, though we must
assume there were consequences when men returned from war without the ability to clean the blood from their hands, when the physical,
quotidian community between the gods and the people was not re-
convened. It was not woman per se who was attacked, but the gods
who were exiled. Perhaps the world as we have come to know it—
impersonal, abstract, detached, brutish—was engendered in that
division.

In a sacred universe, the prostitute is a holy woman, a priestess. In
a secular universe, the prostitute is a whore. In this distinction is the
agony of our lives.

The question is: How do we relate to this today, as women, as
feminists? Is there a way we can resanctify society, become the priestesses again, put ourselves in the service of the gods and eros? As we
re-vision, can we re-vamp as well?

Vamp: A woman who sets out to charm or captivate by the use of
sexual attractiveness.

Re-vamp: To mend, repair, renovate, refurbish, or restore.

What does it mean to re-vamp a society? It means that we must
become vamps again, sexual-spiritual beings, that we must act out of
eros. This means that we must first alter ourselves in the most fundamental ways. We cannot become the means for the resanctification of
society unless we are willing to become the priestesses once more who
serve the gods not in theory and empty practice, but from our very nature. It means that we must identify with eros no matter what the
seeming consequences to ourselves. Even if it seems foolish, inexpedient, even if it makes us vulnerable. It means that we cannot be distracted from this task by pleasure, power, lusts, or anger. It requires a
sincere rededication.

It is, however, exactly this rededication to the principles of the
Feminine that is so problematic. The Feminine has been so devalued
and degraded, has so little power in the world, we have suffered so
much loss of opportunity, have been so oppressed, that it is difficult if
not sometimes seemingly impossible to continue to enact the Femi-

nine in the world without feeling as if we are opening ourselves to further violation. So we are caught in a terrible paradox. To feel powerful, to acquire some gain, we must learn the very masculine modes that oppress us and that are about to destroy the world. In either case we seem to participate in our own destruction. But if we utilize the Feminine, it is possible that the planet will survive, and also the species, and that eventually we will thrive. Without the Feminine and eros, everything is irretrievably lost.

And so let us consider becoming Holy Prostitutes again.

When contemporary feminism was established sufficiently to offer real hope and possibility, women who had formerly considered themselves atheists turned to spiritual matters. The Goddess and goddesses were reinvoked. There was an extraordinary interest in spirituality, myth, rite, ceremony. The spiritual instinct buried in a secular universe erupted.

As part of this new spiritual order, we must engage in two heresies. The second is to re-sanctify the body; the first, even more difficult task is to return to the very early, neolithic, pagan, matriarchal perception of the sacred universe itself. But to overthrow secular thought may be the heretical act of the century. That is why we are in so much psychic pain.

Susan Griffin writes the following in the last chapter, entitled "Eros," in *Pornography and Silence*:

> The psychic is simply world. *And if I let myself love, let myself touch, enter my own pleasure and longing, enter the body of another, the darkness, let the dark parts of my body speak, tongue into mouth, in the body's language, as I enter a part of me I believed was real begins to die, I descend into matter, I know I am at the heart of myself, I cry out in ecstasy.* For in love, we surrender our uniqueness and become world.

If we become world through love, then love is essentially a political act. If we become world reaching to the gods, then love is essentially a spiritual act that redeems the world.

How then do we become Holy Prostitutes? How do we materialize without literalizing the Holy Prostitute? How do we bring her essence into being? How do we restore the temple? How do we change not only behavior but our consciousness as well?

To become the Holy Prostitute is to be willing to endure the agony of consciousness required of the heretic. It is the willingness and ability to hold one worldview when the majority holds another. It is to commit oneself to eros, bonding, connection, when the world values thanatos, separation, detachment. The Holy Prostitute was Everywoman, and she made herself available in the service of the gods, especially to those outside the province of the gods. The contemporary Holy Prostitute must be willing to try to bring the sacred to the one who is defiled; she must be the one who will take in "the other"— the one who makes love with "the other" in order for him to be reconnected to the community. She carries the belief that "the other" does not want to remain an outsider.

These ideas are old and familiar, easy to say, so difficult to enact. Yet when they are transformed from idea to belief within ourselves, transformation outside ourselves follows.

I have done some work called personal disarmament. I ask individuals to consider themselves a nation-state and to impose upon themselves those conditions they would like to impose upon the country. In this exercise they must identify their enemies, their armies, defense and offense systems, secret weapons, and so on. Then after this self-scrutiny, I ask them to publicly commit at least a single act of personal disarmament to initiate the change to a peaceful world. It seems to me that our militarism and defensiveness are signs of our inner fear and aggression. I believe that ultimately it will be easier for us to disarm as a nation if we are disarmed as individuals.

The same scrutiny is essential to the issue at hand. If we built brothel adjuncts to our temples and sent our young girls there at eighteen, it would be ludicrous, it would change nothing; nothing can change as long as we devalue the Feminine, denigrate the body, and disbelieve in a sacred universe. Certainly the sexual revolution has proven this, for it has changed nothing. So it is not sex we are after at all, but something far deeper.

The task is to accept the body as spiritual, and sexuality and erotic love as spiritual disciplines; to believe that eros is pragmatic; to honor the Feminine even where it is dishonored or disadvantaged. These, then, are some of the questions I think it is appropriate for us to ask ourselves:

Whom do I close myself against?

When do I not have time for love or eros?

When do I find eros inconvenient, burdensome, or inexpedient?

When do I find eros dangerous to me?

When do I indulge the erotic charge of guilt?

Where do I respond to, accept, provoke the idea of sin?

When do I use sexuality to distract rather than to commune?

When do I reject eros because I am rejected?

When do I abuse the body?

How do I reinforce the mind/body split?

When and how do I denigrate the Feminine?

When do I refuse the gods? When do I pretend to believe in them?

How often do I acquiesce to the "real world"?

In a guided meditation, I was confronted by a large, luminous woman, approximately eight feet tall, clearly an image of a goddess, though I had never encountered a goddess figure in any of my own meditations. Her hair was light itself. As she came close to me, I was filled both with awe at her beauty and terror at her presence. If I were to take her into me, I knew my life would be altered, I would have to give up many of the masculine modes I had adopted in order to negotiate successfully in the world. The woman was powerful, but her power was of receptivity, resonance, magnetism, radiance. She had the power of eros; she drew me to her.

As she appeared, I was reminded of a statement by a friend. "When it comes to the bell," Dianna Linden said, "we all want to be the clapper, we don't want to be the body; but it is the body which sings." Still, when she appeared, I consciously experienced the terror of the Feminine I had so often read and heard about. I was afraid of my own nature . . .

So, though I have written about it, thought about it, tried to act accordingly, I must admit that I have not been able to fully put on the role of the Holy Prostitute. This fills me with sadness, also awe at the difficulty of the task. But I do commit myself; she is the woman I aspire to be.

Hiʻiaka Chanting

Haunani-Kay Trask

Glistening tree snails
    miraculous light gleaming
        ʻōlapa leaves

    in Pele's uplands.
        Elegant *hāpuʻu*, translucent
           as her eyes. And

      our flitting *iʻiwi*
         nimble beak sipping
           love's *lehua*

        buds. Winter moss
           sponging the earth. Hypnotic
             mist. Hiʻiaka chanting

      on the wind.
           Step lightly, dancer.
               Look up, look up.

About the Contributors

Poet, essayist, and naturalist DIANE ACKERMAN lives and teaches in Ithaca, New York. Her works include *Origami Bridges: Poems of Psychoanalysis and Fire*; *Twilight of the Tenderfoot: A Western Memoir*; *Cultivating Delight: A Natural History of My Garden*; *A Natural History of Love*; *A Natural History of the Senses*; and *The Moon by Whale Light*.

PAULA GUNN ALLEN divides her time between New Mexico and Southern California. Her books include *Pocahontas: Medicine Woman, Spy, Entrepreneur*; *Diplomat*; *The Sacred Hoop*; *Grandmothers of the Light*; and *Off the Reservation: Reflections on Boundary-Busting, Border-Crossing Loose Canons*. She is a former professor of English at UCLA.

SUSAN BISKEBORN is the author of *Artists at Work: Twenty-Five Northwest Glassmakers, Ceramists, and Jewelers*. She has published numerous poems and essays, including "Women at Work" in the anthology *A Road of Her Own: Women's Journeys in the West*. She lives in Seattle with her husband and their daughter, Mary.

MARLENE BLESSING is a poet, essayist, and fiction writer. Her anthology of women's journeys in the West, *A Road of Her Own*, was recently published. She has been a book editor for more than two decades and lives in Denver.

BETH BRANT, a writer of poetry, short stories, and essays, is a Bay of Quinte Mohawk from the Tyendinaga Mohawk Reservation in Ontario, Canada. Her works include *Mohawk Trail, Food and Spirits,* and *Writing as Witness: Essay and Talk.* She edited *A Gathering of Spirit: A Collection by North American Indian Women* and *I'll Sing 'Til the Day I Die: Conversations With Tyendinaga Elders.*

KIM CHERNIN, a poet, mystic, and memoirist, was born in the Bronx to two fiercely committed Marxists. Chernin's books include *Seven Pillars of Jewish Denial: Shekinah, Wagner, and the Oasis of Peace; In My Mother's House: A Memoir;* and *Crossing the Border.*

ALISON HAWTHORNE DEMING is a poet and essayist descended from the great American writer Nathaniel Hawthorne. She has won many awards for her writing, including the Walt Whitman Award from the Academy of American Poets. Her published works include *Writing the Sacred into the Real; Temporary Homelands; The Edges of the Civilized World: A Journey in Nature and Culture; Science and Other Poems;* and *The Colors of Nature: Culture, Identity, and the Natural World.*

SUZANNE EDISON is a landscape designer by profession. She has published articles on landscape design and most recently published a poem in *Scent of Cedars,* an anthology of emerging writers in the Pacific Northwest. She lives with her husband and daughter in Seattle, Washington.

ANITA ENDREZZE, a member of the Yaqui Indian tribe, is an artist, an author, and a poet. Her written works include the award-winning *At the Helm of Twilight; Throwing Fire at the Sun, Water at the Moon;* and *The Humming of Stars and Bees and Waves: Poems and Short Stories.* Her work has been widely anthologized and translated.

DR. CLARISSA PINKOLA ESTÉS is a poet, and a psychoanalyst in practice for thirty-five years. After the massacre at Columbine High

School in April 1999, she served as a post-trauma specialist for the students and community through 2003. In addition to her national best-seller *Women Who Run with the Wolves*, books by Dr. Estés include *The Gift of Story* and *The Faithful Gardener*.

FLOR FERNANDEZ BARRIOS was born in Cuba. She immigrated to the United States in 1970, when she was fourteen years old, and graduated from International College with a doctorate in Transpersonal Psychology. She is currently in private practice in Seattle as a psychotherapist. In addition to her practice, she is a nationally recognized workshop leader on multicultural issues and spirituality. Her books include *Blessed by Thunder* and *The Mask of Oya*. Her writing has also appeared in *Raven Chronicles*, and she was one of the featured writers in *Seattle Arts* magazine.

REBECCA GOLDSTEIN is the author of several novels, including *The Mind-Body Problem*; *Properties of Light: A Novel of Love, Betrayal, and Quantum Physics*; and *Mazel*, and a collection of short stories, *Strange Attractors*. Her work has won many awards, among them two Whiting Awards. In 1996 she was named a MacArthur Foundation fellow. She holds a Ph.D. in philosophy from Princeton University, where her work was concentrated in the philosophy of science. She lives in Massachusetts.

JANE GOODALL has been studying chimpanzees in Gombe, Tanzania, since 1960. She received a Ph.D. from Cambridge University and is one of the world's most honored scientists and writers. Her publications include *The Ten Trusts: What We Must Do to Care for the Animals We Love* with Marc Bekoff; *Through a Window: My Thirty Years with the Chimpanzees of the Gombe*; *In the Shadow of Man*; *The Chimpanzees of Gombe: Patterns of Behavior*; *Reasons for Hope: A Spiritual Journey*; and *Visions of Caliban: On Chimpanzees and People* and *Africa in My Blood: An Autobiography in Letters*, both with Dale Peterson.

MARY GORDON is the author of the novels *Spending, Final Payments, The Company of Women, Men and Angels*, and *The Other Side*. Her nonfiction works include the critically acclaimed memoir *The Shadow Man* and a collection of autobiographical essays, *Seeing Through Places: Reflections on Geog-*

raphy and Identity. She is the recipient of a Lila Acheson Wallace/Reader's Digest Fund Writer's Award and a Guggenheim fellowship. Gordon lives in New York and is a professor of English at Barnard College.

JOY HARJO is an enrolled member of the Muskogee-Creek tribe, an accomplished poet, and, as lead vocalist and saxophone player for the band Poetic Justice, an award-winning musician. A major figure in contemporary American poetry, she wrote the best-selling *How We Became Human: New and Selected Poems* and has earned many honors, including the Lila Acheson Wallace/Reader's Digest Fund Writer's Award and the Lifetime Achievement Award from the Native Writers Circle of the Americas. She lives in Hawaii and teaches at UCLA and the University of Hawaii.

ELIZABETH CAROTHERS HERRON is a poet and fiction writer. Her published works include the poetry collections *Desire Being Full of Distances, Language for the Wild*, and *The Stones the Dark Earth*, and a book of short stories, *While the Distance Widens*. She is a professor of arts and humanities at Sonoma State University.

LINDA HOGAN is a Chickasaw poet, novelist, and essayist, and the author of eleven previous books, including the recent *The Woman Who Watches Over the World: A Native Memoir. Seeing Through the Sun* received an American Book Award from the Before Columbus Foundation; *Mean Spirit* won the Oklahoma Book Award as well as the Mountains and Plains Booksellers Award, and was a finalist for the Pulitzer Prize; and *Book of Medicines* was a finalist for the National Book Critics Circle Award. Hogan has been the recipient of an NEA grant, a Lannan Award, a Guggenheim fellowship, and a Five Civilized Tribes Museum Playwriting Award. She lives in the mountains of Colorado.

CATHERINE JOHNSON is a writer and educator whose essays have appeared in *Scent of Cedars, Teaching with Fire*, and *Nature of an Island*. When not writing, Johnson serves as a full-time faculty member at the Leadership Institute of Seattle (LIOS), where she is committed to the intellectual, emotional, and spiritual development of her students in service of fostering greater health and sustainability in families, organizations, communities, and the world.

MOHJA KAHF is a Muslim poet who was born in Damascus and came to the United States as a child. Her books include *E-Mails from Scheherazad* and *Western Representations of the Muslim Woman: From Termagant to Odalisque.*

RITA KIEFER is a poet and retired professor. Formerly a member of a community of Catholic nuns, she writes poems that reflect her spiritual journey. Her volumes of poetry include *Nesting Doll*, which was a finalist for the Colorado Book of the Year, *Unveiling*, and *Trying on Faces*. Her poems have appeared in *The Bloomsbury Review, Ploughshares, Southern Poetry Review*, and elsewhere. She lives with her husband in Colorado.

MARILYN KRYSL is a poet and fiction writer as well as a feminist and peace activist. She is the former director of the Creative Writing Department at the University of Colorado and a founding editor of the literary journal *Many Mountains Moving*. Her books include the short story collection *How to Accommodate Men* and a book of poetry, *Warscape with Lovers.*

URSULA K. LE GUIN, whose novels, essays, and poetry are widely read and beloved all over the world, is the author of *Changing Planes, The Left Hand of Darkness, Always Coming Home*, and *Unlocking the Air*. Her translation of the *Tao Te Ching* was published in 1997.

DEMETRIA MARTINEZ is the author of two collections of poetry and a novel, *Mother Tongue*, winner of a Western States Book Award for Fiction. She lives in Albuquerque, New Mexico, and writes a column for the *National Catholic Reporter.*

COLLEEN J. MCELROY is professor of English and creative writing at the University of Washington. Her publications include the travel memoir *A Long Way from St. Louie*, the collection *Driving Under the Cardboard Pines and Other Stories*, and several volumes of poetry: *Traveling Music*; *What*

Madness Brought Me Here: New and Selected Poems, 1968–1988; and *Queen of the Ebony Isles* (winner of the American Book Award). McElroy lives in Seattle.

DEENA METZGER is the author of many works, including *Entering the Ghost River*; *Writing for Your Life: Discovering the Story of Your Life's Journey*; *Tree: Essays & Pieces*; *Intimate Nature: The Bond Between Women and Animals* (with Brenda Peterson and Linda Hogan); and the novels *The Other Hand* and *What Dinah Thought*. Her books of poetry include *Looking for the Faces of God* and *A Sabbath Among the Ruins*. She is also known for her exuberant "Warrior" poster that illustrates the triumph over breast cancer.

SY MONTGOMERY is a columnist, commentator, and author of many heralded books, including *Encantado: Pink Dolphin of the Amazon*; *Spell of the Tiger*; *Walking with the Great Apes*; *Nature's Everyday Mysteries*; *Seasons of the Wild*; *Journey of the Pink Dolphins: An Amazon Quest*; and *The Curious Naturalist: Nature's Everyday Mysteries*. She lives in New Hampshire.

NAOMI SHIHAB NYE is a poet, novelist, and anthologist. She is the author of *19 Varieties of Gazelle: Poems of the Middle East*; *Come With Me*; and *Is This Forever, or What? Poems and Paintings from Texas*. Her children's books include *Baby Radar*; *Habibi*; *Salting the Ocean: 100 Poems by Young Poets*; and *Sitti's Secrets*. She lives in San Antonio, Texas.

ELAINE H. PAGELS won the National Book Award for her groundbreaking work *The Gnostic Gospels*. She is also the author of *The Origin of Satan*; *Beyond Belief: The Secret Gospel of Thomas*; and *Adam, Eve, and the Serpent*.

SUSANNE PARI was born in the United States to an Iranian father and an American mother of Protestant and Jewish background. She was raised a Muslim. Her novel *The Fortune Catcher*, a family saga set against Iran's Islamic Revolution, was published in 1997. She lives in Northern California with her husband and son.

MOLLY PEACOCK is Poet-in-Residence at the American Poets' Corner, Cathedral of St. John the Divine, and former president of the Poetry Society of America. She is the author of five volumes of poetry, including *Cornucopia: New and Selected Poems*. Peacock lives in New York City and London, Ontario.

BRENDA PETERSON is a novelist and nature writer and the author of fifteen books, including *Living by Water*, *Singing to the Sound*, the memoir *Build Me an Ark: A Life with Animals*, and the recent *Sightings: The Gray Whales' Mysterious Journey* (co-authored with Linda Hogan). Her third novel, *Duck and Cover*, was selected as a *New York Times* "Notable Book of the Year." She has also co-edited with Linda Hogan the best-selling anthologies *Intimate Nature: The Bond Between Women and Animals* and *The Sweet Breathing of Plants: Women Writing on the Green World*. Her fourth novel, *Animal Heart*, was published in 2004.

JUDITH ROCHE is a poet, editor, arts educator, and arts events programmer who lives in Seattle. She has published two collections of poetry and edited several anthologies and collections, including the American Book Award–winning *First Fish, First People: Salmon Tales of the North Pacific Rim*.

PATTIANN ROGERS is an award-winning poet whose books include *Firekeeper: New and Selected Poems*; *Song of the World Becoming: Poems, New and Collected, 1981–2001*; *Eating Bread and Honey*; *A Covenant of Seasons*; and *The Dream of the Marsh Wren: Writing as Reciprocal Creation*. She lives in Colorado.

SHARMAN APT RUSSELL is the author of *An Obsession With Butterflies: Our Long Love Affair with a Singular Insect*; *The Last Matriarch: A Novel*; *When the Land Was Young*; *Kill the Cowboy*; and *Songs of the Fluteplayer*, winner of the Mountains and Plains Booksellers Award. Her work has also been featured in *American Nature Writers*, *Writing Nature*, and other anthologies. She teaches writing at Western New Mexico University and at Antioch University in Los Angeles.

AMY SCHURING is a poet whose work has appeared in literary magazines such as *Seneca Review* and the anthology *The Nature of an Island*. She is at work on her first volume of poetry and lives in Maine.

BARBARA SJOHOLM is the author of *The Pirate Queen: In Search of Grace O'Malley and Other Legendary Women of the Sea*. She also published, as Barbara Wilson, the award-winning memoir *Blue Windows: A Christian Science Childhood*. She lives in Seattle.

STARHAWK is a writer, an activist, and a witch. She is the author of *The Twelve Wild Swans: A Journey to the Realm of Magic, Healing, and Action*; *The Fifth Sacred Thing*; *The Spiral Dance*; and *Walking to Mercury*.

HAUNANI-KAY TRASK is one of Hawaii's most recognized native authors. She is the author of a best-selling collection of essays, *From a Native Daughter: Colonialism and Sovereignity in Hawaii*, and several volumes of poetry, including *Light in the Crevice Never Seen* and *Night Is a Sharkskin Drum*.

A Native American poet and storyteller, GEORGIANA VALOYCE-SANCHEZ belongs to the Chumash/Tohono and Pima O'odham Nation. She lectures at California State University, Long Beach, in the Department of American Indian Studies and is a member of the California Indian Storytelling Association.

KATE WHEELER'S collection of short stories, *Not Where I Started From*, was a finalist for the PEN/Faulkner Award. She is the recipient of a Whiting Award and has received fellowships from the Guggenheim Foundation and the NEA. She also wrote the novel *When Mountains Walked* and co-wrote *In This Very Life: The Liberation Teachings of the Buddha*.

TERRY TEMPEST WILLIAMS is an author, a naturalist, and an environmental activist. Williams is perhaps best known for her book *Refuge: An Unnatural History of Family and Place*. Her other books include *Red: Patience and Passion in the Desert*; *Leap*; *Desert Quartet: An Erotic Landscape*; and a collection of essays, *An Unspoken Hunger*. Her work has been widely anthologized and has appeared in *The New Yorker* and *The Nation*, among other national and international publications. She was inducted into the Rachel Carson Honor Roll and has received the National Wildlife Federation's Conservation Award for Special Achievement. Williams lives in Utah with her husband.

Acknowledgments

So many people have offered their visions, insights, and help during the years of reading and selecting the essays and poems for this collection— Elizabeth Wales, Gail Hudson, Kimberly Richardson, Maureen Michelson, Christine Lamb, Dr. Anne DeVore, and Kris Russell, among many others. We are so grateful for the keen-eyed and expert editorial assistance of Vanessa Adams, Tara Kolden, and Rebekka Stahl. Finally, this book would not have come to light without the commitment and grace of our editor, Rebecca Saletan, and her wonderful assistant, Stacia Decker.

Permissions Acknowledgments

Flor Fernandez Barrios, "Carmen," from *Blessed by Thunder: Memoir of a Cuban Girlhood* by Flor Fernandez Barrios. Copyright © 2000 by Flor Fernandez Barrios. Reprinted by permission of Seal Press.

Rebecca Goldstein, "Looking Back at Lot's Wife." Copyright © 1992 by Rebecca Goldstein. Reprinted from *Commentary* (September 1992) by permission; all rights reserved.

Jane Goodall, "Healing," from *Reason for Hope: A Spiritual Journey* by Jane Goodall. Copyright © 1999 by Soko Publications Ltd. and Phillip Berman. By permission of Warner Books, Inc.

Mary Gordon, "Women of God." Copyright © 2002 by Mary Gordon. Reprinted from *The Atlantic Monthly* (January 2002) by permission of the author.

Joy Harjo, "Songline of Dawn," from *A Map to the Next World: Poems and Tales* by Joy Harjo. Copyright © 2000 by Joy Harjo. Used by permission of W. W. Norton & Company, Inc.

Linda Hogan, "The Great Without." Copyright © 1999 by Linda Hogan. Reprinted from *Parabola: The Magazine of Myth and Tradition*, vol. 24, no. 1 (Spring 1999).

Colleen J. McElroy, "Where the Past Takes Us." Copyright © 1999 by Colleen J. McElroy. Reprinted from *New Letters* magazine, vol. 65, no. 3 (1999).

Deena Metzger, "Re-Vamping the World: On the Return of the Holy Prostitute," from *Tree: Essays and Pieces* by Deena Metzger. Copyright © 1997 by Deena Metzger.

Sy Montgomery, "Shamans," from *Walking with the Great Apes* by Sy Montgomery. Copyright © 1991 by Sy Montgomery. Reprinted by permission of Houghton Mifflin Company. All rights reserved.